PENGUIN BOOKS

TO CHANGE CHINA

Jonathan D. Spence's twelve books on Chinese history include *The Gate of Heavenly Peace*, *The Death of Woman Wang*, and, most recently, *Treason by the Book*. He is Sterling Professor of History at Yale University. His awards include a Guggenheim and a MacArthur Fellowship.

To Change
CHINA

Western Advisers in China

by JONATHAN SPENCE

PENGUIN BOOKS

This book is dedicated to Helen with love

PENGUIN BOOKS
Published by the Penguin Group
Penguin Putnam Inc., 375 Hudson Street,
New York, New York 10014, U.S.A.
Penguin Books Ltd, 80 Strand, London WC2R 0RL, England
Penguin Books Australia Ltd, 250 Camberwell Road,
Camberwell, Victoria 3124, Australia
Penguin Books Canada Ltd, 10 Alcorn Avenue,
Toronto, Ontario, Canada M4V 3B2
Penguin Books India (P) Ltd, 11 Community Centre,
Panchsheel Park, New Delhi – 110 017, India
Penguin Books (N.Z.) Ltd, Cnr Rosedale and Airborne Roads,
Albany, Auckland, New Zealand
Penguin Books (South Africa) (Pty) Ltd, 24 Sturdee Avenue,
Rosebank, Johannesburg 2196, South Africa

Penguin Books Ltd, Registered Offices:
Harmondsworth, Middlesex, England

First published in the United States of America by Little, Brown and Company 1969
Published in Penguin Books 1980
Reprinted in 2002

3   5   7   9   10   8   6   4

Copyright © Jonathan Spence, 1969, 1980
All rights reserved

LIBRARY OF CONGRESS CATALOGING IN PUBLICATION DATA
Spence, Jonathan D.
To change China.
Reprint of the 1969 ed. published by Little, Brown, New York.
Includes bibliographical references and index.
1. China—Relations (general) with foreign countries.
2. China—Civilization—Occidental influences.   I. Title.
[DS740.4. s62   1980]   301.29'51'01821   79-24544
ISBN 0 14 00.5528 2

Printed in the United States of America
Set in Fairfield

CONTENTS

ILLUSTRATIONS

ACKNOWLEDGMENTS

My especial thanks go to Thomas Engelhardt, who worked with me on this book as research assistant, as collaborator — much of chapters three and four are his work — and as a sharp and constructive critic. My thanks, also, to Arthur and Mary Wright, and to Robert Lifton, who read the whole draft manuscript and made many useful suggestions; to Jacob Gerson and Adrian Bennett III for making their unpublished theses available to me; to Edward Gulick and Jacob Gerson (again) for reading draft chapters in their fields of special expertise; to Olga Basanoff for making extensive translations from Russian material, which would otherwise have been unavailable to me; to my students Joseph McDermott, Peter Kostant, and John Swem for giving me some useful leads; to Oliver J. Todd for corresponding at length about his career in China; to the archivists of Yale-in-China, Yale Historical MSS, the Yale Medical Library, and the Bancroft Library of the University of California in Berkeley for locating and giving me permission to use large amounts of original material; and to the many others, at Yale and elsewhere, whose comments and advice helped this book along its way.

Everything here is full of opportunities, after all. Only there are, of course, opportunities that are, in a manner of speaking, too great to be made use of, there are things that are wrecked on nothing but themselves.

— FRANZ KAFKA, *The Castle* (Bürgel speaks)

INTRODUCTION

This is a book about Western advisers in China. For over three hundred years, from the 1620s through the 1950s, these men placed their technical skills at the disposal of the Chinese. At the beginning of the period, they brought knowledge of the stars and of planetary motion; at the end, they introduced the Chinese to aerial warfare and the mysteries of the atom.

From the hundreds of advisers who labored in China, I have chosen sixteen. Despite the range of their expertise—among the sixteen were astronomers, soldiers, doctors, administrators, translators, engineers, and even one professional revolutionary organizer—and despite the more than three centuries that their works span, their cumulative lives have a curious continuity. They experienced similar excitement and danger, entertained similar hopes, learned to bear with similar frustrations, and operated with a combination of integrity and deviousness. They bared their own souls and mirrored their own societies in their actions, yet in doing so they highlighted fundamental Chinese values. And they speak to us still, with a shared intensity, about the ambiguities of superiority, and about that indefinable realm where altruism and exploitation meet.

To Change
CHINA

SCHALL *and* VERBIEST:

To God Through the Stars

On July 29, in the year 1644, Adam Schall, a Jesuit missionary residing in the city of Peking, sent a formal petition to the Emperor of China. "Your subject presents to Your Highness," wrote Schall, "predictions concerning an eclipse of the sun that will occur on September 1, 1644, calculated according to the new Western method, together with illustrations of the percentage of the solar eclipse, and the sun's reappearance as it may be seen in the Imperial capital and in various provinces. In some provinces the eclipse comes earlier, in others later. The predictive data are listed and presented for examination. Your subject humbly begs from Your Highness a decree to the Board of Rites to test publicly the accuracy of the prediction of the solar eclipse at a proper time."[1] Schall also offered to repair the astronomical instruments that had been damaged by a fire in the Palace the previous May. The Emperor ordered Schall to report for a public testing of his predictions at the beginning of September, and in the interim to proceed with the casting of the new instruments.

The drama of that September confrontation comes clearly through the official Chinese report of the day's events: "On September 1, 1644, the grand secretary, Feng Ch'üan, was ordered in company with Adam Schall to bring the telescopes and other instruments to the observatory and to command the officials and students of the Calendrical Department and of the Bureau of Astronomy to repair to the observatory to study the eclipse of the sun. Only the prediction calculated by the Western method coincided exactly with the primary eclipse, the total eclipse, the passing of the eclipse, the time, the percentage, the location, and other details, whereas the predictions calculated by the [traditional Chinese] methods contained errors as to the time and percentage of the eclipse."[2] In recognition of his success, Schall was offered the directorship of the Bureau of Astronomy. This was an office of the fifth grade, placing the incumbent in the middle echelons of the nine-grade Chinese bureaucracy. After consultations with his Jesuit superiors, Schall accepted the post. The man of God became a Chinese bureaucrat.

This was no ordinary appointment. It was, rather, one of those rare moments in time when two streams of history converge, and the overtones of that convergence are to be the theme of our story. Before this moment China, secure in her superiority, had never dreamed that anything of value might be found in the West. The Chinese Empire was unquestionably the greatest in the world. The Chinese Emperor was the Son of Heaven, mediator between the spiritual and earthly realms, untouchable and unapproachable in the recesses of his glittering Court. What new techniques could be needed in a country that drew its wisdom from the Sages, controlled one hundred and fifty million subjects with a small and sophisticated bureaucracy, had touched perfection in art and in poetry, and plumbed the mysteries of sea, of earth, of sky? Civil wars, famines, even conquest by alien nomads such as Mongols or Manchus, were simply digressions; order would always be restored, the conquerors themselves would soon be subdued by the civilizing force of Chinese culture. For the Chinese, their country was "The Central Kingdom"; its boundaries were coterminous with "civilization." Those outside the boundaries were barbarians.

Though the Chinese could not conceivably be expected to have seen it — it was to take more than two centuries for the implications to become clear — Adam Schall was a portent. He came from a

Europe that was experiencing a revolution in the fields of faith, knowledge and scientific technique. The Protestant Reformation had destroyed the Roman Catholic hegemony; the astronomical discoveries of Copernicus and Galileo, complementing Columbus's voyage to the Americas and Magellan's circumnavigation of the globe, shattered man's former vision of the earth, and the place of that earth in the universe. From the seventeenth century onward, the Chinese definition of the world was to come under increasing attack. The Westerners were not like earlier barbarians, who could be absorbed by China and learn to accept her values. Instead, their aim was to change China into something acceptable to them, to make China partake of Western values.[3]

Herein lies the significance of Adam Schall's appointment in 1644. For him, membership in the Chinese bureaucracy was not an end in itself: it was a means to a greater end, the conversion of the Chinese people to the Roman Catholic faith. Schall had developed his technical expertise, become an adviser to the Chinese, and finally their employee, all with the encouragement of his Jesuit superiors. Science was to be used to the greater glory of God. The Chinese, for their part, had favored and promoted Schall because it appeared that he might be useful to them as a technician, pure and simple. One side or the other had to fail in their designs.

Schall's presence in Peking, and the particular strategy that he had adopted, owed much to the activities of his Jesuit predecessor Matteo Ricci. Ricci had traveled to China in the late sixteenth century, and after years of frustration in attempting to convert the poor, had decided it would be more practical to win the favor of some Chinese officials or courtiers — to convert, in other words, from the top down. He accordingly concentrated on studying the Chinese *Classics*, so that he could converse with learned men on equal terms, and on demonstrating his prowess in the fields of mathematics, astronomy, cartography, and mechanics. As he had hoped, his skills aroused Chinese curiosity, and some of the curious became his backers. They used their influence on his behalf, and in 1601 Ricci was granted the exceptional favor of being permitted to live in

Peking. Ricci discussed Roman Catholicism with Chinese scholars, and subtly pointed out that many of its main tenets could be found in the Confucian *Classics*; his great learning, and his personal probity, finally enabled him to convert several high-ranking officials to Christianity, and he secured permission to bring some more Jesuits to Peking.[4]

After Ricci died in 1610, his China journals were brought back to Europe by Father Nicolas Trigault, and rapidly went through several editions in Latin, French, Spanish, German, and Italian. Although there had been books on China before — such as Mendoza's *History* based on Spanish and Portuguese accounts[5] — Ricci's was the first to give a carefully written and reasoned description of the attainments of the great civilization on the other side of the earth. His readers learned not only that this China was indisputably the same as Marco Polo's Cathay, and that it was an exotic and colorful land where men ate their food with ivory sticks, drank an infusion of tea leaves, wore shoes of silk embroidered with flowers, and carried fans in the coldest weather; they were presented also with an analysis of a civilization that, despite its strength, might prove susceptible to Western influence. "I am of the opinion," wrote Ricci, "that the Chinese possess the ingenuous trait of preferring that which comes from without to that which they possess themselves, once they realize the superior quality of the foreign product. Their pride, it would seem, arises from an ignorance of the existence of higher things and from the fact that they find themselves far superior to the barbarous nations by which they are surrounded."[6]

The "foreign products" to which Ricci referred were such items as the clocks, the map, and the spinet which he had introduced to the Chinese Court; the "higher things," on the other hand, were the doctrines of Christianity, and it was going to be hard to convince the Chinese of the superiority of an alien religion. Ricci described the caution with which he and his fellow Jesuits had proceeded in this delicate field:

In order that the appearance of a new religion might not arouse suspicion among the Chinese people, the Fathers did not speak openly about religious matters when they began to appear in public. What time was left to them, after paying their respects and civil compliments and courteously receiving their visitors, was spent in studying the language of the country, the methods of writing and the customs of the people. They did, however, endeavor to teach this pagan people in a more direct way, namely, by virtue of their example and by the sanctity of their lives. In this way they attempted to win the goodwill of the people and little by little, without affectation, to dispose their minds to receive what they could not be persuaded to accept by word of mouth, without endangering what had been thus far accomplished.[7]

This language must have rung oddly in the ears of European readers attuned to the rigors of the Inquisition and Counter-Reformation, but nevertheless many of them were intrigued.

One who listened was Johann Adam Schall von Bell. Born into a wealthy and noble Cologne family, Schall had entered the Jesuit order in 1611, at nineteen, and was studying in Rome when Trigault arrived there on his mission. The two men met. Schall was convinced by the posthumous message of Ricci that he had found his true vocation; he applied for permission to serve his God in the Far East and it was granted. Opposite Schall's name in the 1616 list of Jesuit students his superiors entered the brief notation: "Is going to China."[8] Trigault, in turn, was struck by the talents and enthusiasm of the young student, and asked that Schall be permitted to accompany him on his recruiting tour of Europe. But permission was not granted. It was more important for Schall, his superiors insisted, to finish his current course of studies. Accordingly it was not until October 1617 that he finally left Rome for Lisbon, where a fleet on which he could take passage for China was being assembled.

In Lisbon Schall joined twenty-one Jesuits who had been selected for China service, 614 other passengers and crew, and some ten thousand live poultry, on the ship *Nossa Senhora de Jesus*. They sailed on April 16, 1618, and despite the fact that they were "stowed like herrings among the goods, luggage and provisions," training for the future started as soon as they were on the open sea. Under Trigault's direction they pursued their studies: mathematics on Tuesdays and Fridays, the Chinese language on Wednesdays and Saturdays. In addition, Schall was one of a small group who worked at astronomy, since his superiors had noted Ricci's recommendation that if the Jesuits could attain the skills necessary for correcting the Chinese calendar "this would enhance our reputation, give us freer entry into China and secure us greater security and liberty."[9]

Schall's vessel reached Goa on the western Indian coast on October 4, 1618. The five and a half months' voyage had been costly. Forty-five of the passengers had died from fever, among them five of the Jesuits. Two more Jesuits still in a weakened state died in Goa. Here the surviving passengers learned for the first time that in 1616 the Jesuits living in China had been arrested and ordered to leave China forever, their church and residence in Nanking had been razed, and Christianity formally banned. Fortunately the orders had not been forcefully pushed through, and several Jesuits had stayed on, hidden by Chinese converts, both in Peking and the provinces.[10]

Schall and the others determined to press on, and finally reached Portuguese Macao on July 15, 1619. In Macao, Schall was once again put to work at the Chinese language, this time under the direction of Father Valignoni who had been expelled from China during the persecutions. He was still there in June 1622, when the Dutch attacked the Portuguese settlement and were beaten off, partly by the accuracy of a cannon fired from the Jesuit residence. Sometime in the late summer Schall and three other Jesuits crossed quietly into China and set out for the north. Leaving the party in Hangchow, Schall joined Father Longobardi, who had remained in hiding during the persecution, and on January 25, 1623, the two men entered Peking, taking up residence in the small house near the southwest city gate where Ricci once had lived.[11]

Schall described their arrival as follows: "I remember how while still a young man, I accompanied the aged Father Longobardi to Peking. He and another father presented a petition to the Emperor, in which they said simply that they wished to stay in the capital to work on the bronze cannon."[12] Though the fathers still technically under the ban of expulsion received no reply, added Schall, they stayed on in Peking on the pretext of awaiting an Imperial edict granting them permission. Behind these curious proceedings lay the fact that certain important changes in the Chinese political scene had occurred which indirectly favored the Jesuits. Shen Ch'üeh, the official who had been responsible for launching the 1616 persecution, was briefly out of favor; and in 1621 Manchu tribesmen, north of the Great Wall, had inflicted severe defeats on the Ming armies. This gave influential Chinese officials, among them the Christian converts Hsü Kuang-ch'i and Li Chih-tsao, the chance to bring the Westerners' technical accomplishments to the embattled Ming Emperor's attention. They urged that cannon be brought from Macao to be used against the Manchus in the north, and suggested that the Jesuits be employed as advisers. The cannon arrived, but unfortunately two of them exploded, killing several Chinese bystanders, and Shen Ch'üeh used this incident to renew his attacks on the Christians, though unable to get them again expelled from Peking, or to prevent them preaching in the provinces.[13]

While the Ming dynasty fought for survival on its frontiers, and in the capital a ruthless eunuch and his faction struggled for power with reformers in the Confucian bureaucracy,[14] Schall followed Ricci's advice and calmly began his astronomical work. Astronomy and calendrical science had great politico-religious importance in China, since the Emperor was regarded as the mediator between heaven and earth, and the calendars issued in his name were followed unswervingly both in China and the tributary states on her borders. Throughout the vast Chinese Empire sowing and harvest, festivals and funerals, political decisions and judicial assizes, almost all facets of life ran to the rhythm of the lunar months and auspicious days recorded by Peking. Errors in the calendar accordingly took on a portentous significance, and in times of dynastic weakness they could call in question the Emperor's right to the title Son of Heaven. If the Jesuits could only prove that Chinese calendrical science was inaccurate, they would gain great prestige. To reassure critics in Europe who were ignorant of this background, and protested that too much time was spent in such occupations, Schall wrote: "There is nothing surprising in the fact that the Jesuits apply all their energies to the reform of astronomy, since it is a purely scientific occupation, not at all out of place for religious men."[15] What he meant by this was that though it was, of course, surprising for a missionary to be devoting all his efforts to astronomy, it seemed to be the sole channel through which the Chinese could be brought to God. For only if the Jesuits earned official appointments through their technical abilities could they hope to be brought into the Imperial bureaucracy; this would win them the friendship of influential Chinese scholars, and give them the power and the opportunity to make mass conversions.

Schall established his reputation by correctly predicting the eclipse of October 8, 1623. The effect of this was heightened when he predicted the eclipse of September 1625, and wrote his first book in Chinese on astronomy, which he disarmingly described as "a little treatise on eclipses, in two sections, which I composed to practice my Chinese writing style during my first stay in the Imperial City." In 1626 he produced a Chinese treatise on the telescope, concentrating on its usefulness to astronomy, but not neglecting to point out that it could also be useful in time of war.[16]

Though Schall's skills were gaining him important contacts in Peking officialdom, in 1627 his Jesuit superiors posted him to the northwestern province of Shensi. Schall, who had grown used to the comparative security of astronomical work in Peking, found the work of conversion among a hostile local populace truly arduous. Perhaps, indeed, his superiors thought that it would be good for the young man to get away from science in the city and have a severe testing in the field. In a confidential report to the head of the order in Rome, Longobardi wrote of Schall at this time: "Talent good; judgment good; prudence mediocre; experience limited; progress in letters good. Temperament: naturally good, sanguine, gay, not yet wholly mature. He knows how to deal with people, but as yet not suited for the position of superior."[17]

Despite his inexperience, Schall threw himself into his new task with his customary energy, and by 1629 he had made friends with several local officials, baptized numerous converts, and succeeded in erecting a fine church topped with a golden cross in the provincial capital of Sian.[18] But Schall had no chance to follow up these initial successes, for in 1630 he was abruptly summoned back to Peking.

In his absence Hsü Kuang-ch'i, the Christian convert and staunch supporter of the Jesuits, had been made a vice-president of the Board of Rites, a position near the summit of the Imperial bureaucracy, and in 1629 he had proved successfully that the Western methods of astronomical calculation were superior to those of the Chinese and Mohammedan astronomers presently employed by the Court. He was ordered to head a newly formed Calendrical Department and to staff it as he wished. He selected his friend and fellow convert Li Chih-tsao and the two Jesuits Longobardi and Terrentius.[19] Here was the first chance of a toehold in the official bureaucracy for which the Jesuits had waited. Terrentius (Johann Schreck), a brilliant astronomer and mathematician, had been a member of the Cesi Academy with Galileo. Understandably upset by the Pope's 1616 injunction forbidding him to defend the Copernican heliocentric theories, Galileo had refused to give the Jesuits help in predicting eclipses. But Terrentius was in regular correspondence with Kepler, the other great European astronomer of the time, and thus eminently qualified to attempt a synthesis of available knowledge and to lead the Jesuits to a position of dominance in the Chinese technical bureaus.

Jesuit hopes for such triumphs received a setback when Terrentius died suddenly in 1630. Schall was recalled from Shensi to take his place. Though not as great a mathematician as Terrentius, Schall's knowledge of Western astronomy was enough to put him far ahead of the Chinese and Mohammedan opposition. He had at his fingertips the latest techniques, fruits of the European revolution in the sciences: new methods for predicting eclipses, geometrical analyses of planetary motion, the concepts of a spherical earth and the division of its surface by meridians and parallels, advanced algebra, and such aids to precision as the telescope and the micrometer screw.[20] Thus it didn't really matter that because of Church dogma the Jesuits didn't bring the most developed heliocentric theories to China; they already had the technical edge over the Chinese.

Taking up work where Terrentius had left off, Schall set about examining the Chinese astronomical calculations and found them wanting: "In the Chinese ephemerides, vulgarly called a calendar," he wrote, "we found an 'alternative' placed beside almost every day, which didn't please us much; and in the other calendar used to show the planetary motions we noticed right away a large number of mistakes which stemmed from their faulty calculations." Accordingly he resolved to offer the throne "a complete astronomy book"; he worked five years on it, producing a work in three parts, one on planetary theory, one on fixed stars, and one of tables to aid calculation.[21] Unfortunately his superior and protector, Hsü Kuang-ch'i, died in 1633. Schall, never very tolerant of human frailty, was ill at ease under the new director, Li T'ien-ching. "Li was a fine man," wrote Schall in one of his terse pen-portraits, "but too peace-loving, and in those areas where he should have fought a bit he yielded." "Those areas" were virtually the whole field of calendrical calculation and astronomical observation; under Li's direction there was incessant squabbling among conflicting factions in the bureau. Schall had to fight constantly in defense of his own methods, and to preserve his independence, since "I knew perfectly well that the moment the Chinese mathematicians got involved my projects would come to nothing." Somehow he still found time to deal with problems of hydraulics and optics, and even to repair the spinet that Ricci had long before given to the Wan-li Emperor. For good measure he wrote out — in Chinese — a complete guide to spinet-playing.[22]

Taking advantage of the entrée to the Court that the repair of the spinet had afforded him, Schall offered the Emperor two gifts which he had brought from Europe with him in 1618 but never before had had a chance to present. One was an illuminated life of Christ, on fine parchment, to which he had added a Chinese commentary; the other, a representation in wax of the adoration of the Magi, finely colored. The Emperor accepted the gifts, and was reported to be delighted with them. Schall did not see the Emperor in person —

such opportunities were only to come after his 1644 promotion into the Chinese bureaucracy — but in the palace negotiations that preceded the presentations he was able to meet some of the Court eunuchs and to convert them. These eunuchs, at Schall's bidding, carried the Christian message into the forbidden quarters of the Emperor's palace. Here lived the Emperor's wives and concubines, with whom only the Emperor and castrated males might converse; some of these palace women were in fact converted, though it hardly seems possible that they received sophisticated teaching from their recently converted eunuch associates. Nevertheless, Schall felt that such roundabout tactics were justified, since one never knew which favored concubine might not bring the Emperor himself to see the light. He pointed out, to a possibly skeptical European audience, that God's grace was clearly manifest in these transactions: Chinese concubines grew more beautiful and rose in the palace hierarchy after baptism, while those who mocked God's word developed unsightly blemishes, and fell from favor.[23]

All this shows the ambiguity of Schall's position. He was sure of his superiority over the Chinese technicians, but was constantly having to prove it. He was convinced of the truth of his own religion, yet at the same time he knew that the Chinese considered their own civilization far superior to his. He hoped ultimately to convert the Emperor, but was barred from his presence and had to use eunuchs as his spiritual intermediaries, making exaggerated claims for their few successes. At times the dynamic missionary was transmuted by the heavy confidence of the Chinese into an artisan and errand boy. Members of the bureaucracy, whose conversion he also richly desired, shrewdly gauged his waxing or waning influence.

Schall had learned from Matteo Ricci, and confirmed through his own experience, that the Confucian bureaucrats were a well-educated elite, proud of their sophistication. Methods of conversion that had been successful in the ruder societies of Latin America or Southeast Asia would not work in China. Thus, though Schall was a forthright man, he was horrified by the brash tactics of two Franciscan friars who appeared in Peking in 1637. He wrote to a friend after Chinese guards had expelled the friars: "There came to this capital two Fathers of Saint Francis, determined to be martyrs or to convert the emperor and all the Chinese. Neither of them knew how to speak Chinese . . . both of them wore their habits. . . . Each of them carried his crucifix in his hand and wanted to begin preaching." But when the guards appeared, Schall continued sarcastically, "no thought of martyrdom came to them then. They surrendered their crucifixes with little or no protest, and with clasped hands uttered more than enough 'laoyes' which means 'Señor! Señor!,' concluding with a 'Dimitte nos in pace.' . . . It is better to die in bed than to become a martyr in this fashion."[24]

Unlike the eager friars, Schall followed contemporary Jesuit theory and did as little as possible to upset the members of the Confucian elite or to disturb their existing beliefs. The quickest way to achieve conversion in China would be conversion from the top; to succeed, he must do the Emperor's bidding at all times and gain the respect of the Chinese who mattered. Schall therefore endeavored to live like a Confucian official. He worked hard at the Chinese language, studied the Confucian Classics, wore the long robes of the Chinese scholar, and lived in considerable style. To translate the word "God" he used accepted terms for "Deity" and "Lord of Heaven" culled from the Chinese literary heritage, assuring his European critics that there were theistic elements in the Confucian canon that made such usage legitimate. Furthermore, he accepted the idea that the rites which the Chinese performed in honor of their ancestors or of Confucius had purely civil significance, and that Chinese converts to Christianity might continue to practice such rites without being condemned as heretical.

By these methods Schall and his fellow Jesuits were able to gain the confidence of influential Chinese, and had made several thousand converts in China by 1640, including fifty palace women, forty eunuchs and over one hundred others in the Emperor's entourage.[25] It seemed that finally Schall was breaking through to the Emperor himself. His presents had been accepted, his astronomy praised, and he was given new and important duties. The threats of war from the

Manchu tribes, now united and organized into a hostile state on China's northern frontiers, led the Emperor to issue an edict in 1642 ordering Schall to devote his energies to the casting of cannon for use in campaigns against the Manchus.

Schall protested that he only had a book knowledge of cannon-making; nonetheless, he was given an open area of land, supplies and laborers, and told to get on with the job. The work was simple enough, Schall found, commenting rather contemptuously that "all these things which are quite ordinary to Europeans seem extraordinary to the Chinese who have no experience of them."[26] The commission brought him the status of a mandarin and commensurate power over his underlings. Taking advantage of this, he ordered his workers to kneel at an altar in the foundry before starting work. After twenty large cannon had been successfully cast, he was ordered by the Emperor to make another five hundred, each weighing only sixty pounds, to be carried by infantry soldiers into action. Schall noted caustically that such cannon would inevitably be abandoned by the fleeing Chinese troops and fall into Manchu hands. Presumably he kept his scepticism to himself, since his military advice was increasingly sought; in 1643 he was ordered to submit designs for improved fortifications in Peking, and in 1644 was sent to check the northern defenses. He reported that the situation appeared hopeless.[27]

The situation was indeed hopeless, and Schall had to stand by as the bandit army of Li Tzu-ch'eng swept into Peking in April 1644 with fire and sword, and the Ming Emperor committed suicide in his palace. It must have seemed to Schall that his whole life's work was going up in the flames of the burning city. For twenty-one years he had been at the bidding of the Ming Emperor and labored to impress the Ming bureaucracy. Now the dynasty had been overthrown, and he and the other Jesuits would have to start again. But Schall was not one to give up easily. The first priority was to protect his property from the looters who roamed the streets. "I knew that the Chinese were not very brave," he recalled in his memoirs, "but I knew not yet where their rage might lead, nor what had caused this unusual tumult. So I grasped a Japanese sword and posted myself at the great door before the main hall, ready to bear or break the charge. All then happened as I had hoped. For those who were on the roof, seeing me thus armed and determined, and adorned besides with a beard which would have been sufficient for all of them, began to apologize, shouting that they were looking for robbers and since there were clearly none in the house, they would withdraw immediately."[28]

The second priority was to get in touch with Li Tzu-ch'eng, since even if he was a bandit, he was also the leader of a victorious army, and there was always the chance that he might prove to be the founder of a new dynasty. So Schall reported to the bandit leader's palace and was granted a long interview; presumably he offered his services, but he gives us no record of what transpired, save that the meeting was cordial and he was offered wine and food.[29]

Li Tzu-ch'eng in turn was routed by the Manchu armies from the north, and Schall seems for the first time to have called in question the whole Jesuit strategy of conversion through technical work. "I had already taken the decision," he wrote, "to abandon the calendar and astronomy in order to concern myself solely with religion." He must have felt that the Ming overthrow was God's warning to him personally. But when Li Tzu-ch'eng's soldiers, fleeing from the Manchus, set fire to the area in which Schall lived, the house where he had stored all his mathematical books was spared, although the leaves of the trees all around it were scorched and burnt. Schall seized on this as renewed evidence of God's blessing: "I could not stop myself thinking that such an extraordinary action of fire on such dry materials must be a good augury."[30] So in June, when the Manchus had consolidated their hold on the city, he offered them his services.

Schall's position was a strong one. The Manchus had founded the Ch'ing dynasty and were anxious to consolidate their claims as the holders of the Mandate of Heaven, the true heirs to the Ming. To do this, they had to prepare accurate calendars and predictions on the Chinese model, and prove they were not simply northern barbarians. Schall's work in the Calendrical Department was well known. His

P. IOANNES ADAMUS   SCHALL COLONIENSIS
INGRESSUS HOC TYROCINIUM 21. OCT. 1611.
INICÆ MISSIONIS DECUS ET PRÆSIDIUM
OBIIT PEKINI 15. AUG. 1666. ÆT 75

Adam Schall in Peking, wearing the embroidered White Crane plaque, insignia of Chinese Civil Officials of the First Rank. The oil painting was probably made from life in 1660. *Courtesy Verlag J. P. Bachem, Cologne.*

two main rivals were the Ming and the Mohammedan astronomers, but he had already proved that his expertise was greater than theirs, and as a Westerner he was a free agent, owing no loyalties to the defeated dynasty. Fully aware of this, Schall had even had the temerity to petition the Manchus for continuation of his special privilege of living in Peking, since he was "a foreigner like you," and his petition had been granted.[31] It was at this point that he threw out the challenge to the rival schools of astronomy and forced them to a direct confrontation. The Manchu Emperor accepted the evidence of Schall's superior skills and made him director of the Bureau of Astronomy.

Now that Schall had become an established official in the Ch'ing bureaucracy he had to make the most of his new position, and he did so in a number of ways. He performed feats of astronomical calculation and mechanical expertise which, at little cost, boosted his own image. He accompanied his official astronomical pronouncements with moralistic observations calculated to curb the young Emperor's sexual excesses and errors of judgment.[32] His fame could be brought to aid fellow missionaries: "Throughout the Empire my name was so spread that almost all knew of me. It was often useful to my companions, situated elsewhere, to say they were my brothers or friends."[33] He acted as the interpreter for foreign envoys arriving at the capital, even if, like the Dutch, they were enemies of his faith. "The upshot was," Schall wrote, "that if something occurred that no one dared to handle, the courtiers said 'Let Father Adam deal with it.' "[34]

The purpose of all this activity was, once again, to speed the conversion of the Chinese people. In the early years of the Ch'ing dynasty Schall was on good terms with senior Chinese officials, Manchu generals and princes, and in contact with many women of the palace including the Dowager Empress. But as always, progress was frustratingly slow. As he wrote to a friend in 1651: "To sum up in a word what I think of the Tartars — they are not yet sated with rape and murder, and have not yet abandoned lewdness in shamefully abusing their captives. I live amongst them, I have daily dealings with them. Very often I offer them the doctrine of salvation, but I have to beware of casting my pearls before swine; not, I should add, just to those who seem totally hostile, but even to those I think ready to receive it. Nevertheless, I get nowhere."[35] It was not until the mid-1650's that he began to draw near to the greatest and most elusive prize, the Emperor himself.

The regent Dorgon, who had been de facto ruler for the boy Emperor, died in 1650, and in 1651 the Shun-chih Emperor, now thirteen years old, took the reins of government in person and carried out an extensive purge of Dorgon's henchmen. He seems to have truly admired and trusted Schall, whom he called *ma-fa* (grandfather), constantly waiving palace etiquette on his behalf. Schall was excused from the customary prostrations, given Imperial permission to adopt a son (Shun-chih was distressed that the celibate Schall had no heir), permitted to hand over his official memorials in person, granted land on which to build a church in Peking, and allowed to sit in the Imperial presence. He was given an honorary title of the first rank which placed him in the top echelons of the Ch'ing bureaucracy, and his ancestors were posthumously ennobled.[36] Schall claims that at the peak of his favor, in 1656–1657, Shun-chih visited his house on twenty-four occasions, often unannounced, and talked with him informally late into the night. They discussed astronomy, government, the Christian religion, and much else; Schall was struck by the young Emperor's intelligence and eagerness to learn, and felt they shared a mutual esteem, yet conversion never came. As Schall wrote sadly, "most men, especially these orientals, hold deep in their hearts something that faith in God has as yet been unable to remove." In Shun-chih's case the greatest barrier was chastity, or rather, monogamy; he couldn't answer Schall's subtle question of why it was that European husbands with one wife should often have more children than a Chinese with ten concubines, but he still showed no inclination to give up his luxurious palace life. He also remained an inflexible determinist, convinced that the stars in their courses controlled his destiny.[37]

Perhaps Schall's insistence began to weary Shun-chih. Certainly by 1658 he was spending less time with Schall and more with a small group of Buddhist monks who had won his confidence.[38] Old and disappointed, Schall found that these balmy years had been but a brief respite, and he became once more "a skiff in mid-ocean," as he put it.[39] His enemies took the opportunity to close in.

These enemies were of two kinds, Chinese astronomers and Catholic missionaries. Though the astronomers brought his downfall, it was the missionaries who first gave him trouble. At issue was Schall's whole policy of cultural adaptation. It was not merely that he lived like the Chinese: a European visitor to Peking in the 1650's described him as being "shaved and clothed after the Tartar fashion," and "carried by four men in a Palakin or Sedan, attended by several considerable persons on Horse-back."[40] To many, he seemed also to think like the Chinese, and to be far too tolerant of their pagan rites. His policies had serious theological overtones, and even fellow Jesuits thought he was making too many concessions. Furthermore, Schall was often intemperate and moody: "on the exterior a rather harsh man, very irascible and morose after the German fashion," wrote one contemporary.[41]

Dominicans and Franciscans, who were entering China in some numbers and believed in a life of poverty and conversion of the poor, were often jealous of the Jesuits' influence, and attacked both the Jesuits' religious position and their lavish style of life. Owing to their protests, the Jesuit practices were condemned by the Archbishop of Manila in 1635, and in 1645 the Pope issued his own prohibition. Another condemnation was handed down by a committee of five theologians of the Roman College in 1655. The Jesuits marshaled their defenses, and persuaded the Pope to withdraw the prohibition in 1656; this prompted the Dominicans to return to the attack with renewed vigor.[42]

All this controversy placed Schall in an awkward position, especially as many of these friars also condemned his work in the astronomical bureau as being grossly superstitious. "The case was," wrote one Dominican who was in Peking with Schall, "that Father Adam being president of the College of Mathematics, had the charge of, as well in Political as Religious respects, assigning lucky and unlucky Days for every thing they are to do (tho some excused the said Father as to this particular)." He summarized Schall's duties as being to choose "days and hours for everything except eating, drinking, and sinning."[43] A Franciscan gave even broader criticisms: "The Jesuits have selected purely human means to spread the faith, in direct contradiction to the means used by the Apostles, recommended by Christ Our Lord, and employed by all those who subsequently worked to spread the Kingdom of God — with the exception of said Jesuit Fathers. Using their own means the Jesuits in the Oriental missions set themselves before the heathen as men of wealth and influence, even as men of power and nobility. From this it follows that they are unwilling to allow missionaries of other orders to enter the territories in which they are preaching, lest the heathen, after seeing these obedient, poor and humble men, should turn against the Jesuits who would be shamed and confounded."[44]

Schall could have ridden out these storms with his customary bravado, but he was unable to handle the persistent hostility of the scholar-astronomer Yang Kuang-hsien, who became the spokesman for the anti-Christian literati. The tempo of the attack increased after Shun-chih died in 1661. Schall's Chinese adversaries finally resorted to the accusation of high treason. As they memorialized in 1664:

The Westerner Adam Schall was a posthumous follower of Jesus, who had been the ringleader of the treacherous bandits of the Kingdom of Judea. In the Ming dynasty he came to Peking secretly, and posed as a calendar-maker in order to carry on the propagation of heresy. He engaged in spying out the secrets of our court. If the Westerners do not have intrigues within and without China, why do they establish Catholic churches both in the capital and in strategic places in the provinces? During the last twenty years they have won over one million disciples who have spread throughout the Empire. What is their purpose? Evidently they have long prepared for rebellion. If we do not eradicate them soon, then we ourselves rear a tiger that will lead us to future disaster.[45]

The charges were investigated, and though Schall with the aid of the newly arrived Jesuit Ferdinand Verbiest was able to prove that he was innocent of astronomical errors, he was found guilty on the other charges and sentenced to death by dismemberment. Because of his age, this sentence was altered to flogging and banishment, and even those punishments were not carried out because of his meritorious services in the past. Instead, Schall, partially paralyzed and unable to speak as the result of a stroke, was allowed to stay on under house arrest in his Peking residence. He died there peacefully in 1666, at the age of seventy-five. But Catholicism was proscribed, the churches were closed, and the other missionaries banished to Macao and Canton. Many of them had not regretted Schall's fall. Two jokes popular in Macao at this time summarize their attitudes: "One Adam having driven us out of Paradise, another has driven us out of China"; "Father Ricci got us into China with his mathematics, and Father Schall got us out with his."[46]

Schall could forgive his Chinese persecutors on the grounds of his own interpretation of their national character: "Such is the desire for vengeance among the Chinese, a passion so inordinate that, even amidst public disasters, the ineffaceable memory of what they consider an affront, and the tenacious rancor of their private hatreds, leads them to forget themselves as long as they might bring harm to others."[47] He found it harder to forgive those of his own faith and background whom he considered too narrow-minded and shortsighted to see the point of what he was doing. "I thought to myself of all the work that for over twenty years I had given to the reform of astronomy, and I wished that it should not be lost. For it was to astronomy that I was indebted and I hoped for similar results for my successors. At the same time I saw to my great sorrow that this work was held in contempt by those who above all should have encouraged it."[48] There could be no clearer summary of the way that Adam Schall, man of God, had been edged aside by Adam Schall, Chinese astronomer.

*   *   *

Schall, sword at the ready, had routed the looters of Peking by a display of physical courage. His successor as de facto leader of the Jesuits in China, Ferdinand Verbiest, eluded his first enemies by guile. En route to China in the winter of 1656, Verbiest's vessel was attacked and boarded by pirates before it had even left the Mediterranean. He hid, and watched in alarm as the pirates stripped the Jesuits and passengers to their shifts, removing all their valuables — even crucifixes and breviaries — before herding them into the stern. Sizing up the situation, Verbiest took evasive action: "When I saw my fellow fathers in disarray, with their clothes flapping loose, this divinely inspired idea came to me: that I should despoil myself of my own accord, or rather tear open my clothes in the same way so that they were all awry, hanging loose and untied at the neck, chest, wrists and knees, to make me look like the other Fathers who had already been despoiled of all their possessions. Thus it was that I eluded the pirates' sacrilegious greed, and was able to preserve my treasures with me intact. For each pirate, when he saw me all dishevelled like the others, thought that I must have been robbed together with the rest. In this way I wandered free and untroubled through the whole ship and made my way to the stern."[49]

Such was the caution and quick thinking of the man who was to pick up the threads of Schall's life and endeavor in a truly remarkable way. Ferdinand Verbiest was born in 1623, the son of a bailiff on a great estate in western Flanders. He was educated in Jesuit schools in Courtrai and Bruges, and entered the order in 1641. After some years of teaching grammar, Greek, and rhetoric at Brussels, he was sent to complete advanced studies in theology at Seville and Rome. A brilliant intellectual, enjoying the confidence of his superiors, he could have looked forward to a distinguished life in the highest circles of Catholic Europe. Instead, from an early age, he badgered the General of the Order for a posting to a foreign mission. His requests were all firmly turned down until finally in 1655 his tenacity bore fruit. "I approve your praiseworthy desires," wrote the Jesuit General Goswin Nickel, "I hope that they will be realized, and that your entry into China will bring salvation to the souls of many."[50]

After pirates had rudely interrupted his first journey, Verbiest made his way to Lisbon and sailed for the Far East in the spring of 1657, reaching Goa in the autumn and Macao the following summer. Early in 1659 the Chinese authorities allowed him to enter China, and he took up his missionary duties in Sian, Shensi province, where Schall had worked thirty years before. For eight months Verbiest labored, apparently with success, though as yet he was not an expert at the Chinese language; then in February 1660 the Shun-chih Emperor summoned him to Peking, to assist Schall in his astronomical work. Verbiest lived in China for a further twenty-eight years, but he was never again to work simply as a missionary among the Chinese people. Like Schall, his energies were to be absorbed by the world of science and the Court of the Emperor.

The first real test of Verbiest's astronomical ability came during the persecutions of 1664, and he acquitted himself well. Ordered by the tribunal to estimate the exact time of a forthcoming eclipse of the sun, the Chinese astronomer Yang Kuang-hsien estimated 2:15, the Mohammedan astronomer Wu Ming-hsüan 2:30, while Verbiest with the help of the stricken Schall, claimed it would not occur till 3 o'clock. Lenses had been set up so that the sun's image was projected into a dark room — the first two calculations having proved erroneous, almost exactly at 3 o'clock the first shadow appeared. This triumph was not enough to sway the judges, and Verbiest was condemned to flogging and banishment. However, this punishment and Schall's sentence of execution were both commuted, and the two were allowed to stay on together under house arrest in Peking, though now they had no official position, and their enemy Yang Kuang-hsien had been appointed director of the astronomical bureau.[51]

After Schall's death in 1666, Verbiest was still under house arrest. Feeling that Schall, despite his setbacks, had been on the right track, Verbiest devoted his enforced leisure to astronomical studies; as he wrote in a letter dated April 1668, "instead of earthly news I send herewith news of the Heavens."[52] He was waiting for the political situation to change and when it did he moved fast and effectively.

By late 1668 Emperor Shun-chih's son K'ang-hsi, now fourteen, had taken over the throne in person, punishing his regents and their followers for their excesses. At the same time it was becoming apparent that the calculations made by Yang Kuang-hsien and Wu Ming-hsüan in the astronomical bureau were often inaccurate. In December, repeating Schall's move of 1644, Verbiest challenged the two astronomers to prove their skill by calculating the length of the shadow that would be thrown by a given object at a given time of day. Yang and Wu were unable to complete the experiment, but Verbiest's calculations proved exact. Then on December 28, Verbiest received an order from K'ang-hsi to check the calendars that his rivals had submitted. At the end of January 1669 Verbiest replied, pointing out several major errors that had been made by the Chinese and Mohammedan astronomers; he ended with a broad-based summary of the role of the calendar in China. It is hard to remember that this is a Belgian Jesuit, not a Chinese official, speaking: "The virtue and the power of our Imperial Majesty has spread far and wide, so that many scores of nations are tribute-bearers and the nations which follow our Imperial calendars extend for several myriads of miles. From the Imperial Capital of our Empire the authority radiates to the four corners of the earth. In such an immense territory how can we endure an inaccurate calendar that can nowhere measure the real length of day and night, the correct time, or the real solar periods all year round?"[53]

The Emperor ordered the princes and senior ministers to investigate Verbiest's charges and submit a report on their findings. The ministers replied that Verbiest seemed to have been right and Wu Ming-hsüan wrong. The K'ang-hsi Emperor found this conclusion too vague, and issued an angry edict which showed that he intended to settle these astronomical squabbles once and for all:

Earlier when Yang Kuang-hsien accused Schall, the princes and ministers in the state-council determined clearly on what points Yang Kuang-hsien was right and accordingly approved his suggestions, and on what points Schall was wrong, and accordingly considered how to discontinue his calculations. You have not now carefully investigated why formerly the state-council decided to abolish the Western method nor why you now decide to restore it without further investigation of Ma Hu, Yang Kuang-hsien, Wu Ming-hsüan and Verbiest before memorializing to Us. This is improper. We order you to deliberate this matter again![54]

Verbiest and Wu Ming-hsüan were ordered to carry out a final round of competitive experiments, by calculating the precise height and angle of the sun as it would appear at a given time. All instruments had to be in place two weeks early, and the astronomers then fixed them in position, and covered the movable parts with strips of paper on which they laid the imprint of their personal seals. Thus it was impossible to tamper with the forecasts. Verbiest's calculations proved precise, and in late February 1669 he was appointed director of the astronomical bureau. Yang Kuang-hsien and Wu Ming-hsüan were arrested.

Verbiest moved confidently into the field of calendar reform, exposing his predecessors' errors and insisting that they be corrected immediately even though the calendar had already been printed. After lengthy ministerial debates, K'ang-hsi agreed to this request. At the same time Verbiest impeached Yang Kuang-hsien for having falsely accused Schall five years before; Schall and his fellow workers were vindicated and their titles and honors were posthumously restored, while Yang was condemned to death.[55]

This success, however, was as paradoxical for Verbiest as it had been for Schall: increasing technical duties deflected him from his spiritual endeavors. He not only had little time to convert the heathen, he even had to give up his personal devotions. As he wrote in August 1670 to his closest friend Philippe Couplet: "Last year I hoped that the pressure of business would gradually decline as the months passed, but I am still overwhelmed with work, to the point that the Father Superior has to dispense me — and this has not been a rare occurrence — from reciting my breviary."[56]

Verbiest worked on the calendars, directed his bureau staff, and

Le Pere Ferdinand Verbiest.

Ferdinand Verbiest, in Chinese Winter Robes without insignia, points approvingly at some of the instruments that enabled him to be so successful as Director of the Astronomical Bureau from 1669 to 1687. The engraving appears in Du Halde's *History of China*, Paris, 1735.

built large and complex instruments for the Imperial observatory;[57] but the "pressure of business" to which he referred was not entirely due to the demands of astronomy. Much of his time was taken up with trivia. At the K'ang-hsi Emperor's request he spent weeks on end perfecting a system of pulleys to lever giant stones over a rickety bridge, making gay sundials and a water clock, building pumps to raise the water in the royal pleasure gardens, and painting tiny trompe l'oeil figures to be viewed through a prismatic tube. Verbiest described one such object, a little landscape, with horses and birds in the foreground, which could be enjoyed as a painting in its own right. "But when viewed through a prismatic tube, one could see in it only a tartar's head and body, down to the belt, dressed in robe and summer hat. All were amused at seeing this image."[58] He was proud of these activities, and described them at length in his letters, for of course these activities would turn out not to have been trivial if they led to the supreme goal — conversion of the Emperor. Verbiest was optimistic that the K'ang-hsi Emperor, having been impressed by astronomy and delighted by mechanics, would swing to the faith behind the science. "Thanks to Divine Providence we hope that this [Imperial] favor will grow, and will finally bring our joy to a peak. But we must still be patient, wait for the suitable moment, moving little by little along the way which will lead to the difficult and important goal."[59] So Schall had hoped and waited for his Emperor.

But like Schall, Verbiest also had his enemies. These included Jesuits in Peking, many years his senior, who resented his growing prestige. When Verbiest asked his superiors in Europe for more money to meet the costs of his scientific establishment and the inevitable payments and bribes of life at the Manchu court, he wrote in Flemish so that other Jesuits would be unable to read his letter. He was convinced that he was on the right track, and determined that his colleagues should not thwart him: "All the favors that we have obtained up to now have been given by the Emperor as payment for services rendered in the field of mathematics. Right there is sufficient reason to let me continue and to give me resources."[60]

Verbiest's knowledge of Chinese grew good enough for him to act as interpreter for visiting foreigners. When the K'ang-hsi Emperor ordered him to the palace to serve as his tutor, Verbiest also learned Manchu so that they could converse informally, and finally wrote a Manchu grammar to help other missionaries in learning the language. Under his direction K'ang-hsi studied the principles of astronomy, worked through the *Elements of Euclid* (which Ricci had translated into Chinese long before), moved on to spherical trigonometry, and finally to practical experiments in astronomical observation and terrestrial measurement.[61]

How close the two men really were, and how much of this new knowledge K'ang-hsi comprehended, is a moot point. Verbiest wrote of the Emperor's intelligence and the affection between them, while other missionaries believed that the Emperor followed little of what was going on.[62] But certainly some real personal contact took place, and new assignments and rewards came to Verbiest. An edict of 1674 ordered him to cast "light but effective cannons, convenient for transportation" to be used in the suppression of the civil war that had erupted in South China.[63] Verbiest made 132 heavy cannon; their success in the field brought an order for 320 light cannon. In 1682, with victory assured to the Imperial forces, Verbiest was given the title of vice-president of the Board of Works, because "the cannons whose casting he had directed were good and strong."[64] The bailiff's son from Flanders had become a senior member of the Chinese bureaucracy.

Favor and obligation naturally overlapped. Thus Verbiest, chosen by the Emperor to accompany him on one of his Imperial tours to Manchuria, described his role as follows: "I was to be always at the Emperor's side, so that I might make in his presence the necessary observations for determining the state of the heavens, the elevation of the Pole, the grade of the terrain, and to calculate with my mathematical instruments the height and distance of the mountains. He could also conveniently ask me to tell him about meteorites, and any other problems of physics or mathematics."[65] Verbiest was given ten horses to carry the equipment and lodged each night in a tent near the Emperor's. Choked by the dust of the marching army, exhausted by each day's hard riding so that "during the trip I was so tired each night on reaching my tent that I could not stand upright," there was no respite for Verbiest from the honors he had earned: "I would have excused myself several times from following the Emperor, had not my friends advised me to the contrary and had I not feared that the Emperor might notice my absence and take it badly."[66]

This tenacity brought its small rewards, as on one night in the mountains when a chosen group sat with the Emperor at the edge of a stream. Verbiest describes the scene: "As it was a beautiful night, and the sky was clear, K'ang-hsi asked me to give him the Chinese and European names for the stars appearing on the horizon; he himself named first those that he had already learned. Then, taking out a little celestial map that I had given him some years before, he began to calculate from the stars what hour of night it was, taking great pleasure in showing those around how much skill he had acquired in science."[67]

Such moments kept Verbiest's hopes of conversion alive as other business pressed upon him. Not only did he continue with astronomical writing, preparing tables "for 2,000 years into the future" at K'ang-hsi's request, he drew up new tables of the latitudes of cities in Manchuria which K'ang-hsi ordered adopted in all future Chinese maps.[68] As vice-provincial of the order in China he worked for all missionaries; Franciscan friars, for example, repeatedly praised his disinterested help and the influence he could bring to bear to save them from persecution.[69] He pushed for the development of a native Chinese clergy, and supported the efforts of French missionaries to enter China, although he knew this would anger the Portuguese. He urged the development of an overland route from Europe to China through Russia. His tact was certainly greater than Schall's, his talents as multifaceted, and success seemed within his grasp. But at the peak of his accomplishments and prestige, in 1687 at the age of sixty-four, he was thrown from his horse and suffered serious internal injuries. He died the following year. K'ang-hsi ordered a state funeral and sacrifices to be offered in his name, and the Jesuit was taken to his final rest in splendid Chinese style:

In front was a banner-picture twenty-five feet high and four feet wide, ornamented with festoons of silk. At the bottom was a piece of red taffeta, inscribed with [Verbiest's Chinese] name and his dignities, in gold characters. Before and behind were bands of musicians and standard-bearers. Then came the Cross, in a large niche, ornamented with columns and various silk ornaments. Several Christians followed, some with flags and others with wax tapers in their hands. Then came the image of the Virgin Mary and the child Jesus holding a globe in his hand. A picture of the guardian angel followed, with more flags and tapers and then a portrait of Father Verbiest, habited as an official, with all the honor conferred on him by the Emperor. We [his Jesuit confreres] followed immediately after in white mourning, according to the custom of the country, and at intervals we expressed our grief by loud weeping, according to the manner of the people. The body came next, accompanied by officers appointed by the Emperor to do honor to the remains of the famous missionary. They were on horseback. Among them were the Emperor's son-in-law and the captain of the guards. The procession was closed by a party of fifty horsemen."[70]

There seemed no reason why Verbiest's death need interrupt the steady pattern of missionary successes in China, and at first all went well for his successors. Rewards were heaped on the Jesuits who worked as mediators between China and Russia in drawing up the 1689 Treaty of Nerchinsk. An "edict of toleration" of the Christian religion was issued in 1692 after Jesuits had cured K'ang-hsi of a dangerous malarial fever by using quinine. The Jesuits were given land inside the Imperial city to build a church, and were commissioned by K'ang-hsi to undertake a full cartographic survey of his empire. K'ang-hsi remained affable and generous to the missionaries, often singling them out for special notice when he toured the provinces. Jesuits were regularly appointed to direct the Bureau of

Astronomy, and their place as technicians of influence within the regular bureaucracy seemed assured.[71]

All these hopeful signs proved illusory, however, and the problems that had once plagued Schall flared up again: factional fighting between missionaries became increasingly bitter, leading in 1705 to the despatch of a papal emissary who managed to split the Jesuits in China irreparably and to alienate the Emperor.[72] The hostility of influential Chinese officials increased, and persecution of Christians became common in the provinces. There was now no European with the influence (and no Chinese official with the inclination) to stop them. In the eighteenth century, K'ang-hsi's son and grandson condoned open persecution of Christians, and Christianity was declared heterodox, though missionaries continued to serve at court as astronomers, as the makers of fountains and curios, or as painters and builders.[73] Finally, in the 1770's, the maligned and discredited Jesuit order was abolished in Europe, and fresh waves of violent persecution in China sent the remaining missionaries into exile or hiding. The first calculated attempt to win over the Chinese through Western technical expertise had clearly failed.

Yet despite these setbacks, Westerners remained optimistic concerning the opportunities that China offered. Missionary accounts kept alive the image of the Chinese Emperor as a possible subject for Christian conversion, insisted that his mandarins were enlightened bureaucrats already on the path to truth, and described each act of persecution as a prelude to ever greater triumphs for the Faith. Theorists like Voltaire and Adam Smith used examples from China to reinforce their critiques of their own societies; others responded in a more light-hearted manner, embracing the gay extravagances of "Chinoiserie" which brought pagodas into British gardens, willow-ware to Western dinner tables, and Manchu pigtails to the heads of both King George III and George Washington.[74]

Western analysis of China was, in fact, inaccurate and sentimental. Confident of the superiority of their expertise and sure that China needed them, the first generations of Western advisers had simplified China to suit their purposes, had failed to understand the strength and impermeability of the Confucian moral structure, and had dismissed the hostility they often encountered as a temporary aberration.

Looking back from our own vantage point to the time of Schall and Verbiest, we can see that on balance it was the Chinese who had gained from the exchange. They had used the Westerners' skills when it suited them, and paid a fair price, but had offered little else in return. What did not concern them they had shrugged aside. By the early nineteenth-century Western religion was but a blurred memory. As the widely read scholar and eminent official Lin Tse-hsü put it in 1840: "It appears that the Jesus-religion preached by Matteo Ricci was Catholicism, whereas the Jesus-religion preached afterwards by Verbiest was Christianity. The two terms 'Catholic' and 'Christian' must express some such difference."[75]

But the Westerners were not to dismiss the matter so lightly. The convergence symbolized by Schall's appointment had become an integral part of Western thinking. In China lay opportunity, and expertise was still the key. "It was a star that long ago led the Three Kings to adore the True God," Verbiest had written in 1674. "In the same way the science of the stars will lead the rulers of the Orient, little by little, to know and to adore their Lord."[76] Just because this particular forecast had proved overoptimistic, there was no need to abandon the strategy. There was no need to abandon it, indeed, even if one sought to bring the Chinese to other gods, through other sciences.

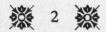

PETER PARKER:

Bodies or Souls

There had been grandeur enough in the Jesuits' plan to bring the Chinese to God through astronomy, but their efforts seem positively restrained when they are contrasted with the forceful Protestant evangelists of the nineteenth century. Driven onward by new visions of progress, humanitarianism, and commercial expansion, the prophets reared in the industrial revolution groped for a new rhetoric and wider worlds to conquer. "When I contemplate the subject," wrote the American Protestant missionary Peter Parker after his first sojourn in China, "and its magnitude expands into all its importance and moral grandeur, the exclamation is irrepressible, — Oh! that talent might be enlisted adequate to guide and foster the interest, and conduct the mighty enterprise to a successful consummation! . . . To liberate man from physical, mental, and moral vassalage, and to disseminate the blessings of science and Christianity all over the globe, are sufficient for the mightiest intellects, and most benevolent hearts."[1]

Yet Peter Parker was, in his own way, following a Jesuit strategy to reach the Chinese. He had simply substituted modern medicine for the science of the stars. The parallel emerges clearly from a speech that Parker made in England, in 1841. "The objects he had in view," noted a British newspaper reporter covering the event, "were, first, to enlighten the empire of China in the sciences of physic and surgery; and secondly, having opened the way by their means, to spread among the vast population of that country, the blessings of Christianity. He went on to show the defective and erroneous state of medical science in that country. He then proceeded to adduce a number of cases that had fallen within his own experience, showing the great value of hospitals in that country, not only in the advancement of science amongst the nations, and in the practical benevolent effects, but in conciliating the good feelings of the natives, and thereby clearing the way for the introduction of Christian principles among them."[2]

The road to China was long for Parker, as it had been to the Jesuits, and like them he was only able to travel it because he had received advanced education and was strengthened by personal devotion. Born in Framingham, Massachusetts, on June 18, 1804, Parker was the only son of a poor farmer. He was raised in strict Protestant surroundings which filled him with a sense of his own spiritual shortcomings. Not until he was sixteen did he find a certain peace, when he underwent conversion and for the first time felt "willing to acquiesce in the will of God."[3] But he remained chained to the farm, his father being partially paralyzed and in debt, until a married sister gave the family an annuity which permitted him to leave home with a clear conscience. He enrolled at Amherst College in 1827, but in his third year there grew restless. Harvard tempted him until he learned that "the situation of the college was such as to render it not desirable for pious students."[4] So he transferred to Yale.

Yale and the city of New Haven enchanted him. It was the "Eden of America," he told his mother. Local benevolent societies gave him free books and bedding; he found comfortable lodgings at fifty cents a day; and the students were friendly. Lack of money was a problem since he must not "lose reputation and influence" among his more opulent classmates; but serving as a waiter in the dining hall would bring in enough to pay for all his board.[5]

In his late teens Parker had felt vague yearnings to take the Christian message overseas, to go "to some place never before trodden by Christian feet, and where the sound of the gospel has never been heard."[6] As he settled in at Yale, local religious services began to work on his senses and strengthen his belief in his missionary vocation: "If I am not deceived, there is no subject which so much interests my whole soul as the condition of the heathen. May it not be that the Great Head of the Church does intend me for this benevolent cause?"[7] He made himself write out his qualifications and motives for seeking the missionary life and found the results encouraging. He was, he concluded, diligent, quite intelligent, forgiving, tolerant, healthy, patient, devout, without pressing obligations to his family, and seriously concerned with the wretchedness of the heathen.[8] By September 1831 his choices of missionary field had narrowed to two, China and Smyrna, and faculty counselors encouraged his conviction that there was important work to be done in both areas. He also began to think of becoming a medical doctor, and after being assured that in his case the instruction would be "gratuitous" and the other expenses "trifling," he started a course of medical studies. At the same time, after due reflection and prayer, he entered the Yale Divinity School. Mother and sisters wept, but lauded his ambition.[9]

He made his new desire for a missionary life known to the American Board of Commissioners for Foreign Missions, which at this time was a clearinghouse for Protestants seeking overseas service, and politely managed to suggest that by rejecting him the commissioners would run counter to God's will.[10] In reply, the American Board encouraged him to concentrate on China, and he joyfully complied.

Parker's first introduction to his chosen field seems to have been the article on China in the *Encyclopaedia Americana*, which he studied with "much interest" in early 1832. In this article he read an outline of Chinese history and learned that the Chinese were "a slavish, industrious and commercial people," that their agriculture was varied and "in a very flourishing condition," their army large but weak, that "in intellectual improvement, this nation has long been stationary," and that in recent years they had "frequently suffered from internal commotions." He learned further that the Catholics had lost their former privileges through "their inconsiderate zeal," and that though China "treats all [foreign countries] as its vassals," there was a bustling international trade, China importing rice, cloth, glass, furs, and sandalwood, and exporting tea, sugar, silk, minerals, lacquer, rhubarb, and musk. Lastly, he discovered that despite the peculiarities of their language "the Chinese understand each other perfectly well" and that thanks to the labors of Morrison and Remusat in compiling dictionaries and grammars the "auxiliary means are not now wanting for those who are desirous of learning this curious idiom."[11]

What the article did not tell him was that population pressures had pushed the Chinese peasants to the very margin of subsistence, that in the late eighteenth century the appalling corruption of the Ch'ien-lung Emperor's favorite, Ho-shen, had driven the regime to the verge of bankruptcy, weakened Imperial authority, and demoralized the bureaucracy, that the Ch'ing armies had proved almost incapable of putting down the increasingly frequent peasant revolts, and that foreign governments were growing impatient with their "vassal" status.[12] The author of the article also omitted one major fact of which he must have been well aware, namely that Britain and America were balancing their trade by exporting vast quantities of opium to China. In 1829, for example, the British exported twenty-one million dollars' worth of commodities to China, of which opium accounted for over ten million dollars; in the same year the Americans did four million dollars' worth of trade, of which over a quarter was in opium.[13] Had Parker known of these grim realities he would have had a clearer idea of the problems he would face in China. As it was, he continued his studies in happy ignorance, while far off on the China coast the British opium runner Captain Innes jotted down: "Employed delivering briskly. No time to read my Bible or to keep my journal."[14]

By the time Parker traveled to Philadelphia in September 1833 for the anniversary celebrations of the American Board of Commissioners for Foreign Missions, his medical and divinity studies were well advanced and he was already regarded as an expert in the China field. He preached no less than three times on the Sunday after his arrival and was active and happy all week. One of his congregation, struck by his zeal, donated two hundred and fifty dollars "to be appropriated to Rev. Peter Parker, missionary to China, when he shall go."[15] It seems to have been Parker's first material windfall, bringing China a giant step nearer, and though he added devoutly "not unto us, not unto us, but to God be all the praise," he clearly felt the lure of this new and bustling world, and saw the opportunities it offered. If he moved to Philadelphia, he reflected, "I shall greatly extend my acquaintance, and prepare to exert greater influence upon my own country when I have left it forever."[16] The "unspeakable privilege of pleading the cause of the heathen"[17] seemed to demand new tactics, but upon returning to New Haven he was stricken by painful fevers which he saw as a judgment from God:"I trust I shall live and not die. Even in the most distressed hours, I have had happy presentiments that I shall yet reach the field of my labors. I do not know that I shall cultivate it long; but I am persuaded I shall see it; and labor in it for a time."[18] The "happy presentiments" were startlingly fulfilled. Three weeks after his seizure he met the wealthy and devout China merchant D. W. C. Olyphant, who offered him free passage to China in his ship *Morrison,* which was to sail from New York in June 1834.

Parker accepted this as his destiny, though after his recent illness he realized the voyage might be his last. As he wrote dramatically to his sister Harriet: "The trying moment is near; the time when we must say farewell — a long farewell till we meet in yonder world. But stay, we will not weep and break our hearts, for this moment is fraught with pleasure too, I assure you. It is for the sake of Christ you part with your only brother; it is that he may bear the tidings of your Saviour's love to the millions of China . . . that he may be instrumental in scattering the light of the 'glorious gospel of the blessed God' in the benighted portions of the earth."[19]

In the meantime, there were the final practical details to be attended to. As packing and preaching continued unabated, he found time to pass his final examinations in New Haven and to receive the degree of Doctor of Medicine in March 1834; two months later, in Philadelphia, he was ordained as a Presbyterian minister.

At a farewell ceremony in the Bleecker Street Presbyterian Church of New York, the Prudential Committee of the American Board of Commissioners for Foreign Missions gave him instructions for his China ministry. Their words sound like a formal warning to Parker, a warning that he should not follow the paths of a Schall or a Verbiest and allow technical expertise to interfere with his spiritual goals: "The medical and surgical knowledge you have acquired, you will employ, as you have opportunity, in relieving the bodily afflictions of the people. You will also be ready, as you can, to aid in giving them our arts and sciences. But these, you will never forget, are to receive your attention only as they can be made handmaids to the gospel. The character of a physician, or of a man of science, respectable as they are, or useful as they may be in evangelizing China — you will never suffer to supersede or interfere with your character of a teacher of religion." He was also urged to spend two or three years "of close and unremitted study" of the Chinese written and spoken language, to learn the local customs, to decide on a base of future operations, and to search out "well-qualified native assistants."[20]

In reply, Parker reiterated his awe and gratitude at the chance offered to him, and his solemn realization that he would probably never return, but added a passage in which he summarized his real goals and answered his critics: "I wish to be useful. I would not throw away my life as some, not appreciating my motive or understanding my prospects, have insinuated. I desire, in just that capacity which God pleases, to do good that shall remain for eternity." He closed on a note of ringing patriotism: "America must do much in this work. The greatest honor is that I go forth as a missionary of Jesus Christ. Yes, I glory in being a follower of the once despised Nazarene; yet I may say, I am happy to hail from America!"[21]

He sailed from New York on June 4, 1834. It was a fine sunny day and the spirits of all aboard were high. As they beat down

towards the open sea, they joined in singing the hymn that a friend
had just composed for Parker:

> *Heaven's softest breezes woo thee*
> *Across the Indian Sea,*
> *God's grace be given to thee,*
> *Till China shall be free;*
> *Free through the Lord of Glory*
> *Who died that she might live;*
> *Free by the Saviour's story*
> *Her darkened sons receive.*[22]

Where the European Jesuits had failed, how could American Protestants not succeed? For Parker knew that "My Father is at the helm, and Christ Jesus, the hope of glory, is the anchor of my soul."[23]

Yet Catholic and Protestant alike, once out of sight of land and sailing on true course to the land of their dreams, fell into a rhythm of activity dictated by the magnitude of the task ahead. Like Schall on the ship *Nossa Senhora de Jesus* two hundred and sixteen years before, Parker on the *Morrison* organized religious services and took to his books, plunging into Remusat's *Chinese Grammar* and brushing up on *Anthers on Surgery*. He felt an elation he could not control, "I am among those who stand upon the pinnacle of the world, a spectacle to millions, both of the friends and the enemies of Christ";[24] but he was also distracted, and unhappy that "my new society and new scenes have diverted me from my holy walk with God."[25] The endless distractions on that holy walk were to mar the rest of his life.

On October 26 he set foot in Canton, and was warmly greeted by the Westerners in the city. These Westerners were few in number and restricted by the Ch'ing government to the "Thirteen Factories" outside the city of Canton proper. In this tiny area, under a quarter of a mile long and two hundred yards wide, Parker found about two hundred missionaries and traders, the bulk of them British, but there were perhaps thirty Americans and a handful of Germans, Dutchmen, French and Danes. Though food and living quarters were good, the foreign community lived under irksome restrictions: they could not be accompanied by their wives, could not bear arms, ride in sedan chairs, row on the river, or enter Canton city. On three days a month they might walk in the flower gardens across the river, but only in small groups and accompanied by a Chinese interpreter who was responsible for their good behavior.[26] It cannot have seemed a very promising base for the mass conversion of China, but it was all there was.

Here Parker met some fellow spirits: Elijah Bridgman, who had reached Canton in 1830, the first American missionary to do so, S. Wells Williams, and others whose fervent meetings in the factory rooms of D. W. C. Olyphant gave that area the name "Zion's Corner."[27] However, before Parker could make definite plans for the future, he fell sick. Since there was a pressing need for him to learn Chinese, he was sent to more comfortable quarters in Singapore, to study the language and practice medicine there till he recovered. He felt friendly with the Chinese people, he wrote to a friend in New Haven; he had gained a good reputation through his medical skills, and was getting the feel of the life. "Tho alone, I seldom feel solitary, and with a Chinese teacher on either hand I do not often think I am eating with chopsticks and with them taking my food from the same plate. I have conformed to their mode of living so far as I deem expedient."[28]

The work exhilarated him, but almost immediately the demand for his technical skills began to deflect him from his spiritual goals. "I read last evening my instructions from the Board, and not without grief to find that, in the deep-growing interest I have felt for the sick and dying among the Chinese, I have in a degree deviated from those instructions, to be thorough in my attention to the language, and have become involved in medical and surgical practice in a manner that I know not how to extricate myself."[29] The dilemma began to obsess him, and by June 1835 he was in a profound depression: he felt a "darkness of spirit," he was "floating down the current to perdition," and often withdrew from all human company to weep "by *day* and by *night* in secret places." He felt inadequate for the task before him: "I have *prayed* & *fasted* & labored for years to be *better* for the missionary work and am yet *unprepared*." Worst of all, something seemed to hold him back from caring for the spiritual needs of his patients: "While anxious to benefit the bodies of the hundreds that weekly come to me, I have not yet raised an ejaculation to heaven in behalf of their souls."[30] The problem was clear enough. "Besetting sins. 1. I partake too much of the spirit of the more worldly physician & not enough of the *Christian, minister,* & *missionary* of the cross of *Christ*."[31] He leaped at the chance to return to Canton, trusting to "dedicate my life afresh to the cause of my Redeemer, into whose image I wish to be transformed."[32]

Back in Canton, however, Parker was plunged more than ever into his specialized medical work, and in November 1835 the Canton Ophthalmic Hospital with space for forty in-patients was opened under his direction in rented rooms in one of the factories. In his first quarterly report Parker justified the apparent narrowness of the medical field chosen: "Diseases of the eye were selected as those the most common in China, and being a class in which the native practitioners are most impotent, the cure, it was supposed, would be as much appreciated as any other."[33]

The hospital was an immediate success. Over nine hundred patients (of whom nearly a third were women) were treated in the first three months. The first operations were on cataracts and other eye diseases, but Parker also operated increasingly on abscesses, tumors, and cancer. There is no doubt that his skills as a surgeon were extraordinary, and modern physicians have written of his work with awe.[34] Here, one example must summarize the whole. In his first report on the Canton hospital, Parker dealt at length with "Case no. 446, Dec. 27th. Sarcomatous tumor. Akae, a little girl aged 13." He describes the arrival of the patient: "As I was closing the business of the day, I observed a Chinese timidly advancing into the hospital leading his little daughter, who at first sight appeared to have two heads. A sarcomatous tumor projecting from her right temple, and extending down to the cheek as low as her mouth, sadly disfigured her face." Having taken out minimal insurance from the girl's

A little Chinese girl. Peter Parker removed the one-and-a-quarter pound sarcomatous tumor in an eight-minute operation. This is one of a series of oil paintings that Parker commissioned: they served both as a medical record and as proof of his expertise. *Courtesy the Curator, Gordon Museum, Guy's Hospital, London.*

parents, in the form of a written affidavit that they would exonerate him from blame if the girl died, Parker decided to operate. The tumor, which weighed one pound and a quarter, and was sixteen inches in base circumference, was removed in an eight-minute operation. The wound made by the incision healed perfectly, and after eighteen days the patient was discharged.[35]

Parker commissioned the Chinese artist Lamqua to make paintings of his most interesting cases, and a portrait of a little girl that might well be Akae has come down to us. Her forlorn figure could serve as a symbol for China as she has been seen by many Western eyes from the seventeenth century to the present. There she stands, innocent and in pain, beautiful but disfigured. Her own people cannot help, but they will let her waste away, watching without expression as she dies. But a flash of the surgeon's knife and all is changed. Transfigured by Western expertise, she can take her rightful place in the world and live happily ever after. Why, asked the Westerner, couldn't the Chinese see how simple it all was?

Parker knew he was meant to be concerned with the souls rather than the bodies of his patients, but there never seemed to be time for that. "May 1, 1836. I have so much *labor* to perform for my numerous patients that I have not as much leisure to converse with them and to improve the opportunities that present [themselves] of making known my errand among them. I must therefore be more on my guard lest the adversary by busying me about the body prevent my depriving him of some of these souls."[36] He grew ever busier as Chinese suspicions relaxed before the proof of his skills. In one of his reports he gave a graphic picture of the patients who demanded all his time and energy, and of the assembly-line technique he developed to handle them:

It is difficult to convey to a person who has not witnessed the scenes of the hospital, a just idea of them. He needs to be present on a day for receiving new patients, and behold respectable women and children assembling at the door the preceding evening, and sitting all night in the streets, that they might be in time to obtain an early ticket, so as to be treated the same day. He need behold in the morning the long line of sedans extending far in each direction; see the mandarins, with their attendant footmen, horsemen, and standard-bearers; observe the dense mass in the room below — parents lifting their children at arm's length above the crowd, lest they should be suffocated or injured; stand by during the examination and giving out of tickets of admission to the hall above, where they are registered and prescribed for; in urgent cases being admitted at once, while others are directed to come in five or ten days, according to the ability to attend to them. Upon that floor witness one or two hundred selected from the hundreds below (many being sent away, some, indeed, irremediable, but still more curable, and deserving attention); officers of various rank, from the district magistrate to the criminal judge of the province, sitting at the table of the physician, with scores of humbler fellow-citizens, seeking the same gratuity at the foreigner's hand.

As the impracticability of prescribing and operating the same day has required a day weekly for surgical operations, (and frequently two days have been requisite) on one of these occasions, too, he should be present. Usually the amputation of limbs, extirpation of cancerous breasts, or excision of tumours, come first in the day; then a company of cataract patients — from six even to sixteen have been operated upon in the same hour. In another room are twenty or thirty affected with entropia and pterygia. Of this division he might observe a dozen patients seated along a bench, the surgeon passing from one to another, performing the operations, a native assistant following with needle and sutures, and a second with adhesive plaster and bandage, availing himself of system and classification for the sake of despatch.[87]

At least all this activity brought financial security. Howqua, the leading merchant of the Chinese organization that held the monopoly of foreign trade in Canton, agreed to let Parker use the factory space rent free. Donations came in steadily from the Western missionaries and merchants. Even the British, who formerly had been "an under current against our efforts,"[38] gave generous credit to the American doctor. The superintendent of British trade, Charles Elliot, wrote that Parker was "advancing the great cause of truth and civilization in this large observed portion of the earth by the safest, the wisest, and the most rapid means," and gave one hundred dollars, promising to match this sum each year.[39]

So good were the omens that Parker and some other Western doctors in Canton determined to institutionalize the work on a permanent base: "Viewing with peculiar interest the good effects that seem likely to be produced by medical practice among the Chinese especially as tending to bring about a more social and friendly intercourse between them and foreigners, as well as to diffuse the arts and sciences of Europe and America, and, in the end, to introduce the gospel of our Saviour, in place of the pitiable superstitions by which their minds are now governed, we have resolved to attempt the foundation of a society, to be called the Medical Missionary Society in China."[40] The Society was founded in 1838 and a branch hospital set up in Macao. To absorption with his own medical work Parker added education, personally directing three young Chinese in medical science and English. He had become a busy and successful doctor, but he still wasn't converting the heathen.

The events of the Opium War enveloped Parker and brought a temporary end to his work. The threat of open hostilities between the British and the Chinese had been growing ever since 1834, when the old East India Company monopoly of trade had been broken, and Western merchants started to push for trade with increasing vigor, roaming along China's coastline. Opium, grown in India, was the most profitable commodity of exchange for the teas and silks of China, and it began to enter China in enormous volume; as the demand for opium grew, the Chinese balance of trade grew increasingly unfavorable, and the outflow of silver alarmed the Chinese authorities and forced them to take action. British merchants, too, began to clamor for an end to the restrictive "Canton system" and the monopolies of the hong merchants; in line with their country's developing free-trade principles they demanded fair tariffs, diplomatic equality, and wider opportunities for trade. Finally, in 1839, the Manchu Emperor sent Lin Tse-hsü as his special commissioner to Canton, with instructions to end the opium evil.[41]

When, in March 1839, Lin Tse-hsü blockaded the foreign traders in the Thirteen Factories in order to force them to give up their opium stocks, Parker was trapped with the rest. He remained calm, however, until the increasing belligerence of the Chinese and British authorities finally destroyed the friendly intercourse he had so painfully established, and his beloved hospital suffered. Parker caught the pathos of the moment in a letter to his sister, dated April 14: "How pained was I to be told that the hospital here must be discontinued! Howqua says that I have been very good to his countrymen, better than he to his parents, but from fear of the consequences to himself, he would not rent me his hong any longer; however, he may alter his mind."[42] Nevertheless, Parker continued to work for peace, offering his services to Commissioner Lin Tse-hsü in the gaining of an "honorable treaty" with the Western powers.[43] Though all British subjects and most Americans had retired to Macao and Hong Kong, Parker stayed on in Canton and his medical skills kept him in contact with the Chinese authorities. In the absence of other doctors he worked increasingly in the field of general surgery. He treated the judicial commissioner's son for epilepsy, was invited by Lin Tse-hsü to give a prescription for the cure of opium smokers, and was finally approached by Lin to treat his hernia.

It may seem curious to analyze Sino-Western relations through the treatment of a hernia, but the negotiations between this young American doctor in a beleaguered city and the most powerful official in China are a graphic illustration both of the gulf between the two nations and of the Westerners' hope that the power of technical expertise would draw disparate elements together. Because of the circumstances and the personal nature of the illness Lin Tse-hsü could not approach Parker directly, nor could Parker afford to make a mistake. In a report, Parker described the elaborate ballet that ensued over "case no. 6565. Hernia. Lin Tsihseu [sic], the imperial commissioner." In July, Lin Tse-hsü sent a message through the senior hong merchant Howqua, requesting "medicine to cure him of hernia." Parker politely countered by sending him, in Chinese, an analysis of the complaint with accompanying anatomical diagrams, and suggesting that a truss be fitted. Lin balked at the intimacy of a personal fitting, and was presumably suspicious of the efficacy of this means; so he sent a friend, who had a truss already, to request another one. Parker reiterated that the truss should be fitted by a doctor. Lin, to double-check, then sent an officer of his private staff, who also suffered from a hernia, to have a truss fitted. Parker obliged, and the officer experienced immediate relief. Finally a man appeared who claimed to be Lin Tse-hsü's brother, and just the same size as the Imperial commissioner. A truss fitted to him would surely fit his "brother." At this ingenuity Parker relented, and the truss was fitted.[44]

Parker noted in his report that "the truss sent to his excellency . . . answered tolerably well," that Lin had praised the hospital in public, and that since the happy outcome "many of his suite have been in daily attendance at the hospital." Soon afterwards Lin Tse-hsü drafted a letter to Queen Victoria in which he requested her help in ending the opium trade, and he asked Parker to check it for him.[45] He also asked Parker to translate some paragraphs from Vattel's Law of Nations.[46] There was a chance that Parker's truss might prove equivalent to Schall's telescope, bringing him real influence in China, and his friends urged him on: "Keep up good spirits in your solitude, Dear Doctor, for you are in a fine position."[47]

Parker had learned "to speak and write Chinese to an extent that occasions me gratitude,"[48] and even as open fighting between the British and the Chinese began in November 1839 he remained complacent about his special role as an expert on international law and medical consultant to the Chinese: "I do not know that I should be unsafe to remain if every other foreigner leaves."[49]

By the summer of 1840, however, his inner pendulum had once

more swung to the opposite extreme. Reflecting on the six years that had passed since he had sailed from New York he was aware that "my Christian feelings are much less ardent now than then." What was he really achieving? He felt "unbelief and despair of reaching the souls of those whose bodys are so confidently and unhesitatingly entrusted to my care. I have ceased almost to *expect* to ever instrumentally correct one of these souls from the error of his way." And, worst of all, it was not only Chinese souls that were in danger, it was his whole personal faith. For a dread moment he seems even to have contemplated leaving the Church. "I am less prayerful, less devotional in my habitual frame of spirit. Ah my soul, when will this deterioration end? Shall it be, must it be, in final apostacy!"[50] In this frame of mind, as British warships blockaded Canton, he sailed from China on July 5, 1840, back to an America which he had believed he would never see again.

But China could not be shaken off. The country was in his bones, and like other Westerners who had lived long in that country he felt uneasy on returning to his native land. "I am not at home," he wrote after a few days in America, "my interests are not here, they are in China."[51] He visited his family briefly, then traveled to Washington, where he met President Van Buren and Secretary of State Forsyth and urged the United States government to appoint a minister plenipotentiary to China to act as intermediary between the British and the Chinese. In January 1841 he preached to the Congress and pointed out that God had clearly blessed the Canton hospital, indeed that "the divine blessing has been so signal upon the institution as to attract the notice of the most casual observer."[52]

Life in Washington was hectic but fruitful, and gradually he forgot his worries. He heard John Quincy Adams "plead the cause of the Africans before the Superior Court," attended President Harrison's inauguration, and married "the best young lady in the world," Harriet Webster.[53] The next few months were a triumphal progress as Parker, still "a young man, tall and fine-looking,"[54] met senators, Supreme Court justices, and the wealthy and scholarly communities of Philadelphia, New York and Boston. To popularize his work and raise funds he traveled to Europe, where he talked cordially with the Duke of Sussex and King Louis-Philippe. The Medical Association of Boston passed a special congratulatory resolution for Parker, and praised "the disinterestedness and personal sacrifices of a missionary, who banishes himself from his own country, as Dr. Parker has done, to labor in a foreign land."[55] Disinterested and self-sacrificing as Parker had been, it was also true that China had made the fortune of the poor farm boy from Framingham.

He returned to China in November 1842, hoping (as he had hoped so often before) that "the resuming of my labors offers a favorable opportunity for forming a new epoch in my life, one characterized by more spirituality, more undivided consecration to the great work of making China savingly acquainted with the Bible and its religion."[56] Once again the opportunity eluded him. The China he returned to was very different from the one he had left. Victorious in their war, the British had signed the Treaty of Nanking with China in August 1842: five ports (Amoy, Canton, Foochow, Ningpo, and Shanghai) were to be opened to British residence and trade, consuls were to be stationed in the same five cities, the old Chinese foreign trade monopoly at Canton was abolished, Hong Kong was ceded, a large indemnity was to be paid, and there was to be a moderate and uniform tariff on imports and exports.[57]

The war had left a legacy of bitterness, and many Chinese did not accept the treaty. Resentment was particularly strong in the Canton area, where a profound antiforeignism had been whipped up by the local gentry during the Opium War. They encouraged the myth that the Cantonese had not been defeated by the British, but had been betrayed by their own treacherous rulers, and they spread stories that showed the Westerners to be an economic and sexual threat. "We shall hack, we shall kill, we shall destroy all of you," ran a gentry placard of 1841. "We shall do our best to flay off your skins and eat your flesh. Let it be now known that we shall massacre you with cruel ferocity."[58] This was still Cantonese rather than widespread Chinese xenophobia, but it was dangerous enough. Conditions remained so unsettled that foreigners, despite the treaty provisions,

Peter Parker at Canton in the 1840's. The Chinese doctor commencing an eye operation is Parker's pupil Kwan Ato. Oil painting by Lamqua, uncle to Kwan Ato. *Courtesy Yale Medical Library.*

could not enter Canton city, and even the factory area was not safe. Savage rioting broke out in December 1842, and Mrs. Parker, who had accompanied her husband to Canton, had to be hurried off to safety as mobs burned and looted the factories. Rioting, often followed by atrocities, recurred throughout the 1840's.

Undeterred, Parker labored on in his hospital, but it brought him less satisfaction than it had before: "God has mercifully reinstated me in my former sphere of usefulness, where I have more work than any one mortal can perform. Never were my professional services sought with more avidity than now. Officers of high distinction seek them, and crowds of all classes; but oh, how I long to be laboring directly for the soul's salvation!"[59] Even his personal devotions suffered and he again had attacks of serious depression from his "neglect of fasting and prayer," and his "icy heart and apathetic spirit."[60]

Parker was now famous, and he paid the penalties. Instead of being able to escape medicine and work for Chinese souls, his language abilities ironically brought him new duties which gave him no time for souls and precious little even for medicine. For in 1844 Caleb Cushing, first minister plenipotentiary from the United States to China, made Parker secretary and interpreter to the United States Mission, though Parker still did not know enough Chinese to write formal documents — he had to speak his Chinese translation aloud while his assistant, who knew no English, wrote it down.[61] Despite these difficulties, Parker accepted the post (which carried a salary of $1,500 plus expenses). He regretted "the temporary suspension of my direct missionary work,"[62] but labored busily with Cushing and Ch'i-ying on drawing up the Treaty of Wanghia. By this treaty the United States, without firing a shot, partook of all the gains won by the British in 1842.[63]

The negotiations were time-consuming and complex, and the "direct missionary work," as Parker knew, was indeed long suspended. But he was absolutely stunned by the American Board's decision in 1845 that in view of the nature of his work they felt that they should no longer support him, and there is real bitterness in his reply to the committee: "Suddenly and unexpectedly deprived of a foundation for support, as permanent, I had supposed, as anything earthly could be, I had no alternative but to seek such means as were available for prosecuting my labors."[64] A friend had warned him that something like this might happen and had urged him to distribute more tracts among the patients he treated, telling them from what mortal sources their blessings came. "You owe it to the patrons, and the Society which supports the hospital, thus to elevate their character for good deeds in the eyes of the Chinese, and by that means advance the cause. But I fear your dilatoriness will retard so desirable a means of action."[65] Friends and admirers of Parker's hurried to his defense, and the issue was joined between those who felt that "the surgeon is himself a preacher and makes his hospital a chapel"[66] and those who had decided that "the experience of the past in more than one or two missions is fitted to awaken doubts as to the value of medical practice as an adjunct of the gospel."[67]

Parker kept largely aloof from these arguments, and was increasingly involved in diplomatic affairs, which grew more complex as trade and missionary activity spread from Canton to the new treaty ports. He was confirmed in his position as Secretary to the United States Mission in 1845 by Secretary of State Buchanan, and in 1846 was made chargé d'affaires of the United States legation.

In this new office he played some part in calming the 1846 riots and began to grow less tolerant of the Chinese, becoming an enthusiastic supporter of the firm measures being taken by the British to guarantee the rights and safety of foreign nationals in China.[68] His new duties increased his prestige and wealth. He paid off loans incurred as a student from the American Education Society, and like the great everywhere began to receive fulsome flattery from his suppliants. "It has often occurred to me," wrote one such, "that you have, in your missionary effort in China, pursued the same course, in one respect, which our Saviour pursued when he came on his mission of love into our world. He commenced with healing the sick, and proving himself the sympathizing friend of those to whom he was to preach glad tidings."[69] It is unlikely that the analogy cheered Parker much. He was constantly worried by his religious shortcomings and desperately overworked, though he was still a courageous medical experimenter and had the foresight to see the benefits of anesthesia, which he introduced to China in 1847.[70] On his fiftieth birthday, having just survived a shipwreck in which many of his companions were drowned, he was able to record with justifiable pride that 52,500 Chinese had been treated in his hospital and that he had been "permitted to preach the gospel of salvation" to tens of thousands of these.[71] But this had not been the real preaching he desired; it involved mainly the distributing of Christian tracts and the murmuring of a few words of goodwill to his patients.

When the new United States President, Franklin Pierce, appointed Robert McLane as Commissioner to China, Parker was chosen to accompany a mission to Peking to seek treaty revision. The negotiations were exhausting and fruitless, and Parker had a breakdown that forced him to Macao for recuperation. He reflected on his first arrival twenty years before and how "then, with me, all was vigor, and hope was buoyant; now I am like a bow too long bent, or like a spent ball; and unless a change of climate and rest for a time shall restore my wonted energy, my work, I fear is nearly done."[72] In 1855 he resigned from his positions and returned to the United States. But his services were still needed, and at the request of President Pierce he returned to China in 1856 as United States Commissioner, with instructions to press for the right of a United States diplomatic representative to reside in Peking and for "the unlimited extension of our trade."[73] Parker's own goals were even broader: to prevail on the Manchu court "to modify its ancient policy so as to afford a government that shall meet the *popular* demand and correspond to the progress of the nineteenth century." Then the current rebellion would end and be followed by "the inauguration of more extended social, commercial, political, and friendly foreign intercourse with that empire, immense in extent of territory and population and inexhaustible in commercial resources."[74] Parker was anxious to forge a "Triple Alliance" with Britain and France in order to bring effective pressure to bear on the Chinese. But the British diplomat, Sir John Bowring, thought Parker's plans "visionary and impracticable," and did all he could to sabotage Parker's mission. He wrote to the Foreign Office that "I anticipate his utter failure, and fear the step he proposes to take will in no respect forward the common object."[75]

Parker not only did fail to gain any of his objectives, but his intransigence also made new enemies. American diplomatic colleagues found him bumptious and vacillating by turns.[76] Chinese officials described him variously as "crafty," "resentful," and "stubbornly adamant," while the Emperor knew of his bellicosity and concluded that "his mentality is inscrutable."[77] The French chargé d'affaires sketched him as "a large man, aged about fifty, with a heavy and painful step, a bulky figure, vulgar features, and a penetrating mind, sly and subtle."[78]

Frustration and unpopularity exacerbated the sourness that Parker had begun to feel for the Chinese. He wrote that they showed "the same disposition to evade obligations, misrepresent facts, and erroneously interpret treaty stipulations, which for years has characterized the correspondence of Imperial Commissioners."[79] Finally he urged that his government should occupy the island of Taiwan to balance Britain's bases in Singapore and Hong Kong: "It is much to be hoped that the Govt. of the U.S. may not *shrink* from the *action* which the interests of humanity, civilization, navigation and commerce impose upon it in relation to Tai-wan, particularly the southeastern portion of it, at present inhabited by savages."[80] Alarmed at his attitude, President Pierce ordered him recalled in April 1857.[81] Parker lived on in retirement in the United States for over thirty years. He died at the age of eighty-four in 1888, the year of the fiftieth anniversary of the founding of the Medical Missionary Society in China. In those fifty years about one million Chinese patients had been treated in the various medical institutions under the society, scores of important medical works had been translated, and dozens of Chinese doctors trained in Western medicine.[82] But during the same period the British and the French had fought two wars with China, staked out claims on China's coast and inland waterways, and faced a series of crises stemming from anti-Western outrages.

In 1837, shortly after arriving in China, Parker had criticized the failures and shortcomings of his Jesuit predecessors: "Had pure Christianity been first introduced we have reason to believe the gospel of the dear Redeemer had been enjoyed not only in Japan but extensively in China and throughout the Oriental world. But now an incalculable amount of prejudice and of downright enmity to the cross must be overcome before the people of the East will listen to the message of the ambassador of heaven."[83] It was a harsh judgment, and a badly oversimplified one. Like the Jesuits, Parker had to learn the hard way that in China even the most precisely calculated means did not necessarily lead to the desired ends. He, who had labored so long at medicine and language in order to make China "free through the Lord of Glory," ended up enslaved by his own skills and incontinently angered by those he had meant to love.

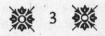

WARD *and* GORDON:

Glorious Days of Looting

Not every Western adviser in China had a religious spur. There were also men who simply had a love of travel and excitement in their bones, adventurers who roamed the world to take what it would give. Such a man was Frederick Townsend Ward, born near the docks in Salem, Massachusetts, on November 29, 1831.

It was not an environment to encourage the contemplative life. "The wharves in Salem in those days," a contemporary recalled, "were lined with ship chandlers' and sail-makers' shops, warehouses, and counting rooms, the sailmakers sitting cross-legged like Turks, sewing the sails with thimbles fastened into the middle of their palm, while the odor of tar and canvas pervaded the premises. The old wharf and sail lofts that fronted the street were favorite resorts of my childhood days and I was never so happy as when allowed to wander about on the old wharf fascinated in watching the loading and unloading of ships that had rounded the point and come lumbering into port."[1]

As a child Ward was mischievous, and as an adolescent, restless. He tried unsuccessfully to get into the military academy at West Point, and then to run away from home to fight in the Mexican War. When he was only fifteen, his father gave up trying to restrain him and let him ship out as a second mate on the clipper *Hamilton*, captained by a relative and bound for China.

Returning from China in the autumn of 1847, he entered a military school in Vermont, where he got whatever book knowledge of military tactics he was later to use. But money was short in his family at that time, and he did not graduate. In 1849 he shipped out again, this time as a first mate. From 1849 to 1858 he wandered the world impatiently searching for wealth and adventure. As he later told the American Minister to China, Anson Burlingame, he "went to sea when a boy, became mate of a ship, and then was a Texas ranger, Californian gold-miner, instructor in the Mexican service, was with Walker [fighting in Central America] — for which he was outlawed by his government — [and] at the Crimea [as an officer in the French army]."[2] Though this account is neither strictly chronological, nor probably accurate, it shows that Ward had few scruples about the activities he undertook, or the causes in which he enlisted.

After ten years of wandering, Ward returned home to try a more normal life. He took a job in his father's office in New York as a ship broker, but he found it too dull and sailed once more for China, reaching Shanghai in the fall of 1859. The China he happened upon was a country in chaos, ravaged by a great rebellion whose leaders called themselves Taipings.

These leaders had developed their power in the southern provinces of Kwangtung and Kwangsi in the late 1840's, drawing recruits from Hakka and Miao minority groups, from secret societies, from pirates driven inland by British patrol vessels jealously guarding the new treaty ports, from impoverished miners and peasants, and from the drifting population on the waterways, unemployed now that the focus of the opium trade had swung from Canton up to Shanghai and the Yangtze valley. The apathy and ineffectualness of the local Ch'ing officials had given the rebel band the opportunity to grow to some thirty thousand men by 1850. Two years later the rebels struck north, gathering hundreds of thousands of recruits along the way. In 1853, after a series of shattering victories, they seized the great city of Nanking and even threatened Peking itself.[3]

At the time of Ward's arrival in Shanghai they were still firmly entrenched in the Yangtze valley, and had routed all the Ch'ing forces sent against them. As rebels, they were a new phenomenon in Chinese history, unlike the peasant rebel armies of the past. Their leader, Hung Hsiu-ch'üan, had gleaned the elements of Christianity from a Protestant missionary pamphlet and had learned in a mystical vision that he was the younger brother of Jesus Christ. His mission, he believed, was to establish the "Heavenly Kingdom of Great Peace" (T'ai-p'ing t'ien-kuo) in China and bring his people back to knowledge of the true God. "My hand now holds both in heaven and earth the power to punish and kill," he wrote; "to slay the depraved, and spare the upright; to relieve the people's distress. My eyes survey from the North to the South beyond the rivers and mountains; my voice is heard from East to West, to the tracts of the sun and the moon."[4]

Hung's troops followed him with fanatical loyalty and were subject to iron discipline. As they advanced across the country all those who resisted were slaughtered, those who surrendered were spared. Hung's followers had to obey the dictates of his religion, which were adapted from the Ten Commandments. The sexes were segregated, opium smoking was forbidden. Land was shared and all surplus paid into a common treasury. Civil service examinations were instituted, based, not on the Confucian canon, but on the new doctrines.[5]

Western observers, initially fascinated by these rebels and sympathetic to their Christian aspirations, felt it would be no misfortune if the Taipings overthrew the Ch'ing dynasty. A British Protestant in 1853 pointed out four "advantages which will accrue to China from success on the side of the insurgents": China would be opened to the dissemination of the scriptures, idolatry would be firmly put down, opium traffic would be stopped, and "China will be fully opened to our commerce, our science, our curiosity, and all the influences of our civilization."[6] A Catholic missionary, though finding the Taiping religion "a compilation of doctrinal rhapsodies, rather than the adoption of a religion transmitted by others," still saw the rebels "as avengers of their nationality" and noted "that they treated me with respect."[7] And these sentiments were generally echoed at home. Marx and Engels in articles they sent to the *New York Daily Tribune* from London wrote, "In short, instead of moralizing on the horrible atrocities of the Chinese, as the chivalrous British Press does, we had better recognize that this is a war *pro aris et focis* [for faith and hearth], a popular war for the maintenance of Chinese nationality, with all its overbearing prejudice, stupidity, learned ignorance, and pedantic barbarism if you like, but yet a popular war."[8]

Desperate to contain the Taipings, the Ch'ing dynasty reluctantly condoned the development of regional armies. These armies were controlled and led by powerful officials in central China; the soldiers were usually peasants, with strong local allegiances, owing loyalty only to their own commanders. Unlike the regular Manchu forces, they were well trained and even well paid as their commanders collected the traditional land taxes and instituted new taxes on commerce, bypassing the national government treasury. Simply to preserve itself, the Ch'ing dynasty had had to delegate enormous powers to these officials. Nor was this the only trouble confronting the Court; other rebellions broke out in the north and west of China; while at the same time the Western powers were brusquely demanding first implementation and then expansion of the terms of the Treaty of Nanking. China's intransigence in this regard precipitated the second Anglo-Chinese War in the late 1850's, and in 1860 after a British representative had been imprisoned and some of his entourage killed, allied forces occupied Peking. On the orders of Lord Elgin, the great Summer Palace of the Manchus, parts of which had been designed in the eighteenth century by Jesuits, was burned to the ground; the Emperor fled. It seemed that the Ch'ing dynasty, wracked by domestic rebellions and invaded by the West, would surely fall.[9]

Stifled by an office in New York, Ward thankfully turned to this disputed China of 1859. It was just the place he had been seeking, one that offered enormous opportunities to a young adventurer. Only twenty-seven years old, "quick, nervous and animated in his movements, and his thick raven hair hanging over his shoulders like an

Indian's,"[10] he must have seemed an odd-looking figure against a Chinese backdrop. He immediately set about finding employment. His first post was as a mate on a Yangtze steamer serving local trade. When Taiping forces threatened Shanghai in the spring of 1860, he transferred to be "first officer of the American-built Gun-Boàt 'Confucius', commanded by an Englishman named Gough. The steamer was one of a considerable fleet of larger and smaller craft extemporized to meet the exigency by the business-men of Shanghai, whose mouth-piece in dealing with the Imperial Government was Taki, a native Banker of great prominence and wealth."[11]

Ward decided to exploit the situation. In May 1860 he approached Taki with the following proposal: why shouldn't the Shanghai merchants, whose lives and property were threatened, form a privately financed anti-Taiping army under Ward's command? After some consultation, Taki agreed to this novel and daring scheme. The Chinese merchants contracted to pay Ward $100 a month for each enlisted man, $600 a month for officers, and to pay a lump sum for every town captured, on a sliding scale from $45,000 to $133,000 according to the size of the town concerned. The merchants also agreed to furnish food for Ward's force and funds with which he could buy arms.

In the force itself, Ward planned to use Chinese only as guides and interpreters, raising his troops elsewhere. This decision was in line with the feeling common among treaty-port Westerners that the Chinese were cowardly and inferior beings. As one young English officer in Hong Kong at this time observed: "I am afraid we bully them a good deal. If you are walking about and a Chinaman comes in your way, it is customary to knock his hat off, or dig him in the ribs with an umbrella. I thought it a shame, and remonstrated with the fellow who was with me today for treating a poor beggar of a Chinaman in this way; but he assured me that if you make way for them they swagger and come in your way purposely. The French soldiers treat them even more roughly than we do."[12] The result of this attitude was that a Westerner considered any European to be superior in battle to ten or fifteen Chinese soldiers, a view common to

Westerners even in the present century. Ward would learn his lesson much sooner.

Having chosen two lieutenants, Edward Forrester (who had been with Ward in Central America) and Henry Andrea Burgevine (a Southerner who, like Ward himself, had arrived in China as the first mate on a clipper ship), Ward began to comb the Shanghai waterfront for recruits. In those days, as many as three hundred ships could be found anchored in the harbor; so it was not a difficult matter to induce layover sailors and navy deserters into joining a high-paying military adventure. Having given three weeks' training to a motley force of about two hundred men, Ward decided to attack Sungkiang, a walled town held by the Taiping forces, about thirty miles southwest of Shanghai. With no artillery to breach the walls, he counted on surprise to bring him victory. But, as Ward was to recount later, his men, by drinking all night, had raised "such a hell of a noise," that the Taipings were more than ready for them. Ward was forced to retreat with heavy losses and pay off his force. His first attempt to form his own army in China had ended in fiasco.[13]

Undaunted, he returned immediately to Shanghai and, despite the ridicule of the foreign community, began recruiting a new force, this time on a more rational basis. First he accepted the service of Vincente Macanaya, a young Filipino soldier of fortune with a great following among the Manilamen on the docks of Shanghai. Macanaya was able to bring with him about two hundred of his followers. To these Ward added half a dozen Western drillmasters (mostly deserters from the British navy) and a small amount of artillery. By the middle of July 1860, he was back in front of the walls of Sungkiang. With the help of accurate artillery fire, and after fierce hand-to-hand fighting with the Taiping troops, the city was taken.

The reward money for the capture of Sungkiang and the possibility of future looting drew more recruits from the Shanghai waterfront. With his newly bolstered force and his newly bolstered confidence, Ward decided to attack Tsingpu, a larger city in Taiping hands. But he had overestimated the abilities of his troops. At Tsingpu he found a well-armed Taiping force behind strong walls, led by another European mercenary, an ex-British first lieutenant named Savage. Ward's force was mauled in two assaults, and he himself was badly wounded. He lost his artillery, his gunboats and his entire provision train. It was the worst defeat of his career in China, and when he returned to Shanghai to rebuild his army, he was met with hostility and scorn. The Shanghai *North China Herald* commented in August 1860: "The first and best item . . . is the utter defeat of Ward and his men before Tsingpu. This notorious man has been brought down to Shanghai, not, as was hoped, dead, but severely wounded in the mouth, one side and one leg. . . . He managed to drag his carcass out of danger, but several of his valourous blacks were killed or wounded. . . . It seems astonishing that Ward should be allowed to remain unpunished, and yet not a hint is given that any measures will be taken against him."[14]

It seemed that Ward's China career was finished. Taki was unwilling to support him further. The commander of the British naval forces, Admiral James Hope, was furious that Ward had encouraged his sailors to desert. The foreign community in Shanghai was openly contemptuous. Ward was still without an army and recovering from his wounds when, on May 19, 1861, he was arrested by Admiral Hope for having defied the Allied declaration of neutrality in the civil war. At his court hearing, Ward insisted he was a naturalized subject of the Ch'ing government, but this claim was untrue and Hope ignored it, imprisoning him on board his ship the *Chesapeake*. In June 1861, the *North China Herald* noted: "[Ward's] force is now disbanded. Some have probably suffered capital punishment at the hands of the Chinese, some have fallen in action, some are expiating their offences against our laws in common jails, and some few have escaped it is hoped with sufficient examples before them never to again engage in such an illegitimate mode of earning a livelihood as enrolling themselves in such disreputable ranks as those of a Chinese Foreign Legion."[15]

Yet the self-righteous hostility of most Westerners in China toward Ward hardly reflected the realities of their position. For, like Ward, the Western powers were "adventurers." They had arrived by sea and settled, by means of guile and coercion, onto the Chinese coast. Moreover, their diplomatic and military representatives had great freedom of action since it took so long for them to request or receive instructions from their home governments. Often they were out to get what they could for themselves or their own countries by any means possible, and accordingly their loyalties went not to the Ch'ing dynasty but to whatever groups in China best promised to forward their interests. The constant friction inherent in this situation had led twice in thirty years to open warfare with the Chinese government. From their point of view the Ch'ing had "paid" them well enough, but they would have been willing to support the Taipings, had the Taipings offered them greater benefits. In addition, early missionary accounts of the Taiping's "Christianity," had impressed most Westerners, and positive reports of their discipline and order (order being one thing congenial to trade) had also influenced Western public opinion.

The Westerners were further encouraged when a new Taiping leader, Hung Jen-kan, came to the forefront in 1859. Hung Jen-kan tried to bring the Taiping religion closer to conventional Protestant tenets and to reestablish contact with the Western powers. He drew up an ambitious program of "modernization," planning to introduce railroads, post offices, banks and insurance to the rebel-held areas.[16] But Hung Jen-kan lost out in a power struggle among rebel leaders, and in 1860 fresh Taiping forces began to approach and menace Shanghai, spreading chaos in the surrounding areas and prohibiting trade in opium. Western opinion began slowly to undergo a change. This change was indirectly linked to the successful ratification of the Treaty of Tientsin in 1860, which gave the Western powers the right to open new treaty ports and to trade along the Yangtze River (much of which was controlled by the Taipings). With these new rights, Westerners began to feel that it was, in fact, the Taipings who were delaying the Western advance and endangering Western economic interests in Shanghai. The stated Western policy of "neutrality" in the Chinese civil war came slowly and fitfully to be an active "neutrality" in favor of a quiescent China under the Ch'ing dynasty. The

Ch'ing, in turn, began unwillingly to cooperate. "It is just that there is a danger (fear) that if we do not make them our allies they may be used by the rebels. The harm in that would be incalculable," said Prince Kung, new chief minister of the central government.[17]

But in May 1861, Ward, under arrest in a cabin on the *Chesapeake*, had yet to feel the effects of this change in policy. Contriving to escape dramatically — leaping at night through a porthole, and being whisked away by a waiting junk to cries of "man overboard" — his only recourse was to hide out with the remnants of his Sungkiang garrison. Later that summer Admiral Hope, now of a different mind, having visited the Taipings in person in an unsuccessful attempt to obtain a guarantee for the security of Shanghai, invited Ward and his lieutenants to a conference on board the *Chesapeake*, assuring them of safe conduct. At this conference, Ward offered the admiral a new plan. In his escapades he had learned from the Taipings themselves that Chinese soldiers, well armed, well trained, and well led, made fierce fighters. Thus "he abandoned the enlistment of deserters and turned his attention to recruiting a native force to be commanded by European officers and patiently drilled in the European School of Arms." This was a revolutionary, and to Westerners in Shanghai a laughable, project. In return, the admiral "winked at the fact that there were still a number of British deserters employed as drillmasters at Sungkiang," where Forrester and Burgevine had held together a nucleus of the old force during Ward's imprisonment.[18]

Ward worked fast and efficiently with his new Chinese recruits, who were mostly local Kiangsu men. "After a little training they learned their drill thoroughly, became fairly good marksmen and knew how to handle and care for their English muskets and Prussian rifles. Commands were given in English. The Chinese readily learned these commands, and the bugle calls. Artillery practice baffled them at first, but after some instruction they made rapid progress in it and before they were ready to take the field many of them had become expert gunners. . . . The whole force was well-clad and well-equipped. It wore a uniform something like that of the Zouaves or the British Sikhs."[19] The most promising of the Chinese soldiers were made noncommissioned officers. The Manilamen were brought up to their former strength, and Ward used them as his personal bodyguard. In the autumn the new army won its first victories. Admiral Hope was so impressed that he agreed to keep Ward supplied with arms, artillery and ammunition. By winter 1861 Ward had a force of about three thousand men under his command, with adequate artillery, steamers for transport, and the active support of the British authorities in the area.

His former Shanghai critics were now all behind him. "The Whilom *rowdie* companion of *ci-devant* General Walker, of Nicaraguan memory," a Western supporter of the Taipings wrote sarcastically, "mercenary leader of a band of Anglo-Saxon freebooters in Manchoo pay, and sometime fugitive from English marines sent to weed his ruffians of their countrymen, suddenly became the friend and ally of the British and French Admirals, Generals, and Consuls. The surprise of Ward can only have been equalled by his gratification upon finding his very questionable presence, and still more doubtful pursuits, patronized and imitated. No doubt, at first he felt considerably elated and vastly astonished at the idea of filibustering having become such an honorable and recognized profession."[20]

In December 1861 the Taipings captured the treaty port of Ningpo, and Admiral Hope decided to take strong action. He visited the rebel capital of Nanking, and demanded guarantees that other treaty ports would not be attacked. Since he, in turn, refused to give any guarantees that the Manchus might not use the treaty ports as military bases, the Taipings rejected his demands. In January 1862 they advanced again on Shanghai, with the apparent intention of cutting off supplies and stirring up a rising inside the city. Admiral Hope ordered British and French forces to cooperate with Ward's army, and some Ch'ing troops, in clearing a thirty-mile zone around Shanghai. To justify his total abandonment of the British "neutrality" policy, Hope declared that "these Rebels are Revolters not only against the Emperor, but against all laws human and Divine, and it seems quite right to keep them away from the Treaty Ports."[21] It was within this zone that Ward's trained Chinese force, later named the "Ever-Victorious Army" by the Chinese government, did its fighting, normally as an auxiliary to British, French and Ch'ing troops.

Ward proved a brave and effective leader of men within the limits of his opportunities. The governor of Kiangsu, Li Hung-chang, wrote that "Ward who valiantly defends [Sungkiang] and [Tsingpu], is indeed the most vigorous of all [the foreigners]. Although until now he has not yet shaved his hair or called at my humble residence, I have no time to quarrel with foreigners over such a little ceremonial matter."[22]

Ward affected an extreme casualness in action. He "wore, in his brief military life, no uniform or insignia of rank, the European dress to which he adhered in battle sufficiently distinguishing him from his men, and he was almost always seen either in the close-fitting English frock-coat which came in with Prince Albert, or in the loose, blue serge tunic much worn by residents of the tropics." He always stood out in battle and, as one observer recalled, "I never saw Ward with a sword or any arm; he wore ordinary clothes, — a thick, short cape, and a hood, and carried a stick in his hand, and generally a Manila cheroot in his mouth."[23] The use of this "stick" (actually a riding crop) and his own bravery nourished among his men a feeling of his invincibility, despite the several wounds he had received.

Moreover, in spite of the thinness of his military training, Ward understood the kind of tactics that were needed in the fighting around Shanghai. This area was a particularly difficult one. As a contemporary British journalist described the situation:

It is simply impossible to seize the cunning, cruel cowards [the Taipings], in the labyrinthine lanes of the Delta. All around they have spies on our movements, and know, as well as we do what these are, so they are comparatively safe in continuing their incendiary tactics within a few hundred yards of our column; then off they escape through ditches and across fields, where it is impossible to get at them. This the rascals are perfectly aware of, especially if pursued by foreign soldiers, encumbered with their heavy equipment. Hunting grasshoppers in a hay-field with fox-hounds would be a more sensible occupation than sending soldiers about a country intersected by a network of creeks, in the expectancy of catching swift-footed and slippery-skinned Tai-pings.[24]

Ward made every attempt to acquire steamships and pontoons to give his troops mobility along, and control of, the waterways. In addition, through careful training of his Chinese troops and the judicious use of as much artillery as he could get his hands on, he tried to minimize these disadvantages. It was this use of the gunboat and artillery which Ward's successor Gordon was to pick up and employ to such effect.

The war itself was fought with great cruelty, savagery, and callousness on both sides. Ward's lieutenant, Edward Forrester, recalled the moment when Tsingpu was lost to the Taipings and he was captured: "I suddenly realized that the insurgents were in possession and were making quick work of my people. Borne aloft over their front ranks were the heads of my officers fixed on spears. . . . The rebels were showing no quarter and were fighting like demons. In an incredibly short time my men were entirely annihilated."[25] The city was retaken by government forces, he added, and Li Hung-chang, "when told that there were a great number of high rebel officials among the prisoners, expressed much satisfaction at their capture. He sent the mayor of Sung-Kiang to me the next day with full authority 'to cut, kill or take away those captured.' The scene that followed surpasses description. So many hundreds were beheaded that the streets again ran with blood; but even the European officers in my command agreed that the measure was necessary in dealing with such fanatics."[26]

A British report of one battle states that "the rebels ran from the fortifications and came to a stand in the main street. . . . Upon this, the field-piece from the "Impérieuse," in charge of Lieutenants Stuart and Richardson, swept them down with grape and canister shot; after this their retreat became a flight, when the party of marines and Chinese detached to cut them off did considerable execution, some 900 or 1,000 having been killed and wounded. .... After all was over, the village was set on fire, and the foreign troops embarked for Shanghai."[27] A reporter for the *China Mail* lyrically recounted another attack: "The scene was now most picturesque. A shell had set fire to part of the city close at hand; the early morning sun was shining pleasantly upon the fields, rich with ungathered crops, and the French band played as the troops scaled the walls."[28]

Ward and his men, despite official recognition of their role, remained an independent band of adventurers out for plunder. Plunder also was the preoccupation of both the regular British and French troops as well as the troops of the Ch'ing armies. One newspaper, reporting on the aftermath of an allied expedition to which Ward's Ever-Victorious Army was attached, stated:

As the houses were ransacked, great quantities of valuable jewels, gold, silver, dollars, and costly dresses were found, which was fair loot to the officers and men. One blue-jacket found 1,600 dollars, and several soldiers upwards of 500 each, while many picked up gold bangles, earrings, and other ornaments and pearls set with precious stones. It was a glorious day of looting for everybody, and we hear that one party, who discovered the Ti-ping treasury chest with several thousand dollars in it, after loading himself to his heart's content, was obliged to give some of them away to lighten his pockets, which were heavier than he could well bear — a marked case of *l'embarras des richesses*. The rebel stud of ponies was well supplied also, and many of the soldiers rode back with their booty.[29]

Ward was doing well out of the war, but he could see that his position with the foreign community — which had tried to run him out of town only one year before — was tenuous. Accordingly he moved with great skill to consolidate his position with the Chinese. In February 1862 the governor of Kiangsu reported that "Ward has informed the Taotai and the American Consul that he wishes to become a Chinese subject and change to Chinese dress."³⁰ The following month Ward married Chang Mei, the daughter of Taki, the Shanghai banker who had helped to finance his forces. The marriage ceremony was carried through in Chinese style, with Ward arriving on horseback dressed in his Chinese official robes. Communication between bride and groom must have proved difficult, since Taki knew only "pidgin" English and his daughter probably knew none at all, while Ward had only a smattering of spoken Chinese and knew nothing of the written characters.

Ward returned to the battlefield soon after the wedding, having spent little time with his bride. It is unlikely that this was any marriage of love; it appears, rather, to have been a practical step on Ward's part to bind himself closer to the Chinese and to gain direct financial backing from his father-in-law. The two men went into business together, and by the spring of 1862 Ward had become "joint owner with Taki of two American-built gun-boats. And, with other gun-boats chartered by them . . . he was now a Chinese Admiral as well — fitted out an expedition against the river pirates."³¹

By making these very graphic gestures, Ward consciously mortgaged himself to the Chinese. He had realized that to prove his loyalty to his Chinese employers he should fit himself as much as possible into the Chinese system. On March 17, 1862, he and his lieutenant, Burgevine, were naturalized as Chinese citizens; both received the button of the fourth class in the Chinese official hierarchy, and Ward was also granted the honor of wearing a Peacock's feather. Only nine days later both men were awarded the button of the third class.³² Having won a series of victories near Shanghai, Ward also received the rank of brigadier general in the Chinese army. It was at this time that his force received by Imperial decree the title Ever-Victorious Army. In May 1862 Governor Li Hung-chang was told by the Emperor that he should "fraternize" with "Ward and others who seek both fame and fortune," and go "even to the expense of making small rewards."³³

In addition to the satisfaction of becoming a general, an admiral,

Frederick Townsend Ward, oil painting by an unknown Chinese artist, and his wife Chang Mei, daughter of the Shanghai financier Taki. *Courtesy the Essex Institute, Salem, Massachusetts.*

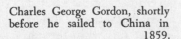
Charles George Gordon, shortly before he sailed to China in 1859.

and an official in the Chinese hierarchy, Ward's "small rewards" fo
loyalty included his becoming a rich man. But of all the benefits h(
received, the most important, and least tangible, was the new statu
he gained both among the Chinese and in the Western communit)
in China. On the Chinese side, the governor of Kiangsu, Li Hung
chang, badly overestimating Ward's influence with foreigners, com
mented that "Ward commands enough authority to control th(
foreigners in Shanghai, and he is quite friendly with me. . . . Ward
is indeed brave in action, and he possesses all sorts of foreign
weapons. Recently I, Hung-chang, have devoted all my attention to
making friends with him, in order to get the friendship of various
nations through that one individual."[34]

Though Ward did not control the foreign community in Shanghai, it was true, ironically enough, that by becoming "Chinese" his
status in the foreign community increased enormously. By the summer of 1862, this restless ex-first-mate, gold-miner and soldier of
fortune could mix not only with the high levels of Chinese officialdom, but with foreign consuls, merchants, and ministers (though he
felt more at home in his military camp at Sungkiang). As with all
men exiled from their homes, this sort of recognition must have been
extremely important to him, and he used his money to improve his
image. The American Minister to China, Anson Burlingame, wrote
to President Lincoln:

> General Ward was a man of great wealth, and in a letter to
> me, the last probably he ever wrote, he proposed through me to
> contribute ten thousand taels to the government of the United
> States, to aid in maintaining the Union, but before I could
> respond to his patriotic letter he died. Let this wish, though
> unexecuted, find worthy record in the archives of his native
> land, to show that neither self-exile nor foreign service, nor the
> incidents of a stormy life, could extinguish from the breast of
> this wandering child of the Republic the fires of a truly loyal
> heart.[35]

By the summer of 1862, Ward had more than three thousand men under his command, as well as trench mortars and artillery. His new-found status had gone to his head, and he began thinking in more grandiose terms. He drew up plans to expand his force to twenty-five thousand men and to take Soochow, a key city in Taiping hands beyond the thirty-mile zone. On August 14, 1862, he had an interview with Li Hung-chang, in which he discussed the rebel capital of Nanking itself, besieged for years by large Imperial forces. As Li reported their conversation to Tseng Kuo-fan, the commander of the troops in front of Nanking and creator of the provincial Chinese armies which were slowly strangling the rebels: "Ward has seen me today, and urges me to transfer him to help attack [Nanking]. He says that he could arrive there in three days, build forts in three days, and recover the city in another three days — without fail. After victory, the wealth and property in the city would be equally shared with the Government's troops; and so forth."[36] But on September 21, 1862, while attacking Tzeki, ten miles northwest of Ningpo, Ward, standing in full view surveying the position, "put his hand suddenly to his abdomen and exclaimed, 'I have been hit.' "[37] He died that night, and received the full honors of a Chinese general at his burial. His dog, "a great shaggy black-and-white creature" which died a few days later, was buried near him.[38]

Though Ward was only thirty years old when he died, he had managed to forge for himself, in a chaotic time and by whatever methods were at hand, a personal and financial success of imposing stature. He had, as well, managed for the first time to train Chinese troops to fight in the more effective European manner; had provided a model for Li Hung-chang's own Huai army; had impressed Li with the possibility of China's strengthening herself along Western lines without relying on foreign nations and foreign troops; had helped to clear a thirty-mile radius around Shanghai of Taiping rebels; and had built up the foundations of a force that was to be more effectively used by his famous successor, Gordon. Yet, in the overall picture, the results had been small. He had defended a city of more importance to foreign interests than to the Chinese. He had, even then, lost many battles, and the Taiping rebels soon returned to the areas he had "cleared." He had not truly altered the course of the civil war which was being decided around the rebel capital of Nanking by Chinese troops without any foreign advisers. And he had died before having a chance to enjoy what he had won for himself.

"Poor old Ward," one young British officer wrote home to his mother on visiting Sungkiang, "is buried here in Chinese fashion — his coffin over-ground. This place was his headquarters. He came out to China as mate of a ship, outlawed from America, and has died worth a million and a half. He was often wounded, and people had the idea he could not be shot."[39]

*   *   *

As the merchants of Shanghai turned to Ward to protect their city, an expedition of 41 warships, 143 troop transports, and 16,800 British, French, Sikh and Indian troops, was advancing on Peking to enforce the Treaty of Tientsin and place Western resident ministers in the capital of the Central Kingdom. When the Chinese executed some twenty captured members of the allied expedition, Lord Elgin, in October 1860, ordered the destruction of the Ch'ing Emperor's magnificent summer palace just to the northwest of Peking.

Charles George Gordon, a young captain of the British Royal Engineers, helping to direct the destruction of that complex of two hundred buildings, wrote home to his mother:

[We] went out, and, after pillaging it, burned the whole place, destroying in a Vandal-like manner most valuable property which would not be replaced for four millions. We got upwards of £48 a-piece prize money before we went out here; and although I have not as much as many, I have done well.

The people are civil, but I think the grandees hate us, as they must after what we did to the Palace. You can scarcely imagine the beauty and magnificence of the places we burnt. It made one's heart sore to burn them; in fact, these palaces were so large, and we were so pressed for time, that we could not plunder them carefully. Quantities of gold ornaments were burnt, considered as brass. It was wretchedly demoralizing work for an army. Every body was wild for plunder.[40]

But a month later, a bored Gordon wrote to his sister: "My Dear Augusta, we are all of us getting sick of Pekin, a dirtier town does not exist. I am sure one ride thro its filthy streets ought to content any enthusiast."[41] The only consolation seemed to be that, by not arriving in China until late September, Gordon had found himself "rather late for the amusement, which won't vex mother."[42]

One can imagine that his mother, daughter of a merchant whaler, had already had quite enough vexation from this fourth of her five sons. Born on the twenty-eighth of January 1833, Charles George Gordon had embarked on a military career at an early age, as his family wished. But there was something a little too headstrong about him; he seemed always to be getting into one scrape or another. In military academy he had butted the senior colonel down a flight of stairs; and later, just before graduation, he had beaten one of the younger cadets over the head with a hairbrush, losing his chance to be in the Royal Artillery like his father and grandfather. And when he had gone to the Crimea in 1855, as a royal engineer, he had done things in his own way, criticized his superiors, exposed himself too much to enemy bullets and had been wounded. Even worse, he had liked it all and wouldn't come home, complaining when peace came: "We do not, generally speaking, like the thought of peace until after another campaign. I shall not go to England, but expect I shall remain abroad for three or four years, which *individually* I would sooner spend in war than peace. There is something indescribably exciting in the former."[43]

Gordon took the next best course. He went off first to Bessarabia to help a frontier delineation commission and then on to Armenia in 1857 for the same type of work. Yet his admiration went out to those very people who paid no attention to the frontiers he was delineating. "We met on our road a great number of Kurds. . . . they are as lawless as ever, and go from Turkey to Russia and back again as they like. They are fine-looking people, armed to the teeth, but are decreasing in numbers. They never live in houses, but prefer tents and caves."[44] When, in 1858, Gordon did return home, he found he rather liked the tents and did "not feel at all inclined to settle in England and be employed in any sedentary way."[45] So, in late 1858, he was back in the Caucasus with an Anglo-Russian commission, again helping to define frontiers and make peace, a job to which he admitted "I am naturally not well adapted."[46] Back in England again in 1859 and promoted to captain, he volunteered for the British force gathering at Shanghai to enforce the Tientsin treaty. On July 22, 1859, he left for China.

Shortly after Gordon's arrival in Peking, and the looting of the Summer Palace, the Treaty of Tientsin was ratified; the Emperor returned to the capital, a new group of ministers more willing to deal with the West took over control, and the invading army was withdrawn. But pending the payment of indemnities and to ensure the carrying out of the provisions of the treaty, a garrison of three thousand men under the control of the British general, Staveley, was left in Tientsin. Gordon was assigned to this garrison as head of the Engineers with the job of constructing barracks for the troops and stables for their horses as well as surveying the neighboring areas. He was to spend the next eighteen months at this job.

Despite the fact that the "indescribable" excitement of war was lacking, young Gordon found a very describable satisfaction in peacetime life abroad. "Do not tell anyone," he confessed to his sister Augusta in October 1861, "but I do not feel at all inclined to return to Great Britain. I like the country, work and independence; in England we are nondescripts, but in China we hold a good position and the climate is not so bad as it is made out to be." In addition, he was able to travel widely in north China, often to areas rarely before visited by a Westerner, informing his sister, "I shall go to the Great Wall if I can in a short time, and thence send you a description and eventually a brick from that fabric."[47] So Gordon waited for his opportunity in Tientsin, rather than on the Thames, sending home boxes of sables, vases, jades, and enamels, with instructions stating "A to my father, B, C and D for general and fair distribution amongst the 'tribe' of Gordons, E and F to my father, G to Aunt Amy . . . P, Q and R to my mother . . . Y to Henry. . . ."[48]

In the spring of 1862, Gordon was ordered to Shanghai where the British forces had been committed by Admiral James Hope to clear the Taiping rebels from a thirty-mile zone around that city. According to the commander of the land forces, General Staveley (the brother-in-law of Gordon's older brother Henry), "Captain Gordon was of the greatest use to me. . . . He reconnoitred the enemy's defences, and arranged for the ladder parties to cross the moats, and for the escalating of the works; for we had to attack and carry by storm several towns fortified with high walls and deep wet ditches. He was, however, at the same time a source of much anxiety to me from the daring manner he approached the enemy's works to acquire information."[49]

In December 1862, Gordon was promoted to major and given the task of surveying the whole thirty-mile zone in preparation for better allied offensives. The job, perfectly fitted to a man content only working for himself, he did admirably, often advancing with a few men deep into rebel-held territory. In less than three months, his task was completed. This year of surveying work, often under dangerous conditions, brought Gordon into contact for the first time both with the Taiping rebellion and with the difficulties of fighting the Taiping troops in the area of allied operations. "We had a visit from the marauding Taepings the other day. They came close down in small parties to the settlement and burnt several houses, driving in thousands of inhabitants. We went against them and drove them away, but did not kill many. They beat us into fits in getting over the country, which is intersected in every way with ditches, swamps, etc."[50] The rebels left him horrified and brought out the "better Christian" in him as the burning of the Summer Palace had not. "It is most sad this state of affairs, and our Government really ought to put the rebellion down. Words could not depict the horrors these people suffer from the rebels, or describe the utter desert they have made of this rich province."[51]

At the same time, Gordon shared the European's scorn for the fighting abilities of the Chinese and the general character of their ruling classes, a sentiment typified by this poem run in the British humor magazine *Punch* just before he left for China:

> *With their little pig-eyes and their large pig-tails,*
> *And their diet of rats, dogs, slugs, and snails,*
> *All seems to be game in the frying-pan*
> *Of that nasty feeder, JOHN CHINAMAN.*
> *Sing lie-tea, my sly JOHN CHINAMAN,*
> *No fightee, my coward JOHN CHINAMAN:*
> *JOHN BULL has a chance — let him, if he can,*
> *Somewhat open the eyes of JOHN CHINAMAN.*[52]

"These Chang-mows [Taipings] are very funny people," Gordon himself commented; "they always run when attacked. They are ruthlessly cruel, and have a system of carrying off small boys under the hope of training them up as rebels. . . . I saved one small creature who had fallen into the ditch in trying to escape, for which he rewarded me by destroying my coat with his muddy paws in clinging to me."[53] If he thought nothing of the Taipings, he thought hardly better of the Chinese government, and said of the country as a whole, "I do not write about what we saw, as it amounts to nothing. There is nothing of any interest in China; if you have seen one village you have seen all the country." Yet, as with his Bessarabian and Armenian experiences, the people appealed to him. In Armenia, it had been the Kurds, here it was the Chinese peasant. "Whatever may be said of their ruler, no one can deny but that the Chinese peasantry are the most obedient, quiet, and industrious people in the world."[54]

In his personal life, Gordon was a lonely and withdrawn man, ill at ease among his peers and in the presence of women. "He stays with me whenever in Shanghai and is a fine noble generous fellow," Harry Parkes, the British consul wrote to his wife, "but at the same time very peculiar and sensitive — exceedingly impetuous — full of energy, which just wants judgement to make it a very splendid type. . . . We have seen a good deal of each other when he is here, for as he is very shy I try as much as possible to dine alone, and we then tattle on on Chinese affairs all to ourselves."[55] His personality prevented him from relating well to those above him, and scarcely better to those below him (except perhaps the Chinese troops he later had under his command — with whom he could not speak). Drawn to China by contradictory impulses he scarcely understood and haunted by self-doubts, he proved erratic in his friendships, inconsistent in his opinions, and contradictory in his thoughts. "The world," he confided to his sister later in life, "is a vast prison house under hard keepers with hard rulers; we are in cells solitary and lonely looking for release."[56] It was only in non-English lands and on his own that he found a part of that "release."

"The fact is," he commented years later from the Sudan, "if one analyzes human glory, it is composed of 9/10 twaddle, perhaps 99/-100 twaddle."[57] Yet he was waiting in China for just that glory which he often seemed to despise, and in March 1863 his chance came.

Since Ward's death near Ningpo six months before, the Ever-Victorious Army had steadily fallen into disarray. Ward's second-in-command, Burgevine, another American, had been appointed to command by Li Hung-chang at the urging of British, French and American officials. In many ways Burgevine was like Ward. An adventurer who also had come to China as a ship's mate, he was brave in battle, sustaining several wounds, and had hopes of carving out his own sphere of influence. But where Ward had had the perception to attach himself closely to his Chinese masters, Burgevine did no such thing. As described by Gordon, he was "a man of large promises and few works. His popularity was great among a certain class. He was extravagant in his generosity, and as long as he had anything would divide it with his so-called friends, but never was a man of any administrative or military talent, and latterly, through the irritation caused by his unhealed wound and other causes, he was subject to violent paroxysms of anger, which rendered precarious the safety of any man who tendered to him advice that might be distasteful. He was extremely sensitive of his dignity."[58]

Li Hung-chang, now settled into Shanghai, feared that Burgevine, whose popularity among his predominantly American subordinates in the Ever-Victorious Army ran high, was more a danger to the Ch'ing in the Shanghai area than to the Taiping rebels he was supposed to fight. Li was soon complaining that "Burgevine is full of intrigues and stubborn. Wu and Yang [the Taotais] both say that he is not so easy going as Ward."[59] Li would have preferred to disband the Ever-Victorious Army, fearing the defection of its officers to the Taipings, but the foreigners insisted that it be retained to protect Shanghai. So, instead, he set his mind to substituting for Burgevine — the independent adventurer — a British officer for whose loyalty he could hold British officials responsible. Arbitrarily, he ordered Burgevine to take his army away from its base of power at Sungkiang and help with the capture of Nanking. At the same time, he arranged that Yang Fang (Taki) should withhold payments to the army. Burgevine, impetuously doing just what Li must have wanted, refused to move his army and (reported Li) "On [Jan. 4] between 9–11 A.M., . . . brought several dozen of his musketeers quickly to Yang Fang's residence in Shanghai; Yang Fang was wounded on the nose, forehead and chest until he vomited a great deal of blood, and more than forty thousand silver dollars were forcibly carried off."[60]

Li, using this pretext, dismissed Burgevine, and turned to the British. Having already committed themselves to the support of the Ch'ing dynasty, the British government, at the urging of Bruce, their minister at Peking, and Staveley, commander of the British forces in China, agreed to allow British officers to undertake service with the Imperial forces. With this understanding, Staveley and Li reached an agreement whose main points were:

> The force to be under the joint command of an English and a Chinese officer. . . . For the English officer, who was to enter the Chinese service, Captain Holland was nominated temporarily, but Captain Gordon was to take the command when he

should have received the necessary authorisation; he was to
have the rank of Chentai [brigadier general]. For expeditions
beyond the thirty-mile radius the previous consent of the allies
[English and French] was necessary. Chinese were to be appointed as provost marshal, paymaster, and in charge of the
commissariat . . . The strength of the force was to be reduced
to 3000, or even below that number, if the custom house re-
ceipts should fail . . . The force and its commanders were to
be under the orders of the Futai [Li Hung-chang], who was
also to buy the military supplies.[61]

Both sides had achieved their goals. Li had replaced an independent leader of a force whose loyalty to the Empire was doubtful with
a man directly subordinate to him, held in check by Li's control of
the force's money, and guaranteed by British officials. In addition, he
had managed to limit the force's power, reducing its strength by
fifteen hundred men. The British, in turn, had assured the continuing existence of the force defending their economic interests at
Shanghai.

On January 15, 1863, Captain Holland took command, but in his
first major engagement, at the town of Taitsang (recently reinforced
by the Taiping rebels), bad intelligence work, bad reconnaissance,
poor tactics, and a mishandled retreat resulted in a disastrous defeat.
Some 190 men were killed, 174 wounded, and many guns lost. The
force returned, demoralized, to Sungkiang to await its next commander.

In March 1863, having completed his surveying work, Gordon
took command of the Ever-Victorious Army. The day before he left
for Sungkiang he wrote to his mother with some trepidation: "I am
afraid you will be much vexed at my having taken the command of
the Sungkiang force, and that I am now a mandarin . . . [but] I
can say that, if I had not accepted the command, I believe the force
would have been broken up and the rebellion gone on in its misery
for years. . . . You must not fret on this matter. I think I am doing
a good service. . . . I keep your likeness before me, and can assure

you and my father that I will not be rash, and that as soon as I can conveniently, and with due regard to the object I have in view, I will return home."[62] For all his hedging to his mother, Gordon was obviously pleased with himself and in no hurry to return to England.

Yet for a regular officer in the British Army, the force he was to command was nothing to brag about. "You never did see such a rabble as it was,"[63] Gordon wrote later to a military friend. Although the Western officers of the Ever-Victorious Army were "brave, reckless, very quick in adapting themselves to circumstances, and reliable in action; . . . on the other hand, they were troublesome when in garrison, very touchy as to precedence and apt to work themselves about trifles into violent states of mind. Excited by Rebel sympathizers at Shanghai, and being of different nationalities, one half of them were usually in a violent state of quarrel with the other; but this, of course, was often an advantage to the commander."[64] The Chinese troops under these officers were hardly inspired by the recklessness of their commanders. "I can say with respect to the high pay of the officers," observed Gordon, "that there is not the slightest chance of getting any men for less — it is by far the most dangerous service for officers I have ever seen, and the latter have the satisfaction of always feeling *in action* that their men are utterly untrustworthy in the way of following them."[65] When Gordon arrived in Sungkiang on March 25, 1863, the morale of the force was at a low point because of the disastrous defeat at Taitsang. Moreover, the officers wanted Burgevine back, fearing, justly, what would happen to them under the command of a regular officer of the British army. The force was mutinous.

Gordon wasted no time. Assuring all the officers "that they need not fear sweeping changes or anything that would injure their future prospects,"[66] he moved against the rebels on March 31. Militarily, Gordon had been a good choice both for the Chinese and the English. By the end of May, his force had taken several points including Taitsang and was camped in front of the town of Kunshan.

What Ward had done by intuition and hard experience, Gordon

did by training. In front of Kunshan, for instance, he analyzed the situation thus:

Isolated hill, surrounded by wall; very wide ditch. City very strong at East Gate. Every manoeuvre seen at top of hill, and telegraphed to chief [of Taipings]. Determined to surround the city. We have already Chiang-zu, at north, belonging to us. Rebels have only one road of retreat towards Soochow, twenty-four miles. Reconnoitre the country on the 30th May. Found that this road can be cut at Chun-ye, eight miles from Quinsan [Kunshan], sixteen miles from Soochow, point of junction and key to the possession of Quinsan held by the rebel stockades. Detour of twenty miles in rebel country necessary to get at this point. Value of steamer.[67]

Having followed his own plan and captured Kunshan with great slaughter of the fleeing Taiping troops, he added: "Knowledge of the country is everything, and I have studied it a great deal. . . . The horror of the rebels at the steamer is very great; when she whistles they cannot make it out."[68] If he was militarily more effective and efficient than Ward, he followed Ward's path, emphasizing the value of steamers in the delta area, as well as of pontoon bridges, and of heavy artillery. He even emulated Ward's style of entering battle: "Gordon always led the attack, carrying no weapons, except a revolver which he wore concealed in his breast, and never used except once, against one of his own mutineers, but only a little rattan cane, which his men called his magic wand of Victory."[69]

Li Hung-chang was gratified. "Since taking over the command," he reported to Tseng Kuo-fan in April, "Gordon seems more reasonable [than the others]. His readiness to fight the enemy is also greater. If he can be brought under my control, even if he squanders forty or fifty thousand dollars, it will still be worth while."[70] Soon after, his admiration seemed almost unrestrained: "When the British General Staveley formerly stated to your official that Gordon was brave, clear-minded and foremost among the British officers in Shanghai, your official dared not believe it. Yet since he took up the command of the Ever-Victorious Army, their exceedingly bad habits gradually have come under control. His will and zeal are really praiseworthy."[71] Gordon's main accomplishment in Li's eyes was his ability to keep his force busy and ensure their loyalty to the Ch'ing government. He was, as well, pleased at the victories Gordon was winning, victories which were making it easier for the government to support Tseng Kuo-fan's troops besieging Nanking.

But Li had spoken too soon. If Gordon followed Ward's path in military tactics, he did no such thing in dealing with his men. Ward, and Burgevine after him, had avoided disciplining the officers and men of the Ever-Victorious Army when they were in camp, realizing that a group of adventurers were hardly soldiers in a regular army. The Chinese troops were allowed to return to their villages during harvest time; and both commanders had winked at the looting with which the officers supplemented their less than regular pay. But Gordon was appalled by this state of affairs. Almost immediately, he banned all looting (on grounds that Li Hung-chang would make regular payments from that time on); drunkenness in battle was to be punishable by death; trading in opium and women was to be stopped; and all ranks were to be subjected to proper training and regular drill. In addition, to show his disapproval of the behavior of his officers, he lived and messed by himself.[72] He was determined to turn this force of mercenaries into a small regular army.

Gordon's plan soon ran into difficulty. After the victory at Taitsang, his officers insisted on returning to Sungkiang to spend their pay and "prize-money" before heading back into action. Gordon yielded, but once in Sungkiang faced a new threat of mutiny. His men, Gordon commented, were "reliable in action . . . [but] troublesome in garrison and touchy to a degree about precedence."[73] To divert them, he started for Kunshan immediately. He decided to make Kunshan his new base, severing all ties with Sungkiang and the memories that went with it. In his diary, he recorded, "G[ordon] determined to move headquarters there, as the men would be more under control than they were at Sung-keong. Men mutiny. One is shot at tombstone outside West Gate. Mark of bullets still there. Men then desert, 1700 only out of 3900 remain. Very disorderly lot. Ward spoilt them. G. recruits rebel prisoners, who are much better men."[74]

If he had trouble with his own troops, he threw his Chinese superiors into fits of total exasperation. In the wake of the attack on Kunshan, he quarreled with the Chinese general whose troops were supporting the Ever-Victorious Army. Depressed by the desertions, disgusted with his Chinese opposites, and dismayed by the criticism he received from the British press in Shanghai for his part in the "massacre" at Kunshan, he wrote to Li Hung-chang in July, 1863: "Your Excellency — In consequence of monthly difficulties I experience in getting the payment of the force made, the non-payment of legitimate bills for boat hire and necessities of war from Her Britannic Majesty's Government, who have done so much for the Imperial Chinese authorities, I have determined on throwing up the command of this force, as my retention of office in these circumstances is derogatory to my position as a British officer, who cannot be a suppliant for what Your Excellency knows to be necessities, and should be happy to give."[75] He refused to be "soothed" by the normal Chinese practice of giving "rewards."

But Gordon was in some confusion. He did not long wish to remain idle, though to "take the field" again meant a loss of English "honor." Burgevine provided him the pretext for reassuming command. After his dismissal, Burgevine had gone to Peking and, with the backing of the American minister, had managed to get himself reappointed by the authorities there to command of the Ever-Victorious Army. When he reappeared in April, Li reported: "When Burgevine had returned from the Capital to Shanghai full of self-satisfaction, he requested me immediately to reappoint him. I flatly refused and gave the details to Prince Kung. As the Throne and the law should both be upheld, how can they be ambiguous and timid in determining the rights and wrongs? This is discouraging. Yet Gordon is the best character among the British officers. . . . Even if he cannot get rid of the evil habits of the Ever-Victorious Army, these do not now seem to be growing worse."[76] At the beginning of August, Burgevine, disgruntled, defected to the Taipings with three hundred Europeans he had recruited from the Shanghai waterfront, much as Ward had recruited the original Ever-Victorious Army; Gordon, fearing that his own force would desert as well, happily retook the field.

The campaign for Soochow began, with Gordon's force acting in conjunction with a much larger body of Imperial troops. This was to be the crowning goal of all the previous campaigns around Shanghai, since Soochow was the most imposing and heavily fortified city under Taiping control in the area. Li, once again reconciled with Gordon, commented guardedly:

> The officers and men of the Ever-Victorious Army are not really trustworthy in attack and defence. What they depend on is the considerable number of large and small howitzers on loan to Gordon from the British, and the ammunition and weapons constantly supplied [by the British]. So your official is willing to make friends with the British officials, in order to make up what the military strength of China lacks. Nevertheless, Gordon is quite obedient in assisting the campaigns. After the conclusion of final victory, he may not cause any trouble, or if he does, your official can rein him in sharply.[77]

Meanwhile Burgevine, now in Soochow, found he had as little hope of gaining influence under the Taipings as he had under the Ch'ing. The Taipings, on their part, found that Burgevine did not live up to his promises either in providing them with Western military equipment or with effective European troops.[78] Burgevine finally surrendered to Gordon, though he defected again to the Taipings in June 1864. While his predecessor Ward, who had had much the same motivations as Burgevine, had been buried with great honors near a Confucian temple, Burgevine died in Ch'ing hands, "drowning" while government troops were ferrying him across a river.

During the negotiations for Burgevine's surrender, Gordon wrote, "Burgevine is safe [in Soochow], and not badly treated. I am trying my utmost to get him out; and then, if I can see a man to take my place, I shall leave this service, my object being gained — namely, to show the public, what they doubted, that there were English officers who could conduct operations as well as mates of ships, and also to rid the neighborhood of Shanghai of these freebooters. I care nothing for a high name."[79]

Obviously, by the time Gordon reached the walls of Soochow and the Ever-Victorious Army was settled in for a siege of the city, he was once again nearing the point of handing in his resignation. The European press in China (the "public" of his letter) constantly questioned the fitness of a British officer's serving under the Chinese. This bothered him intensely and reinforced his growing personal disillusionment with the side for which he was fighting. "I am perfectly aware from nearly four years service in this country that both sides are equally rotten," he wrote from Soochow in October 1863. "But you must confess that on the Taiping side there is at leas[t] innovation, and a disregard for many of the frivolous and idolatrous customs of the Manchus. While my eyes are fully open to the defects of the Taiping character, from a close observation of three months, I find many promising traits never yet displayed by the Imperialists. The Rebel Mandarins are *without* exception brave and gallant men, and could you see Chung Wang, who is now here, you would immediately say that such a man deserved to succeed. Between him and the Footai, or Prince Kung, or any other Manchoo officer *there is* no comparison."[80]

The fighting under the walls of Soochow proved arduous, the city being held by about forty thousand Taiping troops, and on November 27, 1863, Gordon was defeated. But the city fell on December 5 owing to dissension among the Taiping leaders, most of whom surrendered to the Ch'ing forces. Gordon, refusing his men a chance to plunder the rich city, withdrew his whole force to Kunshan. Li Hung-chang, meanwhile, according to Chinese custom had ordered the execution of the Taiping chiefs who surrendered and whose safety Gordon, as a British officer, felt he had guaranteed. In a hysterical letter, never delivered, Gordon insisted that Li "at once resign his post of Governor of Kiangsu, and give up the seals of office, so that he might put them in commission until the Emperor's pleasure should be ascertained; or that, failing that step, Gordon would forthwith proceed to attack the Imperialists, and to retake from them all the places captured by the Ever-Victorious Army, for the purpose of handing them back again to the Taipings."[81] This, of course, was a preposterous infringment on Chinese sovereignty, but Gordon was too highly wrought to consider what he was saying. When Li's Western secretary Dr. Halliday Macartney entered Gordon's quarters, "he found Gordon sobbing and before a word was exchanged, Gordon stooped down, and taking something from under the bedstead, held it up in the air, exclaiming:

" 'Do you see that? Do you see that?'

"The light through the small Chinese windows was so faint that Macartney had at first some difficulty in recognising what it was, when Gordon again exclaimed:

" 'It is the head of the Lar Wang, foully murdered!' and with that burst into hysterical tears."[82]

Though the initial rage passed, Gordon remained indignant. He withdrew to Kunshan and would have nothing more to do with military campaigns against the Taipings. With him remained his force. Though Gordon was legally no longer in command, having resigned, the Ever-Victorious Army was more of a threat now under this "righteous" English officer than it had been under its previous mercenary commanders. The Chinese resorted to "soothing the barbarian." On January 4, a Chinese official came to Kunshan, bringing an Imperial decree and presents for Gordon as rewards for his share in the capture of Soochow. Gordon refused these presents, including ten thousand taels of silver from the Emperor and captured Taiping battle flags from Li Hung-chang. Gordon's official reply, written on the back of the Imperial rescript, stated: "Major Gordon receives the approbation of His Majesty the Emperor with every gratification, but regrets most sincerely that, owing to the circumstance which occurred since the capture of Soochow, he is unable to receive any mark of H.M. the Emperor's recognition, and therefore respectfully begs His Majesty to receive his thanks for his intended kindness, and to allow him to decline the same."[83] This was an incredible affront to the Chinese.

Li Hung-chang, both fearful of what the mercenary army at Kunshan might do and bewildered by Gordon's actions, was at his wit's end. As early as December 27, 1863, he suggested in a memorial: "I hope that the Tsungli Yamen and the British Minister will reach agreement on Gordon's retirement, and order either that the more than one hundred foreign officers and men in the said Army should all be withdrawn, or that Your official should select and appoint several persons to assist in the command of the said Army."[84]

But Gordon, the English Officer, was once again beginning to waver in the face of Gordon, leader of a mercenary army. His troops, inactive at Kunshan, were again mutinous; his higher officers beginning to quarrel over succession to command. Either he had to forget his English honor and take the field, or lose complete control of his army and his chance for glory in China. His British superiors were as exasperated with Gordon as Li himself. "I beg you to do nothing rash under the pressure of excitement," wrote Bruce, "and, above all, avoid publishing in newspapers accounts of your differences with the Chinese authorities."[85] They urged him to take the field again; and Gordon preserving that "honor" to which he had committed himself, insisted through Bruce that the Peking government agree to instruct Li that "in future operations in which a foreign officer is concerned, the rules of warfare, as practised among foreign nations, are to be observed."[86] Having done this, he met Li, who took full responsibility for the Soochow incident. Gordon was satisfied, and several months later was justifying his return to duty by saying: "That the execution of the Wangs at Soochow was a breach of faith there is no doubt; but there were many reasons to exculpate the Futai for his action, which is not at all a bad act in the eyes of the Chinese. In my opinion (and I have not seen Tseng-kuo-fan yet), Li-Hung-Chang is the best man in the Empire; has correct ideas of his position, and, for a Chinaman, has most liberal tendencies."[87]

If Gordon was pleased, Li was less so. He had too clear an idea of Gordon's character not to doubt for the future. "Although yesterday," Li wrote on February 25, 1864, "Gordon was glad to volunteer, and was commanded to assist Kuo Sung-lin and others in an attack on I-hsing, he can only be treated as a partisan officer, not as a regular. Gordon is brave enough, but not sufficiently patient. As his bad temper suddenly comes and goes, I do not know whether there will be any change later on." In late March, scarcely a month after Gordon had taken the field again, Li added: "As soon as military affairs in Chiang-nan are settled, the Ever-Victorious Army had better be discharged. Gordon does not disagree with this idea."[88] In fact, campaigning had not gone well and the force had suffered a series of defeats at the hands of the Taiping rebels. As Li explained in June, "Gordon has felt rather discouraged. On [April 27], in the campaign of Ch'ang-chou, even when the city walls had been blown up, it was still not possible to effect an entry. Thus Gordon saw that the Ever-Victorious Army was of no use."[89]

The British military authorities, though, were strongly against the disbandment of the Ever-Victorious Army. General Brown was "not for disbanding any portion of the Disciplined Force until we see the fate of Nanking and the retreat of the rebels. I am also for keeping up a corps of disciplined Chinese at Shanghai. . . . It is a great strategical point and should be made the place of a regular canton-ment."[90] But Gordon went his own way. When Li offered him £100,000 to pay off and disband the force, he jumped at the chance. Perhaps he was tired of his role as a mercenary general; perhaps he felt, with the siege of Nanking tightening, that the war was nearing its end; perhaps he simply felt that the force he commanded provided a bad example for the Chinese or a bad advertisement for Western methods; certainly he concurred with Li in his opinion of the force itself. "This force," he wrote at the time of its disbandment, "has had ever since its formation in its ranks a class of men of no position. . . . Ignorant, uneducated, even unaccustomed to command, they were not suited to control the men they had under them. . . . I consider the force even under a British officer a most dangerous collection of men, never to be depended on and very expensive. In my opinion more would be done by a force of Chinese under their own officers, who do not want for bravery when properly instructed. . . . Do not let us try to govern their own men by foreigners but, keeping these latter as instructors, make them create their own officers."[91] His opinions on the force he commanded hardly reflected his opinions on himself. "I have the satisfaction," he commented, summing up his time with the Ever-Victorious Army, "of knowing that the end of this rebellion is at hand, while, had I continued inactive, it might have lingered on for years. I do not care a jot about my promotion or what people may say. I know I shall leave China as poor as I entered it, but with the knowledge that, through my weak instrumentality, upwards of eighty to one hundred thousand lives have been spared. I want no further satisfaction than this."[92]

If he had exaggerated the importance of the local victories he had helped to win, he certainly minimized the "satisfactions" he had received. "Allow me to congratulate you," wrote Robert Hart, the young Inspector-General of Customs. "The Emperor has by a special Edict conferred on you the Hwang Ma-Kwa, or yellow jacket, and has also presented you with four sets of Tetuh's uniform, which, you remember, you said you would like to have. Don't, like a good fellow, refuse to accept these things."[93] Hart should not have worried, for Gordon himself commented, "The Chinese tried hard to prevent me having it; but I said either the Yellow Jacket or nothing; and they at last yielded."[94] Concerning this Yellow Jacket and other honors offered him, he told his mother, "I do not care two-pence about these things, but know that you and my father like them. I will try and get Sir F. Bruce to bring home Chung-Wang's sword, which is wrapped up in a rebel flag belonging to a Tien-Wang, who was killed on it at ChunChu-fu. You will see marks of his blood on the flag."[95] In his role as British officer Gordon tended to deny any desire for honors, wealth or glory; but as a mercenary army leader, in exile from an

England that he felt oppressed him, he accepted them cheerfully enough.

Gordon assembled souvenirs for his parents, but he was in no hurry to return home. Instead for the next five months, he turned to the quieter job of helping the Chinese "create their own officers." He had developed a certain faith in the Chinese — rare in a Westerner in nineteenth-century China — and felt "if we drive the Chinese into sudden reforms, they will strike and resist with the greatest obstinacy . . . but if we lead them we shall find them willing to a degree and most easy to manage. They like to have an option and hate having a course struck out for them as if they were of no account." Even Chinese dislike of the West and Westerners, he excused, saying: "The Chinese have no reason to love us even for the assistance we have given them, for the rebellion was our own work indirectly."[96]

Thanks to dramatic accounts in the daily press, he had become "Chinese Gordon" to an enthralled Western world, the man who single-handedly had put down the Taiping Rebellion. It wasn't true, but that was less important to him than the fact that the excitement was over. Being a drillmaster for Chinese troops became a bore — "too *slow* an occupation to be suited to his active and somewhat erratic tastes," explained a friend.[97] The world was hemming Gordon in, and his spirit chafed. In the fall of 1864 he "remembered" his promise to be back in England by Christmas, and as impulsively as he had come to China, he departed. "The individual," he told his relieved mother, "is coming home."[98]

LAY *and* HART:

Power, Patronage, Pay

As more and more Westerners went to China in the mid-nineteenth century, the qualifications for employment became increasingly stiff, and even those who had lived there for many years had their records reviewed. One American, for example, was told curtly that there was "nothing whatever for you to do in the office at Shanghai, and, as you do not speak Chinese, I cannot put you in charge of a port. . . . There's not the least use in your trying to learn the language; you must be now fifty years of age, and if a man begins *after forty* he can never acquire it. . . . My advice to you is *not* to return to China; you will do best by resigning and asking for your year's allowance. However, you're an *old* servant, and you must think and decide for yourself. It's merely because you have been with us so long that *I make this appointment for you at Whampoa:* it is not a nice place to live at, and there is really nothing to be done there."[1]

Robert Hart, "the small, slender, ironclad autocrat,"[2] who wrote this arrogant letter in February 1869, was only thirty-four years old, but he had already been Inspector-General of the Imperial Chinese Customs Service for five years and was the most powerful Westerner in China. As one of his friends put it, "though the 'I.G.' (as he is called) accepts nominations [to the customs service] from foreign ministers, he allows no dictation or interference, reserving to himself the prerogative of taking or rejecting candidates, by whomsoever they may be recommended. The independence of the service is thus protected, and the high character of its membership secured."[3] The "great I.G." was absolute ruler within his realm. Builder of a scrupulously honest, efficient, revenue-producing, foreign-staffed civil service; unofficial adviser to the newly formed Chinese Foreign Ministery (the Tsungli Yamen); and behind-the-scenes diplomat; he was initially "Our Hart" to the Chinese. During the last thirty years of his fifty years in China, he was the focus of Western social life in Peking, holder of immense patronage and receiver of honors from scores of governments around the world. For "a young Irish lad brought up in a small town — a lad to whom even London probably seemed very far away," it had been a spectacular life.[4] When at his death he was buried not in China, but in the homeland he had managed to visit only twice in fifty-four years, it seemed somehow inappropriate.

The eldest child in the Hart family, Robert was born in February 1835 in a small town in the north of Ireland. His father, whose income was only a few hundred pounds a year, was the manager of a distillery and a very religious Wesleyan. Being both bright and studious, young Hart won a scholarship to Belfast University, which he entered at the age of fifteen. At the university, "holders of scholarships — easily distinguishable by the gold top-knot on their mortarboards — were expected in their conduct to be an example to others, and in the matters of study and attendance at lectures to be above reproach."[5] To retain his scholarship year after year, he intensified the seriousness with which he studied, engaging neither in extracurricular activities, nor in sports. Fortunately, "these amusements he probably missed the less as they were not popular at Belfast, the College being new and without muscular traditions, and the students chiefly young men of narrow means and broad ambitions."[6]

At Belfast, he began to consider his future in a new, if confused, light. He thought first of being a doctor, then a lawyer, and finally, hearing a lecture on China at the age of seventeen, a missionary; but career openings for young men of his background were few and far between. So having won the senior scholarship in modern languages, he returned to Belfast for a year of postgraduate work. At that time, Dr. McCosh, his favorite teacher, reported: "Hart came to me and said, 'You have given me new tastes, which make it impossible for me to go back to my father's mill. Can you find me any congenial employment?' I replied by putting into his hands a call for young men to present themselves in Downing Street as competitors for posts in the consular service in China."[7] It was the sort of good fortune the bright and ambitious young man had been looking for, and he was quick to take advantage of the opportunity. "I was just nineteen when the Foreign Office offered the College a nomination for the British Consular Service in China. Thirty-six of us sent in our names, and there was to have been an examination, but the College Council paid me a high compliment and gave the nomination to me."[8]

It was a gamble. He left England with little more than high hopes and the advice of Mr. Hammond, the Permanent Undersecretary of State: "When you reach Hongkong, *never* venture into the sun without an umbrella, and never go snipe shooting without top boots pulled up well over the thighs."[9] In May 1854, he arrived in Hong Kong. Soon after, he was posted north to Ningpo, where he first seriously began to study Chinese. There he met the Reverend W. A. P. Martin with whom he was to form a friendship that lasted forty years. In his three and a half years at Ningpo as supernumerary interpreter for the British consulate, he had a chance to view the conditions under which Western traders operated in China. In 1858 he was transferred to the consulate at Canton where he formed close relationships with Chinese officials, including the Taotai of Canton, who asked Hart to formulate regulations for the collection of duty at Canton and to supervise their implementation.

Hart refused to do so on his own authority. He offered instead to write to H. N. Lay, the head of the newly formed Chinese Imperial Customs Service operating at the port of Shanghai, asking his help. The result of the ensuing correspondence was that, in June 1859, Hart resigned from the British Consular Service, accepting the post of Deputy-Commissioner of Customs in Canton. Once again he had grasped at proffered opportunity. While it had been a long jump from Ireland to China, from the British to the Chinese service proved a simpler step. The newly formed and quickly expanding customs service not only provided scope for action and possibilities of advancement far greater than was possible in the British Consular Service, it brought Hart into contact with Horatio Nelson Lay. This new contact was to provide a profound impetus and example for Hart's later career.

*   *   *

Horatio Nelson Lay, eldest son of George Tradescant Lay, British Consul at the port of Amoy, was born in London in 1832. "When you have finished your education," G. T. Lay wrote to his eleven-year-old son in 1843, "you must come [to China] and see me, should I not be called home before that period." "Here," he added a year later, "is a fine country, people ready to shew you much attention and an employment both honourable and profitable."[10] But the sudden death of G. T. Lay in 1845 left his family impoverished and forced his sons to withdraw from school well before their studies were completed. Their mother determined that they should, nonetheless, follow their father into the China service. To Lord Palmerston, in the Foreign Office, she wrote, "If you My Lord would kindly recommend the elder one [H. N. Lay] to the notice of Sir John Davis I am sure he would when a vacancy occurred and he thought him eligible grant him something. I regret that the youthful ages of my children will prevent my receiving any benefit from their exertions for the present." Palmerston, though initialing the request "recommended accordingly," grumbled in an interoffice memo about "establishing a precedent for educating at the public expense the younger children of deceased Consuls."[11]

In July 1847, the fifteen-year-old H. N. Lay and his thirteen-year-old brother arrived in Hong Kong to take up the study of Chinese under Dr. Gutzlaff, a celebrated language teacher and missionary. When he was seventeen (just at the time Hart entered Belfast University), Lay joined the British Consular Service as an apprentice interpreter, shifting stations between Hong Kong and Canton. In 1854, Sir John Bowring promoted Lay over jealous seniors to the post of acting interpreter (Shanghai) at £500 a year, since he had made such rapid progress with the Chinese written and spoken language.[12] Soon after, Bowring promoted him to fill concurrently the position of acting vice-consul at Shanghai. It was in this position that Lay had his first substantive contact with Ch'ing authorities, and made his first Western enemies, who dubbed him, bitterly, the "Boy Consul."[13]

Young, hot-tempered, always short of funds, energetic and often arrogant with his Chinese opposites, so fluent in the Chinese language that some Chinese later were to suspect him of being a native Chinese, he was self-assured, most ambitious, and extremely capable. "I have noticed," said one observer, "that Europeans who have been brought up from childhood or from early youth in India, or China, and have at the same time made early acquaintance with Eastern languages, are disposed to treat the natives of these countries with greater rudeness, or, as some would call it, energy, than is usual among other Englishmen in the East of similar social standing. The real cause of this I believe to be partial arrestment of moral development at the boisterous schoolboy stage, owing to a too early acquirement of power among people of a different moral code from that of their own countrymen; but it may plausibly, however erroneously, be argued that it proceeds only from appreciation of the best means of dealing with Asiatics."[14]

In that same year, 1854, the Triads, a Chinese secret society, forcefully took over the Chinese section of Shanghai. Western consular officials, led by the British consul, Alcock, created for the port a temporary foreign inspectorate of customs, in order to fulfill their obligations to the Ch'ing government under the treaty system. It was to be responsible for collecting customs duties from Western merchant ships entering the port. Three inspectors were nominated (one British, one French, one American) by the consuls. The Ch'ing government was powerless to resist such moves. Yet jealous of their prerogatives, the Chinese considered such actions to be an unwelcome interference with their civil administration. Monetarily, however, the effect was salutary for the government. The customs collection, which in Chinese hands had always been subject to "squeeze" by local merchants and officials, the greater part of the money never reaching Peking, proved to be more efficiently handled by the Westerners. The money which was turned over to Peking far exceeded Chinese expectations.

Still, the Chinese resented a system in which the nomination of inspectors was made by foreigners, and were determined to take over the selection and the appointment of these employees, while retaining, at least temporarily, the technical expertise of the Western system. Thus, when the British inspector retired in May 1855, the Ch'ing officials refused to appoint the man recommended by the British consul, and instead turned to Lay, who since 1854 had vigorously supported the Ch'ing cause. This opportunity did not fall unasked and unexpected into Lay's lap. Discovering that an opening would soon exist, Lay began to ingratiate himself with the commander of the Imperial forces in the area, who accordingly pressed for Lay's appointment to this post.[15] On June 1, 1855, Lay took over the British position in the triumvirate of inspectors.

The appointment initially proved pleasing to both parties. By nominating Lay, the Chinese hoped, first, to ensure that primary loyalties were directed to China not to the West; second, to retain the Western expertise which was providing much needed money for their depleted treasury; and third, to control Westerners, through Westerners. As they themselves recounted, the results proved satisfying: "H. N. Lay is the most crafty of the barbarians. In the winter of 1855, the former governor, Ch'i-erh-hang-a, sent an offer to that chief to employ him as Shanghai Customs Commissioner with generous pay. The barbarian still feels grateful and looks out for smuggling for us, so in recent years barbarian customs have been three or four times as much as when the port was opened . . . we must continue to hold him responsible for all the barbarians."[16]

On Lay's part, the entry into Chinese service was a blessing. For a young man only twenty-three-years-old, without a father, almost without a country, and without significant connections, this seemed an unparalleled opportunity for the exercise of power. As Bowring wrote to Lay only one year later: "There is no foreigner in China who has equal opportunities for ascertaining the feelings of the High Mandarins, and probably none who possesses so much of their confidence."[17] In addition, for a man who was still supporting a widowed mother and her three children in England, the increase in salary from about £500 (as vice-consul) to about £1450 (as inspector) was significant. Self-made and self-reliant as he was, Lay hesitated not at all to engage himself.

For the next three years, he directed all his energies to the creation of a model customshouse at the port of Shanghai. "All the old tricks of falsifying official documents and records, of offering and accepting bribes for accommodation rendered, of fraudulent declarations, and of disguised or barefaced smuggling, as well as many new deceptions, of which he had never dreamt, were duly exposed and summarily dealt with. When one considers the rawness and paucity of his staff, the evil traditions in which many of his Chinese subordinates had been brought up, the lack of trained and trustworthy examiners, and of an adequate and efficient preventive staff, and the coldness and opposition of many of the foreign merchants, not to mention the activities of hardened and expert smugglers, both Chinese and foreign, one can realize that the task to which he had set his hand was Herculean." His assertiveness, overbearing presence, and ability to withstand the attacks of his Western compatriots, earned him the new unofficial title of "Junior Autocrat."[18]

While Lay worked rapidly to regularize the customs service procedures at Shanghai, his country, France and America had come into ideological and physical conflict with China. The Western nations simply refused to fit into the Chinese tributary system in return for the "favors" bestowed upon them by a reluctant China. Instead they were insisting on treaty revision, with the goal of making China and the Western nations equals in a world of nation-states, a tenet unheard of in, and unassimilable by, the Confucian world system. The Western nations wanted to have resident ministers at Peking, where they hoped they could deal directly with the court rather than through "soothing" provincial officials, and they wanted an extension of trading rights to further ports and to the inland rivers, particularly the Yangtze. By 1856, they had resorted to force to emphasize the seriousness of their goals, taking Canton (1857), the Taku forts (1858), and pushing on to Tientsin. The Court at Peking, finally realizing the danger, dispatched three of their most venerable officials, Kuei-liang, Hua-sha-na, and that veteran of Opium War negotiations Ch'i-ying, to deal with the "barbarians" at Tientsin.[19]

In April 1858, the British envoy, Lord Elgin, had written Lay: "It would be very satisfactory to me if you could make it convenient to accompany me in the Furious on my present expedition to the North, as I consider that y. acquaintance with the system of the Chinese Customs House and y. familiarity with the language would be of material assistance to me at this conjuncture." With the permission of the Taotai of Shanghai, Lay quickly accepted; but he was never accredited as an official member of the expedition. Elgin simply referred to him as a man who "holds the office of Foreign Inspector at the Port of Shanghae."[20] In fact, Elgin hoped to make Lay's position ambiguous. Thus he would provide himself with a special channel to the Chinese and a special source of information about them.

At Tientsin, Lay was something between interpreter and negotiator. As it happened, Lay's place in the talks (June 6–June 26, 1858) was a great deal more important than his position might have suggested. The envoys being ignorant of China and her language, were heavily reliant on their interpreters.[21] But Lay certainly did not make substantive policy decisions. Instead, he played the aggressive role Lord Elgin designed for him as "the uncontrollably fierce barbarian."[22] Lay, like the powers he represented, fitted the role well. He was young, arrogant, brash, interested in foisting his own ideas on a benefactor who had done him great good, and perfectly willing to threaten the use of force to achieve Lord Elgin's aims. "Yesterday," runs the Chinese account, "the barbarian H. N. Lay tried to force acquiescence and was discourteous to the extreme."[23] Lay would not even abide by the forms prescribed by the Chinese.

As early as the first meeting on June 6, Lay insisted that any negotiations must be preceded by a Chinese acceptance of resident ministers at Peking. When Kuei-liang pleaded desperately that, at the age of seventy-three, signing such an accord would mean the loss of his head, the twenty-five-year-old Lay replied: "The provision will be for your good as well as ours, as you will surely see. The medicine may be unpleasant but the after-effects will be grand. As to your chance of losing your head, the best way of saving it is to accept the clause, and the more I make it appear that you act under compulsion, and in order to prevent an advance on the capital, the more sure will be your personal immunity. The more stern my attitude, the greater the service I render to you."[24] To the Chinese secretary Pien he stated, "if they prefered war, why, they would have it."[25]

The negotiator, Ch'i-ying, meeting Lay on June 11, fared little better. According to Lay and his co-interpreter Wade, Ch'i-ying's conversation "was a perfect clatter of compliments and moral sentiments, delivered with that mixed air of patronage and conciliation which, it may be observed, was considered by the mandarins earlier in contact with us as the true means of 'soothing and bridling the barbarians.'" Suddenly Lay produced one of Ch'i-ying's 1844 memorials to the Emperor (captured at Canton by the British in 1857) in which Ch'i-ying described intercourse with the West in these disparaging terms:

"Certainly we have to curb them by sincerity, but it has been even more necessary to control them by skillful methods. There are times when it is possible to have them follow our directions but not let them understand the reasons. Sometimes we expose everything so that they will not be suspicious, whereupon we can dissipate their rebellious restlessness. Sometimes we have given them receptions and entertainment, after which they have had a feeling of appreciation. . . . With this type of people from outside the bounds of civilization, who are blind

and unawakened in styles of address and forms of ceremony, if
we adhered to the proper forms in official documents and let
them be weighed according to the status of superior and inferior . . . they could not avoid closing their ears and acting as
if deaf." At this turn of events, Ch'i-ying was reduced to tears;
the other Chinese envoys retained a humiliated silence, "but
the two foreigners left highly elated." All the Chinese envoys
could report to their Emperor was: "After we lost Canton, our
old files on barbarian affairs in Yeh Ming-ch'en's office were
looted by the English barbarians, and the traditional methods
[of management] have all been seen through. Our techniques of
control are lost, and our intelligence and courage exhausted."[26]

After bludgeoning and threatening the chagrined and powerless
Chinese envoys (minus Ch'i-ying, who had returned to Peking in
disgrace), on June 25 Lay "came to headquarters with a self-made
treaty of 56 articles and pressed Your slaves to agree to it. His pride
and anger everyone with eyes could see. Not only could there be no
discussion but not even one word could be altered. The gunboats
were close by and if we let him leave, Your slaves certainly had no
assurance it would not cause a rupture. The best they could do was
agree to conclude negotiations within two or three days."[27] The
result, due to Elgin's clever use of Lay, was the Treaty of Tientsin,
signed very grudgingly by the Chinese negotiators and with great
reluctance and bitterness by the Emperor.

From these negotiations and the ensuing Shanghai Tariff Conference, it was agreed to extend the Foreign Inspectorate of Customs
from its base of operations at Shanghai to the other treaty ports. This
new customs establishment was to be headed by a foreigner, chosen
by the Chinese themselves, and given the position of *Tsung Shui-wu
Ssu* — a title translated by Lay as Inspector-General of Customs. In
1859, "Mr. Lay, who by his services as British Inspector has acquired
the confidence of the Chinese Authorities, was placed at the head of
the establishment as deputy of the Chinese Imperial Commissioner

and Superintendent of Trade," reported the British envoy, Bruce, adding: "He is charged with the general supervision of the trading arrangements at the different ports, and with the responsible office of choosing the foreigners who are to carry out the details of Custom house administration."[28] The very man who had rudely badgered the Chinese into agreeing to the Tientsin treaty was once again working for them; in fact had never given up his post of commissioner at Shanghai even while laboring so vigorously in the British interests.

Whom then did Lay represent or rather whom did he think he represented? He had, of course, benefited by the changes and had certainly taken advantage of his unique abilities (knowledge of China, her language and economic situation) to do so. The difference in status as well as salary between being one of three commissioners, and being the Inspector-General of Customs was considerable. Yet his motives were not totally selfish. He seems honestly to have felt that what was in the interest of Britain was equally in the interest of China, however little the Chinese were willing to admit the fact. It was simply that there was a conflict of roles. As a young Englishman, away from his own country since boyhood and forced for years to work in a mainly Chinese atmosphere, under Chinese officials, he no doubt felt the effects of that transformation process by which Chinese civilization had for so many centuries drawn foreigners into its folds. He felt as well the bitter criticism of his own countrymen, the merchants in Shanghai, that by his impartial enforcement of Chinese customs regulations he had become more Chinese than the Chinese. Unlike some other Westerners in China, he strongly reacted to "sinicization" by emphasizing his Englishness whenever, as in 1858, he had the chance.

Throughout his career in China, Lay seems to have considered himself a representative of British interests in China, or at least a middleman between China and the West. Yet Lay's position was so contradictory that constant justification was necessary. At one critical moment later in his life, he explained (and exaggerated) his role between 1858 and 1861 in this way:

I was ambitious of obtaining the position of middleman between China and foreign Powers, because I thought I saw a
way of solving the problem of placing pacific relations with
China upon a new footing. In order to conciliate the support
and disarm the jealousy of our European ministers, I had to
prove that my influence was honestly used in the interest of
all . . . The Chinese Government was too rotten a reed to lean
upon, and the foundations of the structure I was endeavouring
to build up had to be artificially created. My position was that
of a foreigner engaged by the Chinese Government to perform
certain work *for* them but not *under* them. I need scarcely
observe in passing that the notion of a gentleman acting *under*
an Asiatic barbarian is preposterous. I was not a Chinese official, but a foreign adviser without rank, but with a high and
influential position, because trusted in and honoured.[29]

The Chinese probably had a clearer sense of the strange and
contradictory position Lay had placed himself in: "The said barbarian [Lay] was afraid of being disliked by various other barbarians,
so he also accompanied them to Tientsin and made a great display of
violence and ingratiated himself with the barbarian chief in order to
show his public spirit. When he returned to Shanghai he was as
compliant as ever in our employ. 'Who bells (the tiger) can remove
the bell.' "[30]

In any case, even before he was appointed to his new post in May
1859, he threw himself into his job with his usual energy. Over the
next two years, he extended the Shanghai system to other ports
opened by the Tientsin treaty, setting up offices at Canton and
Swatow. The hostility of provincial officials at other treaty ports and
the disturbed state of the country (China being at war both with the
Taiping rebels and the Western powers) prevented further action.

Lay, nonetheless, was a very capable and knowledgeable adminis-
trator. He laid the foundations of an international civil service which
would work effectively into the twentieth century. In this sense he,
not Robert Hart, was the creator of the Chinese Imperial Customs

Service. He established a tradition of honesty and impartiality in administration of customs dues; he picked his staff carefully and skillfully, though heavily favoring Englishmen; and he set up a customs service whose goal was to work for the benefit of China. But Lay's personality limited his successes. He was immature, unable to accept criticism or delegate authority, and vindictive to those whom he considered a threat to his position. He managed in a short time to make many enemies without inspiring any great loyalty in those who supported him. These personal limitations soon enough began to make his own position seem shaky; for, in 1860, Lay was no longer essential either to the British (who for the first time had a glut of young, well-trained, and better-educated "interpreters"), or to the Chinese (who had come to distrust his actions and dislike his arrogance). They were soon to discover Robert Hart.

In 1861, tired and in ill health, Lay wrote to Lord Elgin: "Prince Kung has sent me a Commission as Inspector-General. But the rebellion has gained such strength of late as to threaten now the immediate downfall of the Dynasty. This fact and the state of my health considered have determined me to go home on leave of absence for this year." It was the danger to the dynasty that worried him most, and he added: "Before extending the System, I think it prudent to wait and see what this year will bring forth. From the present aspect of things, it seems certain that the Dynasty must either revive or fall this year. If next year the Tatsing [Ch'ing] be in the ascendant, I shall have a clear field for my operations, while if the rebels are triumphant, I shall have nothing to regret. In the meantime, I shall have an opportunity of explaining at home what the Foreign establishment is."[31] Though Prince Kung, head of the newly formed Tsungli Yamen, was willing to grant leave, he wanted Lay first to come to Tientsin to accept, officially, the title of Inspector-General and to establish a customshouse at Tientsin; for, after the Allied Expedition to Peking in 1860, the Ch'ing government needed money simply to pay the indemnities to the foreign governments, not to speak of fighting the Taiping and other rebels. Lay, however, in his usual high-handed manner, sailed for Europe immediately. "Mr. Lay's inability to come to Peking on account of his health is very unfortunate at this moment," commented Bruce. "It is a great opportunity lost, for the Prince and his colleagues had named him Inspector-General, and had invited him to visit them at the Capital." Robert Hart added that Lay's "departure for Europe at that moment was in opposition to strong remonstrances made by myself and others in what we conceived to be his own and the interests of the infant Service."[32] Lay appointed Hart (who had been Deputy-Commissioner of Customs at Canton since 1859) and one other colleague to exercise general surveillance over the collection of customs revenue and foreign trade at the treaty ports.[33] In addition, he notified Peking that he had told Hart to proceed north to aid Prince Kung.

Hart arrived in Peking on the fifth of June, meeting in the ensuing days, first Wen-hsiang, and then Prince Kung himself. He proved to his Chinese mentors that he had a firm and quick grasp of customs matters. Taking quite a different tack from Lay, he established a firm basis with his new employers by emphasizing — as did the Chinese themselves — cordial interpersonal relationships. The results were astonishing. "The Prince himself became friendly and courteous in the highest degree," reported Bruce, the British minister at Peking, "and the impression produced by Mr. Hart's honesty and frankness was so favourable, that he was urged strongly to remain at Peking to assist the Chinese Government in these questions . . . The Prince always speaks of him as 'our Hart,' and the common answer to any suggestion, which appears reasonable but difficult of execution is 'We could adopt it if we had 100 Harts.' "[34]

During the two years of Lay's leave, Hart had the emphatic advantage of being responsible not to individual provincial officials, but to the officers of the newly constituted Tsungli Yamen at Peking. Thus, he was able to form in those two years what was in many ways a new, centralized customs service. By 1863 he had extended the customs to eight new ports, setting up at each port a skeleton staff drawn partly from among young interpreters working for various foreign consulates, and establishing a uniform customs procedure based on the Shanghai model. At the same time, he did not hesitate

Horatio Nelson Lay, the first Inspector General of Chinese Customs.

Robert Hart, the "Great I.G.," about 1866.

to increase his personal position in the eyes of his Chinese mentors to the detriment of his "Chief."

Away in England Lay felt this, writing petulantly (but accurately) on the matter of buying a fleet for China:

> Without meaning to do so, I fully believe, you reversed our positions. You made yourself Inspector-General, and me your agent. You required me to disburse money belonging to the Chinese Govt. for you, and so vest the ownership of the thing purchased in you. This position I could not accept but I never for one moment, I do assure you, doubted your loyalty to myself, though I did think that your success had carried away your judgement. As to the "credit of setting the project a-going," you have quite misunderstood a remark of mine at the close of my letter of the 9th May. Your letter which it acknowledged was so full of "I's" that I thought that I would say that the idea of a Chinese naval force *had* entered other minds besides your own.[35]

Meanwhile, the Ch'ing government's struggle against the Taiping rebels once again seemed to be taking a turn for the worse. By 1862 Ningpo and Hankow had fallen. Under these conditions, an earlier suggestion that the Chinese purchase a fleet of ships abroad was taken up by the Tsungli Yamen. Hart was urged to work quickly for the acquisition of such a fleet to be used specifically to help crush the rebel forces. On March 14, 1862, Hart wrote to Lay in London commissioning him to buy ships for the Chinese government. Apparently Hart had previously agreed that the fleet, though manned by Western naval officers, would be controlled by a Chinese "high officer." It is quite obvious that the Chinese authorities envisioned an agreement along the lines of that so successfully made with Gordon — a joint Anglo-Chinese operation under the control of a provincial official. But Hart's letter to his "Chief" was ambiguous on this point. In January 1863 a further letter arrived from Prince Kung, giving Lay wide scope in his activities. The key phrase was that in the purchase and equipping of ships, the hiring of personnel, and the retention of moneys to meet salaries Lay was to be left to act "as in his discretion he may see fit."[36]

Even before this authorization reached him, Lay had begun to act. In doing so, he found himself in a strange situation. The country he had left as a schoolboy of fourteen, he had now returned to as a man of power. For the first time in fifteen years, he was no longer in a Chinese atmosphere; he no longer had to please Chinese officials. Never a man, even in China, to think badly of himself, he began to see his power as almost unrestrained. "Do remember in your intercourse with K[ung], my dear fellow," he wrote to Hart in July 1862, "that we have to govern and guide him, and not he us."[37] He proceeded to engage a renowned English naval officer, Captain Sherard Osborn, to command the projected war fleet, telling him: "I should like our vessels to be the finest and best equipped afloat! We'll do the thing thoroughly well or not at all. I hear you say, 'Yes, certainly.' I hope you & I together will do more than any treaties can effect, to open China next year."[38] He then bought and equipped a fleet of seven steamers and one storeship.

Before the fleet left for China, Lay drew up an agreement with Captain Osborn on the control of the fleet, the two key passages of which were: "Osborn undertakes to act upon all orders of the Emperor which may be conveyed direct to Lay; and Osborn engages not to attend to any orders conveyed through any other channel. . . . Lay, upon his part, engages to refuse to be the medium of any orders of the reasonableness of which he is not satisfied."[39] Further, Lay announced that he planned to use this fleet, whose control he had placed exclusively in his own hands, not for the destruction of rebel forces, but to open the Yangtze, suppress piracy and save Britain the expense of maintaining a fleet in China. Lay was obviously working to further British policy in China rather than serving as an obedient agent of the Chinese government.[40]

In May 1863 Lay reappeared in China in advance of the fleet he had hired and took up once again his job as Inspector-General. On June 1 he gave the agreements between himself and Osborn to the

Chinese. The Chinese ministers, fearing the Western barbarians almost as much as they did the Chinese rebels, found these agreements an inconceivable infringement of the rights of China. Among other things, they would necessitate the reversal of the whole modus operandi of the war against the Taiping rebels, a war which was being controlled and run on a provincial level. They would also necessitate the creation of a centralized Imperial navy. To make matters worse, Lay "had not only required that the flotilla should be placed in his hands," reported the American minister, Burlingame, but the Chinese also complained that he wanted "entire control of the customs revenue; that he had been impertinent to them; that he had demanded to be put on a level with the chief officers of the government; that he had requested that large sums of money should be given him, so that at Peking he might maintain more than imperial state; that he had requested a foo [palace] to live in, against the customs of the empire, as none but members of the royal family are permitted to reside in these."[41]

Bruce, the British minister, wrote in November 1863 that it was impossible to doubt Lay had wanted complete control of the customs money and the foreign policy of the empire. "He was to dictate the policy to be pursued; it was to be promulgated to the empire by imperial decree, and to be executed [by the fleet and armies] the expenses of which were to be provided for out of the customs revenue."[42]

While in England, Lay's brashness and self-esteem had clearly led him to overestimate his real power in China. The situation was aggravated when Captain Osborn reached China with his fleet in September 1863. Under the violence of the Chinese response (though Lay had been in Peking since June he had not even been granted an interview with Prince Kung), Lay began making motions toward a compromise on matters of personnel and finance; but Osborn proved adamant, standing on the agreements he had signed before leaving England. He wrote to General Gordon just after his arrival: "I shall advocate at Peking our having joint naval and military powers over all Europeans under arms in China, to be furnished with funds, to render proper accounts — but in no way to be interfered with by Footais, Tootais and birds of that feather."[43] The upshot of Lay's misjudgment and Osborn's stubbornness was that the fleet was returned to England and disbanded.

As for Lay, for some time Prince Kung and his associates had wished to get rid of him, and this incident provided the excuse. Lay had been taken on in 1855 partially through his own initiative, but mainly because he seemed to be a capable man for the job. At the same time, his own personality, as shown at Tientsin in 1858 and again on his return to Peking in 1863, offset his technical abilities, justly placing doubts in the minds of the embattled rulers of China as to just where his loyalties were. After 1861 they came into contact with Hart, who not only proved capable of running the new customs office efficiently, but unlike Lay was able to establish a good working relationship with his Chinese employers.

"Any one who, like Mr. Lay, thoroughly distrusts the Chinese, and believes that the only way to manage, is to drive them, can easily put together facts and arguments sufficiently specious to cause many to coincide in his views," Hart commented early in 1864, "[But] the dictatorial attitude that had proved successful with a Taoutae at a distance from the capital, turned out to be mistakenly applied when assumed towards the high functionaries at Peking. . . . To say, that nothing is to be hoped from the present government because it does not at once turn its attention to the construction of railroads, the laying down of electric telegraph wires, the negotiation of foreign loans, and the introduction of all the appliances that exist among the people by whom it has been thrashed, and for whom it has heretofore had an ignorant contempt, is, to my mind, justified by neither logic nor common sense."[44]

In his turn, as early as 1861, Prince Kung had observed: "Although Hart is a foreigner, yet when he is subjected to consideration he may be called docile and compliant, and much of his language approximates to reason; besides which his covetous anxiety for the extremely large salary of the Inspector-General inclines him to use exertions on our behalf."[45] In the wake of the Lay-Osborn Flotilla,

Lay was paid his salary (plus certain gratuities) and dismissed from the Chinese service. He left China in the winter of 1864, returning only once as a business promoter in 1869, at which time he was the "guest" of Robert Hart.

*　　*　　*

Hart took over. In August 1865, at the request of the Tsungli Yamen, he moved his office from Shanghai to Peking, where he remained, except for inspection tours of the different treaty ports and two home leaves, until his retirement in 1908.

Remembering Lay's bad experience with the Chinese, Hart immediately began to clarify the goals of the customs service. "It is to be distinctly and constantly kept in mind," he wrote, "that the Inspectorate of Customs is a Chinese and not, a foreign, Service, and that as such it is the duty of each of its members to conduct himself towards Chinese, people as well as officials, in such a way as to avoid all cause of offence and ill-feeling. . . . It is to be expected from those who take the pay, and who are the servants of the Chinese Government that they at least will so act as to neither offend susceptibilities nor excite jealousies, suspicion, and dislike. . . . The first thing to be remembered by each is that he is the paid agent of the Chinese Government for the performance of specified work, and to do that well should be his chief care."[46]

In other matters he followed the outlines of Lay's previous Shanghai experiment, taking over and adapting Chinese methods whenever possible. His essential task in these first years of leadership was to reorganize Lay's system into a centralized Customs Inspectorate, responsible not at the local level, but to the office at Peking. In setting up this organization, Hart placed himself indisputably alone in the top position in the Inspectorate. While he, unlike Lay, almost never presumed on the Chinese, within his own organization he was an all-powerful autocrat. "Certain it is," recalled one of his subordinates, "that he kept all real authority in his own hands. His staff were ciphers — one Chief Secretary succeeded another — men came and went — but no one was ever indispensable."[47] A friend noted that from the point of view of the Tsungli Yamen, as long as his loyalty was ensured and his service functioning effectively, "such is the confidence with which he is regarded by that august body that his authority within his own domain is never opposed, nor are any of his acts subjected to revision."[48]

Hart was always secretive about his plans as well as his methods of operating the customs service. As Hart's friend W. A. P. Martin wryly described it:

A peculiar feature of the Chinese customs, to some an attraction, to others a drawback, is that no man is permanently attached to any seaport; nor is there a fixed term of tenure for any post. A principle of mobility, borrowed from the civil service of China, keeps them in constant circulation among twenty-four ports. . . . Its object is to counteract a tendency to local entanglements and to give to all an equal chance of serving in places which, for health or other reasons, are regarded as desirable. Every man must hold himself in readiness for transfer from the day of arrival at a new post, though he may be left there for three, or even five, years. Of his next destination he cannot have the faintest inkling, as there is no order of sequence known to any one — perhaps not even to the autocratic head of the service.

So systematic is this want of system, and so arbitrary the permutations, that some wag has invented a pretty fiction to account for them. The I.G., he affirms, keeps a board hanging in his office, on which the place of every man is marked by a peg, names and places alike being in cipher. The office boy, in taking down his master's hat or coat, brings down by accident a shower of those mysterious pegs, and knowing nothing of their cabalistic markings, puts them up at random. Time and again has an old commissioner, with a bank balance sufficient to beget a spirit of independence, elected to quit the service rather than take up a disagreeable post. This has happened often enough to suggest that the I.G. knows how to get a resignation without asking for it.[49]

Though this system proved eminently effective, it also provoked a great deal of partially just criticism both within and without the service — criticism which grew as the service expanded into new areas and the work load increased without a commensurate delegation of responsibility on Hart's part. There is no question that Hart, a petulant man from a poor background, enjoyed the power vested in him, and people commented that "like the Turk, he could bear no brother near his throne." He was hurt by such criticism, replying: "The Yamen says to me, 'we know only yourself, do what you like; but if anyone does wrong, you'll have to answer for it yourself.' The fellows whom I don't select for special billets or special promotion, don't think of this personal answerability, and the Service generally — seniors and juniors — hate me for exercising the right (or rather, duty, and that an imperatively necessary duty) of choice."[50]

Hart seems to have had a good intuitive approach to people and a strong ability to empathize with others (when those others were not threatening him) — a quality which held him in good stead both in his understanding of the Chinese approach to life and in his choosing of a staff to work under him. This was probably his most crucial problem in the early years of his superintendency. Setting up the central office at Peking, Hart appointed a head commissioner at each port, responsible to him alone. Under that commissioner was both an outdoor staff (to deal with matters of supervision and inspection in the harbors) and an indoor staff (to deal with the technical aspect of customs collection). For his outdoor staff, Hart turned to ex-sailors found in large numbers at Shanghai and Hong Kong. The indoor staff was a more difficult problem and a wide search for talent was made, financial inducements were sizable and promotion opportunities quick. In June 1864, for instance, Hart wrote to the American minister, Burlingame, saying: "I should . . . consider it a very great favour if you could get for me from America three young gentlemen, above eighteen and under twenty-two years of age who have received a collegiate education. I should like men of at least fair average abilities, of good standing in society, and of industrious habits. . . . For the first two years they would be located at Peking to study Chinese. . . . An industrious, hard-working and able man might fairly expect to be a Commissioner in eight or ten years. . . . After the second year in Peking, the Inspector-General would locate each gentleman at the port he might consider the most fitting."[51]

Young men like these led an easy and attractive life in China. As an English student in Peking wrote at this time:

First comes my *Sien Sheng* or teacher, a grey, pig-tailed, old gentleman of most respectable appearance and reverend mien. I have given him a room to live in and I pay him 20 dollars or about £5. Next comes my "Boy" or body servant, of about 25 years of age and with a fair share of intelligence, who performs all the multifarious duties of valet, housemaid and boots; sews the buttons on my shirts, mends the rents in my clothes and is always at my elbow when I want him. He receives the sum of $5 monthly or about £1 sterling. A couple of coolies to sweep the yard, fill and empty my bath, carry me to my sedan chair or perform any duty I like to command, together with my *marfoo* [groom] and my horse, complete the number and fill up the list. . . . Cooks etc. are joint property and included in the mess account which, with wine, beer and everything, does not come to more than £18 or £20 a month. For this you live in capital style, two or three kinds of wine, joints, poultry, game, fish, vegetables and fruit such as Covent Garden could scarcely rival. This is truly a marvellously cheap country.[52]

The wide talent search and such material lures produced an efficient and cosmopolitan staff. "In the selection of men I shall follow the principle to which I have adhered during the last six years in the Customs," wrote Hart in 1867; "that is, I shall employ them just as they may be required without respect to their nationality, provided

individual fitness can be secured, and I shall not aim at exact numeri-
cal proportion, or attempt to provide a representative of every Treaty
Power for every port. The Service will continue to be cosmopolitan
in its general constitution: guided by the requirements of the work to
be done, and by the character and capacity of the individual,
appointments, promotions and dismissals will be dealt out without
respect to nationality."[53] Hart emphasized as well the need to
acquire fluency in Chinese, reasoning that the employees of a country
ought to speak the language of that country.

While the staff of the customs service was officially considered to
be of mixed Chinese-foreign composition, the Chinese in the service
invariably held low positions as clerks, accountants, and copyists. In
this, perhaps, lay Hart's greatest failure. Though willing to prepare a
model for China to use in "progressing" into the modern world, Hart
was in no hurry to train Chinese to staff the customs service. A hard-
headed realist, he had no illusions concerning the final fate of the
service he led. "It should not be forgotten that sooner or later, the
existence of the Inspectorate must come to an end; it may flourish, do
good work, and be appreciated for a time; but the day must come
when the natural and national forces, silently but constantly in
operation, will eject us from so anomalous a position." Hart accepted
this, for with it China would have entered the "modern world" as an
equal of all, would essentially have justified his own life's work. The
Service, he concluded, "will have finished its work when it shall
have produced a native administration, as honest and as efficient to
replace it."[54]

Yet, Hart did not prepare an honest and efficient native administration in his lifetime. The older he grew, the more his stake in
China. The more his stake in China, the more he found it necessary
to preserve the status quo in his own organization. In 1908, when the
Chinese were moving toward taking over the customs service, he
commented: "I had hoped for no change in my time, but Tieh said
yesterday they wish to have a working control established as a going
concern before I disappear, and, as they said — though nobody wants
me to go except those who would like to fill my place — it is known I

cannot hold on for ever, and the disorganisation likely to follow an unprepared-for departure should be avoided."[55]

He also failed to prepare someone to succeed him. What he had achieved had been of his own making, and he was chary about giving it up. "When I analyse my feelings truly," he wrote to a friend, "I am amazed to find how little I want *for myself* or *from others*, and I wonder still further, that, wanting so little, I keep my hand on the plough so long. I fear I could not have acted like Cincinnatus and relinquished the plough of State for that of the farm; — and yet all my longing is for quiet and country life."[56] In a more honest mood he added: "If I were to begin life again I should order my doings on another pattern. I have kept too much in my own hands, and now there is more than my fingers suffice for. Habit is hard to change, and I suppose I shall go on as before."[57] "I have done my fair share," he wrote in 1904. "I have kept things together, formed the Service, broadened its basis, hardened its foundations, and made a fine position for any other man to climb higher from, and I ought to let go. — I am enjoying all the position yields — power, patronage, pay, etc. — and I am its slave, the hardest worked and the least free."[58]

Whatever his methods, Hart created an organization as rare in our time as in his — an international civil service. At the time of his death, the foreign "indoor staff" consisted of 152 British, 38 Germans, 32 Japanese, 31 French, 15 Americans, 14 Russians, 9 Italians, 7 Portuguese, 6 Norwegians, 6 Danes, 5 Belgians, 5 Dutch, 4 Swedes, 3 Spaniards and 1 Korean.[59] His customs service had expanded far beyond its original duties. By 1898 it produced one-third of the entire revenue of the Chinese government. It ran the Chinese Imperial Post Office, and controlled the customs service at the new inland Treaty cities as well as on the coast.

Hart himself became much more than just Inspector-General of Customs. He was instrumental in setting up the T'ung-wen Kuan, or interpreters' school, which, under the leadership of W. A. P. Martin, provided China with its first good translations of Western literature and its first diplomats; instrumental in getting the first Chinese diplomatic missions to visit the West; instrumental in sending the former American minister, Anson Burlingame, to act as Chinese envoy to the Western powers in 1867; instrumental in the 1867–1869 negotiations for the Alcock Convention; instrumental in preventing war between Britain and China in 1876, and in arranging a peace between China and France in 1885. It was through his good offices that the Chinese government was able to float desperately needed loans after the disastrous war with Japan in 1894–1895. The Chinese could indeed feel, as their own saying ran, that they were "using the barbarians to control barbarians."

In addition to creating an effective civil service organization, Hart provided it with a perfect example for hard effective work — himself. Martin has described his schedule: "Almost any day of the year he may be found in his office from 9 A.M. to 5 P.M., with a brief interval for lunch and for siesta, to him no less essential. He allows himself no vacation; never quits Peking, not even to visit the Hills, which he has seen only at a distance; and takes no form of exercise, except walking his garden. For him the monotony of existence is relieved by music and literature. While he is at work the din of a brass band is often heard, suggesting that he drives his quill to the beat of the drum. But no sooner does he drop his pen than he takes up the fiddle-bow, and the brass band is silent."[60]

This tendency towards hard work, evident even in his student days, was exaggerated by his inability to delegate responsibility, by his own conception of the customs service: "The Service which I direct is called the Customs Service, but its scope is wide and its aim is to do good work for China in every possible direction."[61] The increasing personal esteem in which he was held by his Chinese mentors led to his being consulted on a whole variety of affairs quite irrelevant to his actual position. Hart wrote in 1883:

Unless I get through the day's work each day, and the week's work each week — two days' English despatches, two days' Chinese work, and two days' semi-official correspondence, and one day for odds and ends — the time that comes after is very trying; with so many irons in the fire, and so many looms

working simultaneously, and with the public at one door waiting for results, and a Yamen at the other waiting for reports
and advice, my only safety lies in sticking closely to my method.
Method is a wonderful thing. It enabled me last year to read
Lucan's *Pharsalia*, while waiting for my afternoon tea, and this
year I am well on with *Lucretius*. It gives me an hour each day
for 'cello and another for violin; and it enables me to keep work
well up to date.[62]

As he grew older, the workload began to tax his strength and
health. "I am oppressed with work," he complained to a friend in
1898. "If I had four Deputy Inspector-Generals who would take
charge of Customs, Post, Likin, and Lights *and work as I do*, I could
then have some satisfaction and repose; as it is, I am smothered."[63]
In spite of his sympathy for the Chinese, Hart was imbued with a
typical nineteenth-century English concept of progress. Essentially,
he hoped that China would enter "upon a career of improvement,
and . . . step by step, develop resources, create industries, and
achieve progress materially, intellectually, morally."[64] He expected
the customs service to provide the model for this process in China.
When this "progress" seemed after so much effort to be frustrated, as
in 1870 with the refusal of the British to ratify the Alcock Convention and in 1895 with the defeat of China in war with Japan, his
own frustration, his sense of tiredness and dismay came out in most
human doubts, in an inability to justify what he was doing, and in
fits of depression. In 1870 for instance, he wrote, in despair, "I do not
intend to stay out here a day longer than I can help, and unless great
changes speedily come, I don't think there will be much worth stay-
ing for in the shape of successful work. I liked China so long as I was
sanguine of being a useful man in it, but now that they have
squatted down again, — and I find that Chinese form is too regularly
crystallised to admit of much hope of real change, — I tire of being a
mere collector of customs."[65]

For forty years, on and off, he spoke of resigning his posts, of
settling down to a quiet life in the country, and of returning home.

He was obsessed by the idea of returning to Ireland, and the very thought of that country brought on great waves of emotion. Writing to a friend in Belfast, he commented: "Indeed as I write, it is interesting, here, forty years come back again. I suppose it is the same with all who go far from home and work in foreign lands: we never forget, and a sound, or a smell, or a sight brings up cradle days and all the surroundings of Home Sweet Home. I've had to stop here for a minute: the tears fill into my eyes. Fancy weeping in '89 in Peking over recollections in Priest Hill [Belfast University] in '49; but so it is, and it is good to have one's memory roused, and one's heart touched and wakened from the wintryness and worldliness of age."[66] In 1888, he was dismayed to think that "I suppose I shall have to resign, or settle down here for ever." Late in life, his concern over dying in China grew strong: "I don't like the thought of passing away here alone, and so far from friends, but others have to submit to that, and why not I? I have lived long, had excellent health, spent life pleasantly, and I cannot fall out with Heaven for taking me off — if I am to go. But I should prefer to go to Heaven, as I said before, via London, rather than direct."[67]

These sentiments highlight the ambiguity of Hart's position and the reflection of that ambiguity in his own mind. Like Lay before him, he had to meet the bitter criticisms of merchants and even consuls that he was using the customs service to help the Chinese against British interests. On the Chinese side, he faced suspicion of just the opposite sort. Even such powerful officials as Li Hung-chang and Tseng Chi-tse disliked and distrusted him. He was a man caught between two cultures, having to balance both at once, to keep them in proper perspective in his mind. Working under these conditions, we can see this constantly reiterated desire to go home as more symbolic than realizable — an attempt to keep his identity assured. For in his fifty-four years in China, he only went home twice on leave: briefly in 1866, during which time he married the daughter of a doctor in his hometown; and again in 1878 as president of the Chinese government's Commission to the Paris Exhibition, at which time he only spent two weeks in Great Britain, all in London. And,

in fact, what could he expect from an England to which he returned — an England which had offered him few enough opportunities for advancement as a youth and which he had left simply
because it was better for a young Irish boy of poor background to
gamble on the unknown than remain within the very limited known?
He could expect as his biographer, Stanley Wright, put it, "a re-
union with his family and with the few remaining friends of days
long gone by, some public appearances as a nine days' wonder, a few
superfluous honours . . . and the doubtful pleasure of watching
from afar movements and happenings in which he would infinitely
rather be playing a part."[68] Perhaps his old chief, H. N. Lay who
died in 1898 a forgotten man, provided him with an example.

Against this what had China given him? It gave him a position of
such power, before he was even thirty years of age, as most men do
not see in their lifetimes. Apart from the overtaxing work (which
was really his own choice) and a good deal of frustration, China gave
him power, influence, glory, and status. Ironically, it brought him a
recognition from his own country (as well as over a score of other
European nations) which would have been nearly unattainable had
he stayed in Ireland. In 1885 he was offered the post of British
Minister to the Chinese government. "The change from Inspector-
General to Minister was absolutely unsought by me, and if it were
not for the possibility of some good work, and the sentimental glitter
of ending at the Legation, I should infinitely prefer to stay where I
am," which, of course, he finally chose to do.[69] Despite his refusal he
was made Sir Robert Hart. Beyond this, his unrestrained power
within the customs service allowed him to help his friends and relatives. "I have never," he declared, "advanced a worse man over a
better; yet, if promotion is due to one of two men of equal deserts,
and one of them is of my own flesh and blood, it would simply be
unnatural to pass him over."[70]

With such power and, as time passed, the status that accrued to it,
he was able to arrange his life-style as it pleased him. In 1879,
according to his niece, "the Chinese, partly no doubt with the idea of
keeping all the foreigners together and partly for the convenience of

business, presently gave the I.G. a piece of land in this [Legation] quarter [in Peking], and he accordingly moved down to comparative civilization — as we understand it — from his far-away corner of the suburbs." There he built himself his house, "a bungalow — for the Chinese in those days objected to high buildings lest they should overlook the Palace — and built in the form of a letter H, partly from a sentimental connection with his own initial, and partly to utilize all the sunshine and southerly breeze possible. Two fine drawing-rooms, a billiard- and a dining-room, filled the cross-bar of the letter; one of the perpendicular strokes was the west, or guest wing; the other contained his own private offices, a special reception-room, furnished in Chinese style — stiff chairs and rigid tables — for Chinese guests and his living-rooms."[71]

With the bungalow went a large Chinese garden. In that garden, Hart installed his own private band of twenty Chinese youths, taught how to play Western instruments by a Portuguese bandmaster. In addition he made sure that "a young man [in the customs service] who is gifted with some social accomplishment or lucky enough to have an accomplished wife, is sure of being ordered to Peking. The I.G. has thus surrounded himself with a constellation of beauty and musical talent which eclipses any of the ten legations. His house is a rallying-point for the whole foreign community. He . . . gives garden-parties once a week, and dinners, followed by dancing, at least as often."[72] When, more rarely, there was a formal dinner some-where else, "the I.G.'s wife went in state, and as became her rank, in a big green box of a sedan chair with 4 bearers."[73]

He seems nonetheless to have been a shy man in private life, though quite fearsome to his subordinates and even his friends during working hours. As one of his critics put it, "there is no doubt that socially he got on far better with women than with his own sex, but all the same he had the masculine trait of not thinking much of the female intellect. Highbrows had no attraction for him; he liked his women friends to be young and pretty — of the sort that could be impressed and say, 'Oh, Sir Robert!' at the right moment."[74] Hart himself exclaimed, "They come; I know why they all come. It is just

Robert Hart (extreme right) and his Chinese band. His Portuguese band-master, M. Encarnaçao, stands at far left.

to get a sight of the two curios of Peking, the I.G. and his queer musicians."[75]

Yet, for all his status, influence, and power in China, Hart realized, from the beginning what he called his "anomalous position." A loyal supporter of the Ch'ing dynasty, which he believed to be the only immediate alternative to anarchy, as he grew older he watched the rise of nationalist feelings both in and around China. After the Sino-Japanese war of 1894-1895, in which Japan first asserted its rights to be called an Asian power, he commented sadly: "This Japanese development and performance will be one of evolution's biggest feats, and it is only beginning! As it proceeds, the Japs will fall in love with the work, and all the East will feel the strong hand."[76]

He despaired of the government he was supporting. "Poor China", he wrote in the spring of 1899. "Even yet they'll not wake up to the necessity for real reform. They can be hammered and hectored into giving up anything, but no advice — no warning — will rouse them to strengthening their backbone or sharpening their claws." Yet, behind this governmental inertia, he saw perhaps more clearly than any other Westerner in China at the time, greater forces at work; and saw, as well, that those forces were egged on by the very acts of Imperialism by which Europe seemed to be pulling China apart. He summed it up this way:

> The fact is everybody's for exploiting China, and concessions in China are thought to be everything. As well have them in the moon! There is nothing new under the sun, and why should not a South Sea Bubble repeat itself? At the bottom of every scheme there are two things that, to my mind, damn it. The first is that it is forced on China and shows so little respect for China that China will drop it whenever she can; and the second thing is that the framers know next to nothing about the country or the conditions the working of the scheme will meet, and that the paying or buying [Chinese] public exists more in

fanciful estimates than in sober reality, — and so I think all these schemes will be ruinous in the end.[77]

As early as 1894 Hart predicted that "Chinese blood has been well cooled by the training its brain has had the last twenty centuries, but I think it quite possible that one of these days despair may find expression in the wildest rage, and that we foreigners will one and all be wiped out in Peking."[78] In 1900 that "wildest rage" took the form of the Boxer movement, a primitive popular uprising inspired by a Chinese secret society and turned against the foreigner in North China, particularly against the foreign missionaries. Those foreigners who were not killed were besieged for two months in the Legation quarter at Peking, Hart among them. A foreign expeditionary force (composed of the soldiers of twelve nations, including Japan) finally relieved the Legations on August 14, 1900. Anti-Chinese feelings ran high among the Western nations. Contemptuously, the Chinese were termed barbarous and China referred to as the "Yellow Peril." The result was that on September 7, 1901, the Chinese government was forced to sign the Boxer Protocol, granting huge indemnities to the foreign powers, and requiring the destruction of the forts at Taku, the occupation of points between Peking and the sea by foreign troops, and the stopping of importation or manufacture of arms for two years.[79]

For Robert Hart more than other Westerners in China, the Boxer Rebellion was a cataclysm. Personally, he lost almost everything. His house was burned to the ground, his letters from old friends, diaries, possessions of a lifetime disappeared. At the age of sixty-five, he was subjected to the hardships of the siege. Like Schall, left in a ravaged Peking when the Ming dynasty fell, Hart saw the hard work and loyalty of almost forty years end in fire and destruction. He saw both the China and the dynasty which he had so loyally served for some decades worse off than when he began to work. "I am horribly hurt by all that has occurred," he wrote, "but there it is, and we can only try and make the best of it! I hold on to be of use to the Service, to China, and general interests. I think I can be of use, and *only* I in all three directions, at this juncture. Otherwise I'd up anchor and be off."[80] But, like Schall, in the wake of all this destruction, he remained calm; and before the dust had settled, he began again, commenting, "I have had my holiday already. Eight weeks of doing nothing, — what more could a man expect?"[81] With that, he plunged into the negotiations for the Boxer Protocol, hoping to soften Western terms and help once more to shore up the failing Ch'ing dynasty.

It is the measure of the man that Hart, amid the "vengeance" atmosphere of his Western friends and in the face of China's total humiliation, could see so clearly and sympathetically the direction in which events would move. In a series of essays written just after the siege was lifted, he commented: "The Boxer movement is doubtless the product of official inspiration, but it has taken hold of the popular imagination, and will spread like wildfire all over the length and breadth of the country; it is, in short, a purely patriotic volunteer movement, and its object is to strengthen China — and for a Chinese programme." He added, prophetically:

Twenty millions or more of Boxers, armed, drilled, disciplined, and animated by patriotic — if mistaken — motives, will make residence in China impossible for foreigners, will take back from foreigners everything foreigners have taken from China, will pay off old grudges with interest, and will carry the Chinese flag and Chinese arms into many a place that even fancy will not suggest to-day, thus preparing for the future upheavals and disasters never even dreamt of. In fifty years' time there will be millions of Boxers in serried ranks and war's panoply at the call of the Chinese Government: there is not the slightest doubt of that![82]

In gauging China's future relations with Europe, he wrote:

What has happened has been the logical effect of previous doings. Europe has not been ungenerous in her treatment of

China, but, even so, has wounded her: a more tactful, reasonable, and consistent course might possibly have produced better results, but in no case could foreigners expect to maintain for ever their extraterritorialized status and the various commercial stipulations China had conceded to force. As to the future, it must be confessed that Chinese, so far, have not shone as soldiers: but there are brave men among them and their number will increase; if the China of to-day did not hesitate on the 19th June to throw down the glove to a dozen Treaty Powers, is the China of a hundred years hence less likely to do so? Of course common sense may keep China from initiating an aggressive policy and from going to extremes; but foreign dictation must some day cease and foreigners some day go, and the episode now called attention to is to-day's hint to the future. Meanwhile the once crowded Peking is a desert, and the first few days of foreign occupation have seen much that need not have occurred and will certainly be regretted.[83]

Though Hart stayed on for eight years after the siege of the legations, and though his customs service took on even greater responsibilities with the new indemnities to be paid and the new job of controlling inland (Chinese) customs as well as customs in the treaty ports, his prophecies began to prove true for himself. He was old, tired, and in ill health; moreover, the Chinese (by an Imperial edict in 1906) made the first moves toward taking over the customs service from foreign control. New forces were at work in China and he was too old to live among them, though he might clearly see and reluctantly sympathize with them. In 1908, though technically still Inspector-General of Customs (which post he retained till his death), he left China. "The morning of his going, I remember, broke fine and clear," wrote his niece, "and the I.G.'s own band had come of its own accord to play 'Auld Lang Syne.' As the I.G. stepped from his sedan chair at the end of the platform his face wore an expression of bewilderment, but only for a moment. Then he turned to the commanding officer, and saying 'I am ready,' walked steadily down the lines of saluting troops while the bands all played 'Home, Sweet Home.' Just as quietly he said good-bye to the host of Chinese officials with whom he had been associated so long; then turned to the Europeans whom he had known so well, to all of whom he had done many kindnesses, and none of whom could say 'Bon Voyage' dry-eyed. . . . At last he stepped on board the train and slowly drew away from the crowd, bowing again and again in his modest way."[84]

He left at the right moment. A new age was coming and only a new kind of adviser from the West would be able to adapt to its conditions. Hart had been the most powerful Westerner in China for decades and yet the Service he controlled and built up had barely affected the basic structure of the Chinese economy and all his exertions had ended in an event of overwhelming humiliation to China. "It's amusing," he commented in a reflective mood, "to have in my time planted the Customs at Hongkong (England), Macao (Portugal), Mengtzu (Yunnan), Lungchow (Kwangsi), Chungking (Szechuan), Seoul, etc. (Korea), and now Tatung (Tibet). We have helped to keep China quiet and the dynasty on its legs, and I hope this is something; for otherwise I don't see much in return for all the work done and thought expended on it — except that the thought produced the work, and the work has succeeded as work! Our forty years of existence is now a part of history, and our doings are woven into the web of the Universe — but as far as simple facts go, I suppose the same can be said of that 'Ta-ra-ra-boom-de-ay' girl, Lottie Collins!"[85] He died on September 20, 1911, just three weeks before the dynasty he had spent his life supporting was overthrown.

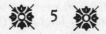 5

MARTIN and FRYER:

Trimming the Lamps

Western advisers in nineteenth-century China, though working without any coherent or coordinated plan, anticipated the patterns of action that in the mid-twentieth century were to be sanctified as "aid to underdeveloped areas." They offered military assistance to the incumbent regime against internal rebels; they pushed through economic reforms to give greater financial stability; and they tried to change the educational structure, in an attempt to make the young more receptive to Western ways.

In China, it was particularly hard for a foreigner to enter the educational sector. To the Chinese, education was the key to social harmony and political stability: from the Confucian *Classics*, hallowed by a tradition reaching back over two thousand years, the young learned obedience, morality, and the norms of acceptable behavior. On the basis of their study of the *Classics*, they participated in the ascending levels of examinations for the civil service. Success in these examinations opened up prospects for a career in government, the major source of wealth and power. To introduce new subjects — such as Western philosophy, languages, or natural science — was to threaten the basis of the Chinese state. Innovation, accordingly, was vigorously resisted.[1]

Resistance did not discourage the Westerners, propelled onward by the dream of making China over into their own image. Of these Westerners one of the most tenacious was an American, William Alexander Parsons Martin. The eighth of ten children in the Martin family, he was born in Indiana on April 10, 1827. His father, an itinerant Presbyterian minister, named this son after two missionaries, brought him up in an atmosphere of strict Calvinism, and took it for granted that he would one day work in the missionary field. For a time young Martin wavered. Study of the sciences at Indiana University made him flexible in his ideas, and he was restless with the rough frontier religion that he was taught at the Presbyterian Theological Seminary. But in the end his parents' wishes prevailed, and at the age of twenty-two Martin sailed for China; he took with him an excellent knowledge of Greek, rhetoric, electricity, optics, and Calvinist theology.[2]

His reception in Canton was scarcely encouraging, but Martin was undaunted. "As we stepped on shore we were greeted by a hooting crowd, who shouted *Fanqui, fanqui! shato, shato!* ('Foreign devils! cut off their heads!'). 'Is this,' I mused, 'the boasted civilization of China? Are these the people for whom I left my home?' But, I reflected, if they were not heathen, why should I have come?"[3] He proceeded up the coast to Ningpo where the Presbyterians had already established a mission, school and printing press. He began immediately to learn the local Ningpo dialect as well as Mandarin.

> With no book or vocabulary to guide me. . . . I was left to form my own system. I took the German, or rather Continental, vowels as the basis, and, with a few modifications, soon arrived at a mode of notation which enabled me to reproduce what I had written down from the lips of my teacher. The idea struck me of teaching him to write in the same way. . . . In a day or two he was able to write separate words, and a week later I received from him a neatly written note inviting us to take a "tiffin," or noonday meal, at his house. Its lucidity and simplicity delighted me, and I exhibited it rather ostentatiously at the breakfast-table. . . . Before the sun had set on that to me

memorable day, in January, 1851, we had formed a society for the purpose of fixing a definitive system for the writing of the "Ningpo colloquial."[4]

Martin began to develop a block-printing system to turn out the "new literature." The hope of conquering the intricate Chinese written language aroused his emotions as religion had never done. "The Chinese," he comments, "saw with astonishment their children taught to read in a few days, instead of spending years in painful toil, as they must with the native characters. Old women of threescore and ten, and illiterate servants and laborers, on their conversion, found by this means their eyes opened to read in their own tongue wherein they were born the wonderful works of God."[5]

In his activities he struck out in all directions with an amazing versatility. Within six months, he was making his first attempts to preach to Chinese audiences and within a year and a half was composing hymns in Chinese. Soon after his arrival, as well, he began studying the written language under a native teacher and completed within five years the "nine chief works which form the basis of Chinese literature. But for distractions, incident to active duty, I might have accomplished this in a shorter time." He also wrote texts for the Chinese on arithmetic and geography, a history of Greece and Rome, and composed his *Tien-tao Su-yuen* (Evidence of Christianity) on which he later commented: "It has, I believe, led to the conversion of many among the educated classes. *Deo Soli Gloria.*"[6] He even organized a small school in which to experiment with his romanization system.

Yet the results were disappointing. The few converts he made came from the mission staff, and their motives often seemed as much financial as religious. His experiments with teaching the Chinese to read through a romanized form of their own vernacular foundered in the face of the Chinese respect for their own ideographic script. And the inflexibility and constraint of life in the mission irked a young man with ideas of his own. As early as 1853 he was looking for new means to open China to Western civilization, Western education, and the Christian God. The Taiping Rebellion seemed to offer the opportunities he sought. "The rebellion is going on apace," he wrote to the Mission Board in New York, "and is not unlikely, from the present appearances, to revolutionize the empire, perhaps rendering all its vast territory open to the preachers of the Gospel." Foiled in his attempt to reach the rebel capital of Nanking, he remained a vocal champion of the rebels, whom he saw as "abstemious, devout and image-breaking" men, and contrasted with the "dissolute and atheistic, or idolatrous Imperialists." He continued to irritate his mission superiors by his willingness to make what they felt were excessive concessions to Chinese culture and by his approach to conversion, which they felt was intellectual rather than spiritual.[7] Finally, in 1858, after he had been refused permission to establish his own mission station in the suburbs of Ningpo, Martin applied for a job as interpreter to the U.S. Minister in China. He was anxious to see Peking, home of the Court and capital of the Empire, which the Jesuits had used as the base for their missionary endeavors.

He was given the post and performed his duties satisfactorily; in an important breakthrough for the missionary cause, he was instrumental in getting a religious toleration clause inserted in the Sino-American treaty. As he had hoped, the work took him to Peking, and he was confirmed in his belief that it would make a promising base for missionary activity. He petitioned his superiors for permission to establish a mission in the capital. When it was not granted, he returned to America for a two-year leave.

He came back to China in 1862, more determined than ever to settle in Peking. Though his own superiors remained adamant, he secured the backing of the British and American ministers for his project, and in 1863, with money borrowed from a friend, he purchased buildings in the Inner City of Peking. Here he established a small chapel and a school. But once again his dreams of wide-scale conversion were not realized — he could claim only six or seven converts a year, and once the initial curiosity had been satisfied, few Chinese, except for the very poor, attended his chapel at all. The

school did little better; Chinese from wealthy families were unwilling
to jeopardize their chances of an official career by studying science
with a foreigner. Most of his pupils were from the poorest classes,
men who found in Martin's offers of food and clothing an escape
from their abject poverty.[8]

Far from deterring Martin, these disappointments gave wings to
his dreams. As he wrote in 1866 after a jarring, slow journey into
Honan by mulecart:

> What better preparation for such dreaming than to arrive
> at a miserable inn with sore feet and aching head after driving
> from five in the morning till nine at night to make out the
> distance of forty miles? . . . Weird fancy waves over you her
> creative wand and old memories mingle with present realities.
> Instead of the shout of your mule-driver and the rumbling of
> his cart-wheels, you hear the shriek of the steam whistle, the
> rush of the train and the click of the telegraph. The dingy
> hovel rises into a stately stationhouse — its carpeted saloons
> thronged by people of all the provinces and the ticket-office
> besieged by an eager crowd. You press to the front, hear your
> money clink on the counter, and are just clutching the coupon
> . . . when the crowing cock awakes you to another day of toil
> and pain.[9]

For men like Martin, Christianity and the scientific "progress" of
the West were inextricably linked. Having failed to make much
headway through preaching to the urban and rustic poor, it was
logical for him to conclude that Westernization must precede, and
would inevitably lead to, Christian conversion. Before Westernization was possible, there must be greater contact between China and
the West: open diplomatic intercourse and more scientific education
on a national, not just a mission-school, scale. But such changes could
only be brought about from the top down, and thus Martin followed
the Jesuit tactic of using his technical skills to gain a foothold in the

bureaucracy. Martin had studied Ricci's career and concluded that "careful to avoid giving offense, and courtly in manners, his science proved to be the master-key."[10]

In the search for his own master key, Martin had the enthusiastic support of Robert Hart, who was just beginning to establish his reputation as Inspector-General of Customs. Hart encouraged Martin to make a full translation of Henry Wheaton's *Elements of International Law;* with the help of Chinese scholars the work was finished by 1863 and presented to the Tsungli Yamen, China's new Foreign Office, that same year. Martin was apologetic about an undertaking that took so much time from his missionary work, but justified it as "not unsuitable for a missionary who feels in duty bound to seek the welfare of the country he has chosen for the seat of his labors," and trusted that it "might bring this atheistic government to the recognition of God and His Eternal Justice."[11]

Chinese officials were initially skeptical of the book's value, writing that "its words and sentences are confused and disorderly; we cannot clearly understand it unless it is explained in person."[12] Prince Kung reported to the Emperor: "Your ministers think that his purpose is two-fold, first to boast that foreign countries also have laws, and secondly, to imitate men like Matteo Ricci in making a name in China."[13] It was a shrewd guess as to Martin's general intentions, and he and his book might well have been consigned to limbo, had it not been for a stroke of luck. In 1864 the Tsungli Yamen officials were able to apply principles drawn from Wheaton to force the Prussians to relinquish a Danish ship that they had captured in China's territorial waters. Prince Kung admitted that "although the said book on foreign laws and regulations is not basically in complete agreement with the Chinese systems, it nevertheless contains sporadic useful points." Among these, Prince Kung emphasized, was the fact that the book suggested "quite a few methods of controlling and bridling the consuls, which may be useful," and he ordered that three hundred copies be distributed among the provincial officials.[14]

This of course was a traditional argument — the old Chinese

principle of "using barbarians to control barbarians," which had been used to justify employment of Ward, Gordon, Lay and Hart. And in 1865 Martin was offered a post as teacher of English in the T'ung-wen Kuan, a school that had recently been established in Peking by Imperial command for the training of interpreters. Martin accepted, relinquishing his missionary salary, and becoming a paid employee of the Chinese government. He believed that his translation of Wheaton might "stand second in influence to the translation of the Bible," and that the teaching post was one with enormous possibilities for influencing the Chinese.[15]

Martin's exuberance was premature. He had been given the post because Chinese statesmen in the 1860's had realized that they were going to have to deal with the West. They therefore sought foreign experts who promised to be loyal and amenable and could be used with profit. Martin was earnest and enthusiastic; he spoke good Chinese; his translation had proved surprisingly useful; and he was friendly both with Robert Hart and the American minister, Anson Burlingame. Furthermore his ideas on education struck a responsive chord in some government circles. The eminent scholar Feng Kuei-fen, studying in Shanghai during the Taiping Rebellion, had made a survey of the fruits of foreign scholarship: he found the religious works "generally vulgar, not worth mentioning"; but "Western books on mathematics, mechanics, optics, light, chemistry, and other subjects contain the best principles of the natural sciences. In the books on geography, the mountains, rivers, strategic points, customs, and native products of the hundred countries are fully listed. Most of this information is beyond the reach of our people." Feng added that the Chinese who passed as "linguists" in the treaty ports were "generally frivolous rascals and loafers in the cities and are despised in their village communities. They serve as interpreters only because they have no other means of making a livelihood. Their nature is boorish, their knowledge shallow, and furthermore their moral principles are mean." He advised that a number of Western teachers be hired to teach their languages to a select number of outstanding Chinese students. Since "all Western knowledge is derived from mathematics," that subject should be made an integral part of the curriculum.[16]

These ideas found favor with powerful officials like Tseng Kuo-fan, Li Hung-chang, and Prince Kung, but they also aroused bitter opposition from countless Confucian scholars who felt that such innovations threatened the moral fabric of society. "Astronomy and mathematics are of very little use," ran the counterargument. "If these subjects are going to be taught by Westerners as regular studies, the damage will be great. . . . The way to establish a nation is to lay emphasis on propriety and righteousness, not on power and plotting. The fundamental effort lies in the minds of the people, not in techniques."[17]

In the face of these hostile arguments, the only way that the new school could operate was by pretending that it was nothing new, and here a defunct school for Russian language, founded in the mid-eighteenth century, proved particularly useful. The "intangible assets" of the Russian school, as Martin described them, "were certain precedents and regulations. The latter were freely copied and the former constantly appealed to, to obviate objection, and to prove that the new departure was no novelty."[18]

This constant harking back to the past was not conducive to the kind of breakthrough Martin had envisaged, and after only a few months of teaching he submitted his resignation: "To be candid," he told his employers, "the care of only ten boys who learn nothing but English is for me too small a business. It looks like throwing away my time." The Chinese persuaded him to stay, promising expansion of the school, pointing out that his students of today might well be the officials of tomorrow, and dangling before him the prospect that one day one of his own students might teach the Emperor English. Rationalizing his decision, Martin wrote: "A view so gratifying to one who regards effective influence for good as the first object in life decided me to stay, though I had gone so far as to offer to find a successor, and had spoken in that sense to Mr. Goodrich. Goodrich, however, declined the place as liable to turn him aside from preaching the gospel. I retained it, as promising to open a field of influence

W. A. P. Martin in Peking, with four of his students.

much wider than I could find in the wayside chapels of Peking."[19] The pursuit of that elusive influence led Martin to sever his last formal ties with his missionary work: in 1867 he accepted the post of professor of international law and political economy in the T'ung-wen Kuan, and turned over his mission to a successor. Only two years later he was appointed president of the T'ung-wen Kuan, and tendered his resignation to the Mission Board in New York.[20]

Martin was determined to make a success of the T'ung-wen Kuan school. A basic problem was finance, since Western salaries were enormously high, by Chinese standards, and Chinese money was only grudgingly made available. This was solved by agreement with Robert Hart, who undertook to supply a lump sum from the customs revenues every year. In Martin's phrase, Hart would supply the oil while Martin trimmed the lamps.[21] Trimming the lamps meant introducing advanced Western sciences; Martin started with physics and mathematics and, as more staff were hired, added departments of chemistry, physiology, and medicine. According to the school regulations all religious instruction was forbidden. More than ever, therefore, Martin had to take the long view of conversion, trusting that the way to Christianity would be opened once China's primitive superstitions had been banished.

To do this, he needed to attract outstanding students and to have them launched on official careers. But the students saw no guarantees that Martin's curriculum would bring official preferment, and directed their energies accordingly. "They pursued their English studies in a very perfunctory spirit, the greater part of their time and energy being given to Chinese," wrote one of their harried teachers. The reason was that only mastery of Chinese would "give them a status and position in the country, while the career to be looked forward to as the reward of their foreign attainments was, at the best, uncertain." Nor were the first students encouraging material: "The few who came were men who had failed in the official career — broken down hacks to whom the stipend offered by the yamen proved dearer than their reputation. . . . They were looked upon by their literary brethren as renegades and traitors to the cause. They felt that they were so themselves." Many of them denied in public that they were enrolled in the School at all.[22]

Martin was not discouraged. On the contrary, he developed new sympathy for the Chinese. He wrote in 1868:

> Never have a great people been more misunderstood. They are denounced as stolid, because we are not in possession of a medium sufficiently transparent to convey our ideas to them, or transmit theirs to us; and stigmatized as barbarians, because we want the breadth to comprehend a civilization different from our own. . . . The national mind has advanced from age to age with a stately march; not indeed always in a direct course, but at each of its great epochs, recording, as we think, a decided gain; like the dawn of an arctic morning, in which the first blush of the eastern sky disappears for many hours, only to be succeeded by a brighter glow, growing brighter yet, after each interval of darkness, as the time of sunrise approaches.[23]

His goal was to speed the new dawn; to achieve this he had to transform the school "from a glow-worm to a lighthouse," so that "millions of aspiring students would soon become as earnest in the pursuit of modern science as they now are in the study of their ancient classics."[24] To this end Martin devoted the next forty years of his life. He developed an eight-year curriculum, designed to cover the major areas of Western knowledge: three years were spent on a foreign language, geography, and Western history; the fourth and fifth were devoted to mathematics; the sixth to mechanics, calculus and navigation; the seventh to astronomy, geology and mineralogy; the eighth to political economy and international law.[25]

The dawn was slow in coming. In his private correspondence Martin dropped the hyperbole that characterized his published writings: "The College may be said to prosper," he told a friend, "as things go in China, i.e. slowly by the addition of now and then a student and now and then a professor."[26] It was sometimes hard to believe that the Chinese had much commitment to Western progress. The telegraph class was a good example. Martin had brought from the United States, at his own expense, "two sets of instruments, one on the Morse system, the other with an alphabetic dial-plate, easy to learn and striking to the eye." Senior officials duly consented to view the wonders, and had a fine morning, "sending bell signals, wrapping copper wire about their bodies, breaking or closing the circuit, and laughing heartily as they saw sparks leaping from wire to wire and setting hammers in motion." But once the novelty had worn off, few were interested in learning how the instruments actually worked; the mechanisms, promise of a new age, were finally "stored as old lumber" in the school's museum.[27]

But the caliber of the students did rise slowly, and they received supplementary duties as interpreters in the Tsungli Yamen and as translators of Western books. By the late 1870's some of the students began to receive minor posts, and several were appointed overseas to the new Chinese legations. Martin became an established and respected figure. In the early 1880's the Chinese government dispatched him to the United States, Europe, and Japan to report on their varied educational systems. In 1885 he was granted the third rank in the official Chinese hierarchy; ten years later he was promoted to the second rank. In Chinese terms he had proved a loyal and dutiful official.

*   *   *

Despite frustrations, a man like Martin could persevere in China, and achieve a measure of contentment, because he believed in the importance of what he was doing. But for others in the same line of work, with no goad except personal ambition, life in China could fall into a wearisome pattern of drudgery and disappointment. Such was the case for John Fryer, who sought wealth and honor in China. As a child in England, Fryer had absorbed his parents' dreams of China, and had watched while his father, a poor clergyman, listened eagerly to returned missionaries and merchants and became deeply interested in the opening of China to the West. "My father," he recalled, "subscribed as much [money] as he was able while my mother for a time adopted rice as a considerable part of her diet." Their son dreamed their dreams: "During my boyhood nothing pleased me more than to read all the books that could be obtained about China. If asked to write a piece of composition the subject I always chose was China. In fact, I was so full of China that my school-fellows gave me the nick-name 'Chin-chong Fy-ung.' "[28]

Attached to a school "attended only by the lowest of the low," and with the family usually short of money, John Fryer built castles in the sky. "When I was sent as an errand boy in the Brewery at Hythe to clean boots and shoes and knives my spirit was so galled that I resolved to work my way up in the world if it was within the range of possibility; and as I washed down the door steps every morning I resolved to make every position a stepping stone to something higher."[29] A government scholarship helped him on his way by taking him from Hythe to the Highbury Training College in London.

Upon graduation in 1860 he accepted a job as headmaster of a small missionary school in Hong Kong, which trained Chinese boys contemplating careers as Protestant ministers. Twenty-two-years-old, and full of hope, Fryer reached Hong Kong in 1861; but on first contact the Chinese failed to live up to his expectations: "One striking feature in the Chinese character is their don't care sort of feeling. If they can get out of doing anything they will, unless they can see a chance of being well paid for it. Anything they do not want to understand they pretend great ignorance of. In fact, unless money is in the way one would take them for a race of idiots."[30]

In Hong Kong, Fryer began intensive study of Cantonese, the local dialect; but in 1863 he accepted a job teaching English at the T'ung-wen Kuan in Peking, in order to learn Mandarin, the speech of the educated bureaucratic elite.[31] Unlike Martin, he was not impressed by Peking. After two years there he sensed opportunities in the bustling commercial city of Shanghai, now free from the Taiping menace, and decided to follow his stated goal of making "every position a stepping stone to something higher" by taking a post offered him as headmaster of the Shanghai Anglo-Chinese School.

Certainly it could not be claimed that teaching — "the dull monotonous task of pedagogue" Fryer called it — was his vocation: "I always detested school teaching. My parents wished me to become a teacher and it was in obedience to their wishes that I did so. Once a schoolmaster always a schoolmaster seems to be the idea in people's minds. It has been difficult to get free from the toil of cramming knowledge into narrow skulls where there was no room for it."[32]

Shanghai in the 1860's was a good place for an ambitious fellow to be. The delta port was the natural focus for the trade of China's greatest internal waterway, the Yangtze, and the distribution mart for the Yangtze valley, one of China's major population concentrations. Divided into two major areas, the Foreign Settlements and the Chinese City, it had become the meeting point for two civilizations. It had all the characteristics of a boom city: vice, opium, and gambling were everywhere — the British consul noted in 1864 that 668 of the ten thousand Chinese houses in the Foreign Settlements were brothels. It was a center for speculation in real estate and business: almost half a million Chinese refugees had entered the city during the Taiping Rebellion, and downtown land which had stood at £50 an acre in 1852 had soared to £10,000 an acre by 1862. To make more money, the Western community had even converted their beloved racetrack into tenements,[33] though they speedily built another one.

A lowly social background was no drawback here. "How many people in Shanghai," Fryer wrote, "do you think would care to have their genealogy sifted?"[34] It was an open, hearty life for a Westerner, and Fryer tried to get the feel of its rhythm. "I shall get in a firkin of beer, and shall take my glass twice a day," he told his presumably horrified parents. "China has cured me of homeopathy and teatotalism. I believe in good exercise, good food, a glass of wine and two glasses of beer a day with plenty of beefsteak and eggs. Now and then a regular clear out with aperient medicine is all that I think one requires."[35] He was even touched by the speculation fever, writing to his brother: "I have more money than I know what to do with just at present, and think next month to send home £250 of tea

for speculation. I might lose it all and I might gain the money over
again. Nothing venture nothing got in every business."[36] But his
nerve failed and the money went into a bank.

In such an atmosphere, teaching the rudiments of the English
language to about twenty Chinese merchants' sons in a missionary-
directed school with a leaking roof became an increasingly unattrac-
tive proposition. Fryer liked to think of himself as a young man in a
hurry, but found he was falling into a rut. "My lot seems already
fixed and I am too old to change," he wrote to his cousin Susy in
1867. "Although I am only 28 I am as old as some men of 38.
Through living so much among Chinamen I have acquired all sorts
of funny habits, and speak English in a way that will afford you
much amusement some day if ever you see me again in England.
People will consider me a most eccentric old fellow." He was getting
"very much like an old hermit," he said, with a bald head, an "unfortunate moustache" and a beard that had begun "to turn fearfully
grey and if it goes on at this rate it will be entirely white in another
year. So much for seven years in this barbarous country."[37] "Really I
live so much out of the world," he told another friend, "that I get no
news worth writing. . . . It is a wretched kind of life to lead in the
midst of such uncertainty. My father's only consolation to me is 'It is
good for a man that he bear the yoke in his youth,' but really I think
I have had a little too much of it, one way and another. . . . I have
little leisure, and take but few walks. That accounts for my getting
the blues very often." And "I am perfectly sick of teaching English."[38] In his annual report he inflicted his irritation even on the
school's director: "Month after month of monotonous and wearisome
labour has to be expended without any very perceptible or flattering
results being produced."[39]

Nor did Fryer plunge into the task of spreading Christianity
among the heathen with the enthusiasm that his superiors apparently
desired. While in England he had considered becoming a minister
like his father, but in China, he contented himself with reading a
text of scripture daily to his pupils. "The introduction of Christianity," he felt, "must be cautiously and gradually brought about, be-

cause in this way it is likely to be tolerated and even to some extent appreciated, whereas by bringing it prominently in the foreground at the commencement, the Chinese would be likely to misunderstand entirely the designs which the Committee have in view in establishing the school." So had Schall, Verbiest and Parker argued. Fryer added hopefully, "the spread of Christianity may perhaps by these indirect means be furthered to a greater extent than at first sight would appear probable," but he didn't seem very sure about it. In any case, he told the school director, he had "no desire at present to be connected with [the Church Missionary Society] whether directly or indirectly."[40] He seemed to relish the concern his attitude was causing; maybe he'd soon be free of the whole business: "I live quite out of the Foreign world altogether, and move in a little Chinese microcosm of my own. 'I am monarch of all I survey; and my right there is none to dispute' — except that dear old Church Missionary Society. Oh how I love and respect it. I shall be sent adrift soon I suppose and goodness knows where I shall float to."[41]

The frustrations made him nostalgic for England. "A nice quiet easy position with a moderate salary in some quiet little country village in the old country with the good lady to keep house for one, would certainly be a much happier state of things than the present." He murmured of "roses and honeysuckle" and of "gentlemen farmers and farmers' wives of the right sterling sort."[42] But he knew this picture was false, that it would be hard to settle down there, and that his prospects were better where he was. "By going abroad," he reflected, "people reap many benefits if they are strong and healthy, but there are many drawbacks. When one has lived abroad six years as I have, it will be like a new world to return home. A year or two will not root out habits and ways which are acquired here in China. Few people can be happy in England after having been long abroad."[43] Returning home would be a confession of failure.

His instinct told him to stick it out in China, to work away at the Chinese language in preparation for the great opportunities that must lie in the future — the next stepping-stones. "I think that my lot is fixed in China. Having studied six years at Chinese, and having acquired some facility in three dialects and the general written language, it would be like throwing away so much time if I gave it all up. And besides what could I find to do in England? And again, China is just now opening up to European civilization. Every year a rapid advance is made. A year or two more, and my knowledge will be invaluable, and people say I shall be worth my weight in gold. Very flattering is it not?"[44]

It was all a question of time and tenacity: "Most foreigners who come to China have the notion that in a year they will master the language. They get a teacher, and pound away vigorously for a week or perhaps a month and then give up in disgust." Accordingly, they made ludicrous mistakes which negated all their endeavors. He told his cousin of hearing a missionary in Shanghai trying to tell his Chinese audience that "Jesus is here also"; the missionary, muddling his tones and aspirates, succeeded only in assuring the puzzled listeners that "Jesus is inside shaving his head." "If I could have my way, not a single missionary should say one word in public till he had lived with the people and studied the local dialect of his mission station at least five years, and passed an examination. Just imagine the ridicule which such people bring on Christianity."[45] Fryer imagined his position was a strong one: "My knowledge of Chinese," he told his sister, "and the fabulous rumours as to my proficiency in different dialects and in Chinese composition, as well as my position as Editor of a popular Chinese newspaper, will enable me to command a good position. . . . I have already a name in China, and that is what many better men than I are striving to get and cannot succeed in."[46]

This "popular Chinese newspaper" was the second string to his bow. Called the *Chiao-hui hsin-pao* (Mission News), it had been founded in 1862 and enjoyed quite a wide circulation among missionaries. Fryer assumed the editorship in 1866 and expected great things. "I mean to make the newspaper work its way, to do a great deal in enlightening China when it gets more widely circulated. I have made up my mind to double the circulation in a year," he wrote to his parents in March 1867.[47] Through articles and editorial comment he tried to interest his Chinese readers in foreign affairs, science, and Western education. He recommended that the Ch'ing government should give young students three years' intensive training in a Western language and then send them to European universities. His articles were picked up and reprinted in newspapers in Canton and Hong Kong and he estimated that "my effusions are read by perhaps five thousand intelligent and of course educated Chinamen, and the illustrations form an attraction to their wives and children."[48] Fryer really enjoyed the newspaper work, to which he was "indebted for amusement as well as improvement," but in the spring of 1868 he suddenly dropped it. "The officials are afraid of the consequences if they were to let me become a recognized servant of the Government while acting as Editor. . . . The matter has lately been pressed upon me again, and it is now added to the terms of a formal engagement which they want me to enter into with them. . . . There is thus no alternative, and so I am reluctantly compelled to resign."[49] The "Government" and the "officials" were of course Chinese. The impatiently awaited opportunity had come. Shortly afterwards Fryer also resigned from the Anglo-Chinese School.

The position the Chinese offered him, which he had accepted with such alacrity, was that of translator of scientific books in the Kiangnan Arsenal in Shanghai. The Kiangnan Arsenal manufactured arms and ammunition, but also incorporated a translation department and schools for training translators and mechanics. It had been developed by Tseng Kuo-fan and Li Hung-chang at the close of the Taiping Rebellion, fruit of the new search for Western techniques that had led to the formation of the Tsungli Yamen and the T'ung-wen Kuan.[50] The Arsenals would supplement the diplomatic weapons hopefully being forged in Peking. As Tseng Kuo-fan wrote in 1862: "If we wish to find a method of self-strengthening, we should begin by considering the reform of government service and the securing of men of ability as urgent tasks, and then regard learning to make explosive shells and steamships and other instruments as the work of first importance. If only we could possess all their superior techniques, then we would have the means to return their favors when they are obedient, and we would also have the means to avenge our grievances when they are disloyal."[51]

Tseng's interest had then spread to the importance of translation. "In addition a school should be established in which to learn translation, because translation is the foundation for manufactures. Foreign manufacturing is derived from mathematics, all the profound mysteries of which can be discovered through diagrams and explanations. It is simply because the languages are mutually incomprehensible that, even though every day we practise on their machines, after all we do not understand the principles underlying their manufacture and operation."[52] Li Hung-chang developed Tseng's arguments, and pointed out how successful the Japanese were being in learning from the West; he warned that "if we have nothing with which to make ourselves strong, then the Japanese will imitate the Westerners and will share the Westerners' sources of profits."[53] Officials in the Tsungli Yamen backed up these arguments, and advised the Emperor: "We should seize the opportunity, at a time when in the southern provinces our military power is in great ascendancy and foreigners are delighted to show us their superior techniques, to make a substantial study of all kinds of foreign machines and weapons in order to learn their secret completely. . . . The friendliness or opposition of foreigners always depends upon the strength or weakness of China."[54]

Much of this discussion was sound: modern arms were one key to Western military successes, translation skills would bring better knowledge of Western mechanics, the Japanese were moving ahead fast and becoming a potential threat to China, and there were plenty of John Fryers around who would be "delighted" to help China forward. But a national "self-strengthening" program would demand a complete reevaluation of the Ch'ing economic and educational system, and to this the Chinese government was unwilling to commit itself. Instead the work was left to the local officials, who often plunged into projects without any understanding of their complexity.

Fryer had been approached in this way in 1867 and had not been convinced. "Feng kept me this morning for above an hour. His ideas seem to be almost absurd. Apparently he hardly knows what he wants to do himself, and has consequently no idea how to set to work. He proposes to take ten of the best scholars from the Taotai's school and let me teach them the principles of the steam engine at the Arsenal. Upon my pointing out the absurdity of such an arrangement he seemed annoyed; but insisted on my going to the Arsenal to look around, promising to send his chair for me. So there the matter rests."[55]

But the offer of a permanent appointment elated Fryer, and stilled his perfectly valid doubts. His horizons, enclosed for so long by schoolroom doors, had opened up again, and that was all that mattered. "Now I have shaken off the yoke I feel like a bird out of a cage," he wrote to his cousin Susy. And although he knew little of science, he plunged into the work in just as piecemeal a fashion as the Chinese, and at first enjoyed it hugely: "My business is to do what is absolute pleasure to me. I always loved Science, but never had time or opportunity to cultivate it. . . . I go at it in real earnest. . . . In the morning I take coal and coal-mining in all its details, in the afternoon I dig into chemistry and in the evening acoustics." His dormant hopes also revived: "I have found a satis-factory anchorage. I may say I never was more happy in my life than I am in my new situation of Translator of Scientific Books for the Chinese Government. It is an honourable and useful position as well as being respectable, and with a salary of £800 a year or thereabouts I can afford to live well. This however is only a beginning of the second era of my life. Excelsior is my motto. I have much higher to climb yet."[56] To his father he wrote even more boldly: "I hope to make it a stepping stone to a high position in China. My ambition knows scarcely any bounds. I have got my post entirely *independently* of any one — consuls, customs, and all I set at defiance."[57]

Before taking this position with the Chinese government Fryer had made one last gesture to the West, writing to Bishop Williams: "Negotiations have been made for my services elsewhere, but since I came to China originally in a missionary capacity I should not feel justified in entering upon purely secular work if a permanent position could be found where my time could entirely be devoted to the work of Christ." He expressed his willingness to work in an inland mission, away from the treaty ports.[58]

The offer was ignored, and Fryer began to enjoy the fruits of his secular work with a clear conscience. He rented "a pretty little house right out in the country" and settled there with his wife Anna. He enjoyed his half-hour ride across the fields in a sedan chair to the Arsenal and the return at dusk. He spent some of his new salary on a telescope and passed pleasant evenings stargazing, and also, he confessed, peering into the lighted windows of far-off houses. In his general exuberance he even took to thumping out an unsolicited musical accompaniment to the devotions of some neighboring Buddhist nuns. His Western neighbors were dropped "because they hardly come up to the standard which I have fixed for my acquaintances." Instead, he shared the cost of a horse and carriage with friends, and began to leave his card in the city. "There is a sort of clique in Shanghai to which I may be said to belong. All are good Christian fellows and in good positions."[59] The Chinese had definitely brought Fryer up in the world.

In the hopes of further advancement, Fryer gave them dedicated service. At first there was a strong measure of condescension in his relationship with his co-workers, even though he professed to admire them: "One younger than the rest has made quite a strong friendship with me and tells me all his affairs as though I were his brother. He is the cleverest Chinaman I ever met, and I am but a child compared to him in many respects. We sometimes argue different points up till midnight. I have taught him to sit at table and behave properly, and really he is a very good fellow for a companion."[60] Initially, also, the work was not very demanding. "I have no competitors for a very simple reason that none can be found up to the mark. I wish I had two or three that I might be stirred up a little and cured of my laziness. Sometimes I only do an hour's work in a day. The mandarins are more like children than men."[61]

Yet at the same time he believed the work offered great opportunities. In urging another Westerner to join the Arsenal staff he pointed out that "it seems to me to be second to none of the various means that are now employed by Missionary Societies — especially as it gives access to the class of Chinese who form the most important part of the Nation and who can be reached in no other way."[62] By the summer of 1869 he felt that the Arsenal "bids fair to become a powerful means for helping forward this venerable old nation and bringing it somewhat into the track of the 'March of Civilization' which we Foreigners like generally to boast about. . . . For my own part I have grown half like a Chinaman. Eight years residence has all but cured me of homesickness. . . . I reckon some of my best friends among the Chinese."[63] If China rose, then he would rise with it.

He was unwilling to jeopardize his new career by any act that might upset the Chinese, as is shown by a grim family example. In August 1869 his wife gave birth to their first child, a son. At the time of delivery she was seriously ill with typhoid fever, and the son died at the age of eight and a half days. His wife, still sick, and distraught at the loss of the baby (as indeed was Fryer himself), was ordered to go away for recuperation by the doctor. This was not possible, Fryer explained to her parents: "The doctor has ordered her to make a sea voyage, but I cannot leave my post to go with her." Instead she moved to a neighbor's house where the air was a little fresher.[64] Her recovery was slow and difficult. Fryer continued his work. He had been scared of applying for a few weeks' leave of absence; the Chinese officials, inured to infant mortality, and with no tradition of recuperative sea voyages, would have been puzzled and irritated by such a request.

Equally striking was Fryer's reaction to the Tientsin Massacre of June 1870. In Tientsin, after the French consul had fired at a Chinese, enraged crowds spread through the city, burning Western churches and business property, and hacking nuns and priests to death. It was known that anti-Western Chinese writers had long been fanning the flames for such an outbreak, issuing detailed and obscene pamphlets which accused Christian priests of copulating with their congregations after the service and committing sodomy in their churches, and nuns of sexually abusing and even eating the children in their orphanages.[65] Most Westerners, unable to see the disruptive effects of their presence on Chinese soil which had caused this violent reaction, were appalled; Martin was to write that the whole area where the riot occurred should have been burned to the ground, confiscated from the Chinese, and made into a French concession.[66] But Fryer expressed sympathy for the Chinese point of view. He wrote to his brother in August 1870: "Foreigners at all the ports are afraid of their lives and are drilling and volunteering and preparing in a way and at a rate which amuses the Chinese greatly. There is nothing for Merchants and Consuls to fear. The danger is to the missionaries and particularly the French, because they render themselves very obnoxious to the Chinese, so that the wonder is there has been nothing of this kind sooner."[67]

Such attitudes seemed to pay off with his Chinese employers, even if they alienated his Western colleagues. The same year Fryer wrote that "my position at the Arsenal is getting rather complicated. There are so many people who have a finger in the pie that it is often very difficult to steer clear of quarrels. In the Arsenal are some ten Foreign Engineers who look on me as an usurper, and are jealous because I have the ears of the officials and can say and do as I please."[68] He still hoped that he would be promoted to some major position in the Chinese bureaucracy; one specific idea he had was that he would "receive an Imperial appointment to establish a Chinese College in London," or at least "get appointed by [the Chinese] government to direct the movement of a body of young men to go to Europe and examine our various arts and manufactures in all their details."[69] The Chinese authorities, however, showed no inclination to give him any kind of controlling position over their own subjects.

Fryer consistently overemphasized his own influence in the Arsenal, and the rewards that his own endeavors would bring. He recounted one incident with Arsenal officials to his brother: "Today they came and asked me to make some chlorate of potash for gun caps and tubes for firing cannon. It was just a day's work and they watched the process very narrowly. When it was complete I let them try it and they were in extasies."[70] Fryer found this a good omen. It did not occur to him that he might be regarded merely as the maker of amusing curiosities by his employers. Similarly, after a steamship which had been assembled at the Arsenal had been successfully launched, Fryer wrote that he knew a "Great Mandarin of the highest class Military rank" who"would do anything just to get me to go with him" on a cruise in the new boat.[71] No invitation was forthcoming.

The Chinese did not give Fryer any major promotions, raises in salary, or large commissions. They merely held him to the work which he had been hired to do. Fryer could no longer complain of idleness. "My work is very hard," he was writing by the end of 1870, "and I have to study much in order to keep pace with the books I have to translate."[72] In the next ten years, working with his Chinese colleagues in the Arsenal, he published at least thirty-four translations: there were nine books on manufacturing, seven on mathematics, six on military affairs, four on navigation, three on engineering and surveying, two each on chemistry and physics, and one on medicine. Between 1880 and 1896 he produced the astonishing total of seventy-four further translations, many on the topics he had already covered, but others in new fields such as geology and meteorology, vocabularies of technical terminology, botany, law, anatomy, and political economy.[73]

Several of the books for which circulation figures have survived sold around a thousand copies, presumably to fairly influential and well-educated Chinese, but Fryer conceded that the total number of copies sold by 1879 — 31,111 — was disappointing: "The numbers sold up to the present time, though considerable, are nothing compared with what might have been expected among such an extensive population. But with no regular means of communication, no postal or railway arrangements, no agencies, and no advertisements or other means of bringing them into general notice or distributing them, it is easy to understand why more have not already been disposed of."[74] Still, the mere fact that the work was being done at all was a matter for congratulation: "The fact that this Translation Department has been established and kept up so long by the Government argues well for the future prospects of China, as it shows that whatever may be the national pride in her antiquated literature, or whatever may be her attitude towards the diplomatists of foreign powers, or the missionaries of foreign religions, she recognized the fact that knowledge is confined to no nation or country. She is therefore willing to be taught even by the 'foreign barbarians' such useful things as she feels she is ignorant of." He trusted that Western knowledge would be insidious, that "the more the celestial mind drinks at this fountain the greater will become its thirst for further supplies,"[75] and consequently the greater its need for Fryer.

Searching for wider influence, Fryer did not restrict his labors to the Translation Department, but tried various other means of bringing Western science before the Chinese. The most ambitious of these was the Shanghai Polytechnic Institution and Reading Room, which opened in 1876, with the goal of bringing "the Sciences, Arts and Manufactures of Western Nations in the most practicable manner possible before the notice of the Chinese." The Polytechnic had a permanent exhibition of scientific and mechanical apparatus, held lectures and classes, and gradually built up a technical library. But it was always short of funds, many of the exhibits failed to materialize, and attendance was extremely disappointing. The *North China Herald* commented that the institution was merely "honored at odd intervals by the visit of some passing stranger who, hearing of its high sounding name, has turned his steps thitherward to find empty halls and . . . incipient decay."[76] Fryer also instituted prize essay competitions similar to the ones that he had run in his Chinese paper in the 1860's; these essays, which were designed "to try and induce the Chinese literati to investigate the various departments of Western knowledge with the view to their application in the Middle Kingdom" drew an enthusiastic response and were often of an encouragingly high standard.[77] He issued a new Chinese periodical, *The Chinese Scientific Magazine,* which carried popular articles on such subjects as the Japanese use of Western technology, power saws, dentistry, the Krupp armament works, and biographies of Adam Schall, James Watt and Benjamin Franklin. The magazine, which

appeared irregularly, had a lively correspondence section, which
seemed to show it was arousing general interest, though one Western
newspaper commented caustically that "to have access in this easy
and gratuitous manner to the knowledge contained in Western books
is a privilege which but few Chinamen can understand or appreciate."[78] Lastly, Fryer was active in trying to standardize the scientific
and technical terminology used in translations. He worked through
the Educational Association of China, founded in 1890, of which he
was general editor, chairman of the Executive Committee, and
secretary of the Publication Committee. Fryer himself undertook to
handle "chemistry, mineralogy, meteorology, lithography, electroplat-
ing, chemical apparatus, philosophical apparatus, founding and
moulding, gunnery, ship-building, mining, engineering."[79]

It is clear that under the general rubric of "bringing science to the
Chinese" Fryer had spread himself very thin. This slightly frenzied
yet diffused method of operating mirrored the times in China. The
"self-strengthening" movement never really took off; indeed, it was
more a succession of experiments than a movement. The various
projects undertaken — the Kiangnan and other arsenals, a few cotton
mills, shipyards, papermills and coal mines, some short stretches of
railroad, a steamship company — remained isolated phenomena. A
real industrial breakthrough would have demanded either efficient
governmental coordination of projects or courageous entrepreneurs
with freedom of action and access to fluid capital. Both were lacking:
the Ch'ing government contented itself with allowing a few individuals to operate under the generalized control summarized in the
phrase "official supervision and merchant management." This meant
that the budding industrialist was dependent on the goodwill of local
officials, hampered by traditional bureaucratic methods of organization, short of capital, and subject to crippling exactions.[80]

When Fryer finally left China in 1896 (to become the first
incumbent of the Louis Agassiz Professorship of Oriental Languages
and Literature in the University of California at Berkeley), it was
clear that China had failed to save herself from foreign encroach-
ments through a scatter-approach adoption of Western science and

John Fryer, dressed as a Chinese Official of the Third Rank. *Courtesy the Bancroft Library, University of California at Berkeley.*

armaments. The Russians were pressing in on the north, the British ensconced in the Yangtze valley, the Germans in Shantung, and the French in southern China. Worst of all, the Chinese had suffered the appalling humiliation of being defeated by the Japanese in the brief war of 1894. Some Chinese intellectuals were beginning to realize that it was not enough to pick over the surface of Western technology. China should look to the dynamics beneath. As the young reformer T'an Ssu-t'ung (who in 1898 was to be executed by the Ch'ing for his disruptive views) wrote to a friend: "What you mean by foreign matters are things you have seen, such as steamships, telegraph lines, trains, guns, cannon, torpedoes, and machines for weaving and metallurgy; that's all. You have never dreamed of or seen the beauty and perfection of Western legal systems and political institutions. . . . All that you speak of are the branches and foliage of foreign matters, not the root. . . . Now there is not a single one of the Chinese people's sentiments, customs, or political and legal institutions which can be favorably compared with those of the barbarians."[81]

Fryer had worked extraordinarily hard for the Chinese for twenty-eight years, but he remained always in a subordinate position. Though it was certainly another stepping-stone, his acceptance of the California professorship was also an admission of defeat in the context of his earlier dreams. The Chinese had taken his best years, and used them as they saw fit. In return they had paid his salary and acknowledged his services by giving him a rank of the third class in their bureaucracy. Once the first excitement had worn off, the life had been no more fun than schoolmastering. His summation of his life's work makes bleak reading:

The work of translating and compiling scientific books is for the time being perhaps about as dull and unthankful a task as any foreigner could engage in, especially in such a secluded place as the Kiangnan Arsenal, and under the depressing influences of the climate of this part of China. Nothing but a strong sense of duty and a firm belief that this kind of labour is one of the most effective means, under the Divine guidance, for bringing about the intellectual and moral regeneration of this great country, has sufficed to render endurable the long and weary years and weary hours of close and continuous application which it has involved.[82]

What had really made the drudgery endurable was, of course, the hopes for advancement. Fryer had told his brother in 1870, "as I aim rather high there is the chance of getting something, even if much below what I aim at."[83] A friendly Chinese official had echoed Fryer's longings in a couplet:

> *May your fame surpass that of Verbiest and Schall*
> *As the electric light exceeds the spark of the glowworm.*[84]

But it was not to be. It took Fryer twenty-eight years to find out that the Chinese were using him, not he them. And when he discovered the unpalatable fact, he departed.

*   *   *

Martin, however, never learned; or, if he did, he didn't care. He stayed on while his dreams collapsed around him. "I am afraid we are tinkering a cracked kettle," Hart had warned him in 1894.[85] The crushing defeat of China by Japan in that year, and the failure of the Emperor's reform attempts in 1898 — he was placed under house arrest by the Empress-Dowager, and his ministers executed or banished — seemed to prove the correctness of Hart's melancholy statement. Yet no one, Martin included, was prepared for the horrors of the Boxer uprising. While Western audiences were rocking in their theaters to the newest mockery of the Chinese soldier —

> *Chinese sojer-man*
> *He wavee piecee fan,*

He shoutee Hip, hoo-lay for Empelor,
He makee hollid yell,
Bangee drum and lingee bell
When Chinee sojer marchee out to war![86] —

the Boxer rebels were massing under the slogan "Protect our country, drive out foreigners, and kill Christians."[87] By 1900 the Boxer movement was receiving the open encouragement of the Court, which had grown alarmed at the ever increasing demands of Western traders, diplomats, and missionaries for special privileges and spheres of interest in China. In June, just fifty years after he had arrived in China, Martin was trapped with the surviving Westerners in the Legation quarter of Peking.[88]

His first feelings were of embarrassment and frustration. "As we looked each other in the face," he recalled of his meeting with Hart in these desperate days, "we could not help blushing for shame at the thought that our life-long services had been so little valued. The man who had nursed their Customs revenue from three to thirty millions, the Chinese were trying to butcher; while from my thirty years' teaching of international law they had learned that the lives of Ambassadors were not to be held sacred!"[89] But as the siege dragged on, he began to feel that dire countermeasures were called for. Like other Westerners, he could not see that the Chinese were desperately responding to force with force. On the contrary, he felt that Westerners were "the victims of pagan fanaticism. Let this pagan empire be partitioned among Christian powers.[90]

After the siege had been lifted by an Allied expeditionary force, the rebels scattered, and the Ch'ing government subjected to a humiliating peace treaty and the payment of a vast indemnity, Martin elaborated on his theme. The Chinese government had outraged humanity, he explained. "By making war on all who hold to principles of human progress, it has placed itself beyond the pale of civilization, and forfeited the respectable position which it formerly occupied among the nations of the earth."[91] The most logical step would be to allow Britain and the other major Western powers to take over the administration of their own spheres of interest, since the Chinese people "were made to be ruled by others" and Chinese independence was "neither possible nor advisable."[92] The United States should take over the island of Hainan, off the southern coast of China. "With what is called by the opprobrious name of Imperialism, I have little sympathy," Martin declared, "but natural expansion or growth is quite a different thing. . . . It is by natural growth that we have expanded our territory to the Pacific, and extended our influence to Japan and China. . . . In China, up to the present time, our political influence has been inconspicuous; but now a great opportunity presents itself, and God forbid that it should pass unimproved."[93]

But Martin had lived too long in China to abandon it now, and he set about picking up the pieces of his shattered projects. First he tried to reorganize the gutted Peking University (of which he had been made president in 1898), until the Chinese government decided to remove all foreigners from the faculty. Then he was invited to found a new university in Wuchang, but the project fell through. Finally he went back to work for the Presbyterian mission station in Peking, aiding in the routine conversion from below that he had abandoned so many years before.

In his old age, he saw the Ch'ing Court begin to press slowly with the reforms in education and government that he had urged in the days of the Taiping Rebellion. His innate optimism reasserted itself; now, surely, China must be on the move: "All kinds of reform are involved in the new education, and to that China is irrevocably committed. Reenforced by railroad, telegraph, and newspaper, the schoolmaster will dispel the stagnation of remote districts, giving to the whole people a horizon wider than their hamlet, and thoughts higher than their hearthstone. Animated by sound science and true religion, it will not be many generations before the Chinese people will take their place among the leading nations of the earth."[94] He was still in Peking when he died, of bronchial pneumonia, at the age of eighty-nine. Though he still could not point to the constructive changes of which he had always dreamed, the Westerners and the Boxers between them had at least accomplished one thing, of that he was sure: "The way has been cleared for the introduction of a new epoch, which may be expected to commence with the twentieth century."[95] Whether this was to be a new epoch in Chinese or in Western terms remained to be seen.

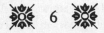

6

EDWARD HUME:

Yale for China

Horace Pitkin, a young missionary from the Yale College class of 1892, was beheaded by the Chinese during the Boxer Rebellion. A number of his fellow alumni "determined to see if possible that Pitkin's sacrifice was atoned for somehow by us as Yale men."[1] These young men, who had been caught up in the great Christian revival on campus at the end of the nineteenth century, were serious, naïve, and dedicated. "As I look back on it now, I am astonished at two things," wrote a member of the class of '98. "One, the consummate self-assurance that we had: just a group of youngsters without experience and without background going out to 'tell the world' what was the matter with it; second, the results that were piled up on so inadequate a basis."[2]

They set about drumming up funds and getting faculty backing. By 1902 they had raised over $17,000, and the Yale Foreign Missionary Society, from which was to spring the project known as Yale-in-China, was launched. "Independent in its management and undenominational in its work," announced the president of Yale at the commencement exercises that same year, "it aims to furnish a center of Christian education in the interior of the Chinese empire and to use all the various means available to that end."[3] The society's own publicity pamphlet emphasized that the mission aimed "to consecrate some part of that energy known as the Yale spirit to the service of God and the good of their fellow men in the Far East."[4]

The organizers of the mission finally chose Changsha, the capital of Hunan province, as the base for their operations. In choosing Changsha the Yale men deliberately turned their backs on the comparative amenities of the great urban centers like Peking and Shanghai, where missionaries and Western schools had already won a measure of grudging acceptance from the Chinese. For Hunan was known as a bitterly antiforeign province, and the city of Changsha was the distribution center for violent antimissionary pamphlets.[5] Besides pamphlets, there were "placards of the most outrageous character," reported the American consul; "pictorial ones so degrading and filthy as to be unfit for any persons to see were placed on the walls so high that ladders had to be used to secure sample ones."[6]

Often it was the local gentry who sought thus to inflame local opinion against Westerners. To descriptions of the missionaries' sexual aberrations, so common at the time of the 1870 Tientsin Massacre, were added economic arguments and calls for action: "They take away the profits of the people without giving them any consideration, planning to possess themselves of our wealth and food. Therefore let all of you who hear my words call out volunteers and begin the killing. Let us kill foreigners and their officials! Put to death the foreign students and foreign children."[7]

Anti-American feeling was particularly strong because of the unscrupulous activities of an American syndicate dealing in Hunanese railway rights.[8] Anti-Ch'ing rebels were also strong in the province, and the revolutionary leader Huang Hsing believed that the secret society members in Hunan were "a bomb full of gunpowder ready to blow, waiting for us to light the fuse."[9] American products were widely boycotted by the Chinese, who were angered at the passage of the exclusion bill forbidding further Chinese emigration to the United States, and the governor-general, Chang Chih-tung, threatened to confiscate any property that was sold, or sublet, by a Chinese to a foreigner.[10] The American consul general summed up the province in 1906: "Everything may be as peaceful as a summer landscape and in half an hour, like a moving tornado, the trouble comes upon you, the numbers growing every moment."[11]

But the Yale Mission members were not deterred, and believed these obstacles could be overcome. They were seeking "the field of the greatest future importance," and didn't mind if this meant "up-hill work for some years."[12] By 1902, after the Boxer Rebellion had been completely stamped out and new treaty rights for inland travel acquired by the foreigners, missionaries hurried to Hunan in answer to the indefatigable missionary Griffith John's call: "Are there not men of means among you who are prepared to come forward and claim the privilege of manning Changsha?"

It was "like the rush into a new diamond field," noted one observer, "men racing past the barriers to stake out claims and work the virgin soil."[13] So many came that one Yale man in China warned that "while the Yale mission is getting together, practically the last great field in China is being divided so that missionary comity will forbid our entering."[14] But his fears were unfounded, and in June 1903 the Hunan Missionary Conference passed this resolution: "That the conference extend a cordial invitation to the Yale University Mission to establish an educational center in Changsha. It recommends the societies working Hunan to entrust the higher education in the province of science, arts, and medicine to [the Yale] Mission, and also to work as far as possible in primary education on lines that conform to the plan of higher education that might be adopted by the Yale University Mission."[15]

The first members of the Yale Mission reached Changsha in 1904. By 1906 they had started the Yale Middle School, which was to be the preparatory school for a projected Yale-in-China College. Though "frankly Christian," the school did "not propose to force Christian doctrines upon its students." The school promised "to broaden the learning of its students, build up character, and train in loyalty to the Emperor and patriotism to the nation." Emphasis would be shared between Chinese and Western learning but particular attention would be given to the English language, "the chief medium of modern education."[16] In the meantime, the Yale Mission was also making plans to start a hospital and medical school. To take charge of this work they invited Edward Hume, a member of the Yale class of '97 and a graduate of Johns Hopkins Medical School, to join them.

Hume was at this time working on plague prevention projects in India, where he had been born and where his father and grandfather had worked long years as teachers and missionaries. He was not initially disposed to accept the invitation to move to China. "India was home," he later recalled, "and I had always intended to work there." Yet in the Yale invitation "were alluring words; 'You will be able to launch a university medical school.' It was the goal I had always set before myself, but it was in India that I had dreamed of realizing that goal. . . . This chance had not come to me in India, for there were government medical colleges already established in the capital cities of the chief provinces. . . . The vision of doing my life work in India began to fade. In China, perhaps, lay the greater opportunity. After weeks of wavering I decided to go."[17]

Hume arrived in China in 1905, aged twenty-nine, and after a year's intensive language study moved to Changsha to found the hospital from which his medical school might one day grow. Despite the undercurrents of anti-Western feeling, the constant threats of violence, the difficulties of renting property, and the primitiveness and isolation of the city itself, Hume was confident that Yale-in-China's work would prosper. "Get hold of the students, of the educated men, — " so Hume wrote shortly after his arrival, "and China will be won!" Won, he explained, to the Western ways and the Western religion that would make the Chinese true citizens of the world; won, not just to technical skill, "but that higher knowledge also, that moral incentive and groundwork of character that comes with the Christian faith."[18] Certainly there would be difficulties: "It is true that the people want education. But it is also true that they would rather *not* get it from the foreigner if that could be avoided."[19] Yet in this very resistance lay Yale-in-China's opportunity, since "the conservative character of the people makes it inevitable that our progress should be slow; but it also gives us a stronger hold as we get well started."[20]

To the outside world Changsha might be a backwater, but to the Chinese of Hunan it was the center of the universe, the capital city for a province of twenty million people, famous for its schools, rich in opportunity. "I began to long to go to Changsha, the great city," Mao Tse-tung later told an interviewer, recalling his boyhood in the 1900's. "It was said that this city was very big, contained many, many people, numerous schools, and the yamen of the governor. It was a magnificent place altogether! I wanted very much to go there."[21] And go he did, as did hundreds of other young and ambitious students.

Yale-in-China hoped it could pluck a few from this number, train them in Western science, humanities, and medicine, and bring them closer to God. There were many avenues open to the evangelical-educators, but Hume had no doubt that "medical work . . . is in general the surest and strongest way of introducing missionary operations in any part of China,"[22] and he determined to follow the very highest Western standards. "It would be a great mistake," he wrote to the Secretary of Yale, "for medical work to be done on any but the most scientific lines. For us that means the standards of Johns Hopkins! Our medical and educational work must be carried on under the strongest Christian influence and under the highest intellectual and scientific standards of teaching and research."[23]

This was not immediately possible, as Hume discovered. His first hospital was an old inn, across the street from the Middle School. Insect powder was liberally sprinkled, walls whitewashed, gutters, doors and windows installed, the pigs moved from their sties in the yard, and the "Yali Court of Medicine" with Hume and an untrained staff of two was ready for business. At the simple opening ceremonies in November 1906, a Chinese pastor read to the curious onlookers the story of Jesus at the Pool of Bethesda, where "lay a great multitude of impotent folk, of blind, halt, withered." Jesus asked one man, who had been ill for thirty-eight years, "Wilt thou be made whole?" Upon receiving affirmative response, Jesus said, " 'Rise, take up thy bed, and walk.' And immediately the man was made whole, and took up his bed, and walked."[24]

It was a forceful and challenging parallel, with complex overtones. For in the Bible story the residents of Jerusalem had not praised Christ for his cure. On the contrary, they had criticized him for ordering a man to carry his bed on the Sabbath. If Hume was to avoid offending Chinese susceptibilities he would have to maneuver cautiously in the thickets of Chinese lore and tradition. Patients were slow in coming. Those who came were wary. For Hume, it was safer not to admit serious patients, lest they die in his dispensary and bring the wrath of the province on his head. The first critical case was sent home when death seemed imminent. Another died, and catastrophe was only averted when Hume and his assistants purchased a coffin costing twice as much as they knew the bereaved family could afford, in order to placate their ancestors. The first important official from the Chinese bureaucracy who came for treatment departed angrily because Hume had felt his left pulse only, and not the right as Chinese medical practice demanded. Even those patients who appeared and saw their treatment through often did so only because all else had failed. Once, after he had watched a Chinese mother desperately calling home the spirit of her unconscious child, a Chinese friend told Hume: "You may be sure, that every time a mother brings an unconscious child to you she has already done all in her power to plead with its soul to return. She comes to the foreign doctor only because she finds her own efforts unavailing."[25]

Still, Hume made progress, whittling away local suspicions by his successful treatment of harelips, cataracts and tumors, and slowly tackling more serious cases. He was a sensitive man, genuinely fond of the Chinese, and eager to learn everything he could of Chinese medical techniques, which he frequently acknowledged were more effective than his own. He respected his patients, and believed that he was beginning to understand their attitudes. He wrote: "In China death came, like everything else, as part of a predestined cycle; night following day, new moon following full moon, winter coming after summer, death after life. Mourning was not a mere show, with sacrifice and wailing, with unbleached cotton garments and abstemiousness; it was a true liturgy of the oneness of life, deliberately adopted and observed through the years, commemorating the beauty and dignity of continuing existence, with its alternating cycles of shadow and light."[26]

Increasingly he was summoned out on house calls to the homes of important Changsha families and even invited to joint consultations with eminent Chinese physicians. Confidence in the hospital grew after the Chinese doctor Hou, trained in the American Presbyterian Mission in Shanghai, joined the staff in 1908. Two years later Hou was joined by Dr. Yen. Yen foreshadowed the new and vigorous China of which Hume dreamed: he had graduated with honors from the Yale Medical School, studied tropical medicine in England, and inspected modern hospitals in Paris, Berlin and Vienna. With the help of these men Hume avoided many pitfalls.

He felt that he was finally getting inside the complex Chinese society. His medical skills seemed to cross all boundaries, to smooth away all antagonisms. He made friends with the local shopkeepers and guild members, talking lengthily with them, and negotiating favorable commercial arrangements in return for medical services rendered. These varied contacts and his medical reputation stood him in good stead during the terrible antiforeign riots of April 1910. Nearly all Western property in Changsha was destroyed, but local residents kept watch over the Yale-in-China buildings after Hume and his colleagues had been forced to flee. He returned to find the hospital unharmed and all his equipment and valuables still in place.[27] The American Vice-Consul commented that all this was "said to be due to the esteem in which Dr. E. H. Hume of the mission is held by the people generally." He added that though government troops had done almost nothing to quell the riots, "the Yale Mission people sent word to the camp and asked for an escort, which was furnished them, but no other foreigner had the slightest assistance."[28]

Sometimes, of course, Hume was mistaken about the motives behind his Chinese acquaintances' friendly gestures. He had been particularly cheered when invited to sit in on meetings of a "literary society" headed by T'an Yen-k'ai, at that time a young political activist pressing the Manchus to push through constitutional reform. Only years later did Hume learn that he had been used as a "cover" at these meetings; T'an told him that "you foreigners hadn't known that these gatherings included only the radicals of the province. After the Western guests went home, the others stayed on to plan for the great day of liberation."[29] The Westerners, T'an explained, had only been invited to allay the suspicions of the authorities.

"The great day of liberation" — the overthrow of the now moribund Ch'ing dynasty — came on October 10, 1911. The Chinese revolutionary Sun Yat-sen had been striving to overthrow the Ch'ing for over a decade, to oust the Manchu rulers from the throne, and introduce a republican form of government in China. Almost a dozen uprisings had been planned and launched; and though all had failed, Sun's revolutionary party had gathered strong support among the Overseas Chinese, among young Chinese radicals, and in the ranks of the younger officers in the Ch'ing armies. The successful October coup, in fact, was the forced response to an accident that occurred while Sun was on a fund-raising trip in the United States. A bomb, apparently ignited by a carelessly dropped cigarette, exploded in the headquarters of some revolutionary conspirators in Wuhan. Government troops came to investigate, and to forestall reprisals a group of soldiers mutinied, and with surprising ease managed to seize the city. Their success spurred on others, and within a month mutinies and risings were taking place throughout China. Totally unable to control the outbreaks, abandoned by their own armies, the Ch'ing were forced to abdicate, and Sun Yat-sen was named President of the new Chinese Republic.[30]

While these dramatic events were bringing an end to the two-thousand-year tradition of Imperial rule in China, Hume himself was seeking funds for his hospital in the United States. "This is the day of opportunity," he wrote on hearing the news. "The Rebellion of 1911 throws wide open the doors of reform and progress in China. It means that educated men, in the modern sense, are to lead the nation hereafter. . . . There will be a tremendously increased enthusiasm for what the West can give unselfishly, in ideals of character, in

Edward Hume (standing, back right) in 1909, shortly after his arrival in Changsha, with Yale-in-China staff. *Courtesy Yale-in-China Archives.*

education and in constructive assistance in any direction."[31] His optimism was given new wings by his former Yale classmate, the millionaire Edward Harkness, who agreed to give Yale-in-China a four-hundred-bed hospital fully equipped, with the following stipulations: "The hospital is to be a center of medical education, for my primary concern is not for medical practice only. It is to be a center that the people of Changsha will regard as their own, to manage and to support. It is to be a project for whose current upkeep I am not to be approached."[32] After this windfall, Hume wrote jubilantly to Dr. Yen: "When you see the hospital plans you will be simply crazy about them because there is nothing in China to approach them."[33]

The original Yale hospital had developed new status after the revolution, when it became the Red Cross headquarters for the Hunan region. T'an Yen-k'ai, in what was to become a familiar warlord pattern in the following years, had taken over the province, killed off the more extreme revolutionaries, and brought his province into the Republic. To prove the progressive nature of his regime, he instructed the Yale hospital to give physical examinations to Chinese students and to work on the development of anti-opium remedies and plague prevention projects. He invited Dr. Yen to become director of public health, and Hume urged him to accept: "Even if we are unable to make headway at first, we shall at least be able to guide the authorities and keep them from doing harm. If we refuse, some hotheaded students from Japan will be apt to step in and set the whole scheme in confusion."[34]

On returning from the United States in 1912, Hume determined to develop his new hospital in cooperation with a Changsha citizen's committee, so that there should be the least possible friction in the community. In this he was in line with the China Medical Missionary Association, which had just resolved that "our aim and hope is that these medical colleges will gradually and ultimately be staffed, financed, and controlled by Chinese themselves."[35] Several of Hume's colleagues in Yale-in-China, however, were extremely sceptical about the advisability of cooperating too closely with the Hunan government, finding it "an extremely doubtful and hazardous solution of the problem" and warning that "in entering into an arrangement that would be more stable, we should probably have to give up the idea of religious teaching."[36] Once again the Western forces were being separated along lines of rivalry that separated the implementing of expertise from the attainment of long-range spiritual goals.

For the moment, Hume's policies won out, and in the summer of 1913, Governor T'an Yen-k'ai, with the support of prominent members of the Hunanese gentry, signed an agreement with the Yale Mission. Yale-in-China would build and equip the hospital and furnish the salaries and expenses of fifteen Western-trained doctors; Hunan would construct the school buildings, purchase the necessary land and provide an annual subsidy. The name chosen for the new medical school and hospital symbolized the new harmony: the literary name for the province of Hunan was combined with the first syllable of Yali to give the word "Hsiang-ya." Control of Hsiang-ya was to be in the hands of a self-perpetuating board of twenty men, ten Chinese and ten Yale appointees. As the first students entered the new nursing schools and the medical preparatory school, Hume wrote joyfully: "It is realizing the educational end for which after all even the doctors of our mission are in China. It means that in cooperation with the citizens of Hunan we are permitted to do that work which China needs and for which we have come."[37]

For several years this Hunanese-American cooperation proved very real and fruitful. Hsiang-ya survived, despite a move by the Peking government to abrogate the agreement and considerable uneasiness among members of the Yale-in-China executive committee in New Haven. Finally in February 1917 the new hospital was completed. "It was the dark of the moon, and we were shrouded in a great blackness as we gathered to watch for the promised great event," recalled Mrs. Hume. "Suddenly as if by the call of some great primeval voice, the hospital burst into light. From every window gleamed rays of the first electric light ever seen in the province of Hunan. With this new promise of light, the dark, tunnelled, city streets and our little oil paper lanterns seemed suddenly to belong to a remote past."[38]

It is splendid language and a splendid vision, beautifully capsuling the Westerner's yearnings for a China in his own image. But as is often the way with visions, it failed to correspond to reality. It is not just that there had, in fact, been an electric power plant lighting Changsha for many years.[39] That is a minor substantive fact, modifying but not shattering the vision. It is, rather, that on all sides of this gleam of Western light, China was being torn apart by forces so powerful that they made the Westerners' efforts poignantly irrelevant.

China's democratic Republic had never been soundly established. The second President, Yüan Shih-k'ai, had exiled Sun Yat-sen and the Kuomintang leaders, made a mockery of constitutional procedure, and finally declared himself Emperor in 1915. But at least he had had the prestige and the military backing to keep some sense of Chinese unity before the world. After his death in 1916, however, large areas of China fell under the control of independent warlords, men with personal armies who also often controlled a territorial base which could be anything from a township to whole provinces. Within their own territories the warlords taxed the population mercilessly, sometimes for decades into the future. The depredations of the armies and the dislocation of communications made famine a constant threat. Army deserters and starving peasants swelled the omnipresent bandit gangs.[40]

Hunan was no exception to this pattern. Eight men controlled the province at different times between 1911 and 1920. "Each acted as if he were an enemy general in military occupation of conquered territory," wrote an observer, and each practiced a "ruthless spoliation designed to bleed every possible source of plunder."[41] Reports of brigandage, and of infanticide, starvation and cannibalism among the peasantry were commonplace; as an American consular official in Changsha put it, "the inhabitants were the victims of a series of exorbitant military taxes at the hands of each faction in turn, in addition to suffering the usual abuses of pillage, rape and fire."[42] T'an Yen-k'ai, whom Hume euphemistically called "our beloved governor" may have been a little better than the others; at least he was fairly honest and appeared "amiable and intelligent."[43] But he was only in office for brief spells (1912–1913, 1916–1917, and in 1920), and even when he was in office he rarely controlled his own province, which like the rest of China was a battleground for "constitutional" armies from the north, "revolutionary" armies from the south, and such independent warlords as chose to take to the field.

Hume just had to keep going in any way possible: "In the hospital our work expanded in spite of the disorders, and although we tried to keep out of politics, it was sometimes almost impossible to avoid being involved. Many of the officials, who were powerful individuals one day and fugitives the next, had been outwardly friends of the Hsiang-ya movement."[44] The hospital became a regular sanctuary for fleeing officers and politicians, while the new men in power would summon the Western doctors to attend them. "We were, in reality, medical aides to the various generals," Hume admitted.[45] It was probably this linkage with the military, the only resource in time of civil war, that brought Yale-in-China safely through. Even the most disinterested doctor could not avoid realpolitik.

In such an atmosphere, control of the students in both the medical school and the Middle School was a difficult business. Within the unsettled country, the intellectual climate was changing fast. Political and literary journals, written in colloquial style instead of the old classical language that had dominated China's culture for millennia, brought the students articles on socialism, the emancipation of women, educational reform, anarchism, and translations of writers such as Ibsen, Zola, Dostoyevsky, and Oscar Wilde. The Chinese had been shocked and disillusioned by the First World War, which seemed to show the bankruptcy of the Western scale of values. They were further infuriated by the Treaty of Versailles which followed it, since they had believed that Woodrow Wilson would use his influence to give back to China the German-controlled areas of Shantung province. Instead, Germany's privileged position was transferred to Japan, unleashing a storm of protest in China.[46]

Students neither knew where to study nor what to feel. Mao Tsetung has described his own feelings and actions as a nineteen-year-old in Changsha at this time. "I began to read advertisements in the papers. Many schools were then being opened and used this medium to attract new students. I had no special standard for judging schools; I did not know exactly what I wanted to do."[47] He registered for police school, for a soap making school, for a law school, for a commercial school, and for a middle school. Finally, in bewilderment and disgust at the false claims made, he went to work on his own in the Changsha Public Library. "There for the first time I saw and studied with great interest a map of the world. I read Adam Smith's *The Wealth of Nations,* and Darwin's *Origin of Species,* and a book on ethics by John Stuart Mill. I read the works of Rousseau, Spencer's *Logic,* and a book on law written by Montesquieu."[48] Such students were shattering their ties to China's past of their own volition, searching for a new answer to China's problems. Their politics were naturally confused. Mao notes: "At this time my mind was a curious mixture of ideas of Liberalism, democratic reformism, and Utopian Socialism. I had somewhat vague passions about 'nineteenth-century democracy,' Utopianism and old-fashioned liberalism, and I was definitely anti-militarist and anti-imperialist."[49]

It was typical of the times that in its attempt to be broad-minded and generous to Chinese students, Yale-in-China gave Mao considerable assistance in developing his reputation as an efficient radical leader. In 1919 after Mao's periodical, the *Hsiang River Review,* had been closed by the governor's orders, he was made editor of the Yale-in-China review *The New Hunan;* and though this review was also soon suppressed, Yale-in-China proceeded to rent him three rooms in which he formed a "Culture Bookshop." Mao established seven branch stores from this base, all selling Marxist books and periodicals; profits were used to finance the socialist youth corps and the fledgling Communist party.[50] Because of his successes as an organizer and publicist, Mao was one of the two delegates from Hunan who attended the first congress of the Chinese Communist Party in Shanghai in 1921.

Unaware of the forces threatening it, Yale-in-China continued to expand. By 1923, when Hume was made its first president, it included the Middle School, the Hsiang-ya Hospital, a nursing school, the beginnings of the College and a medical school. But the expansion was not truly the proof of an inner strength, since the institution was not moving as fast as the China around it. When one Yale-in-China teacher said that he knew "nothing that will knock the bottom out of the bottomless superstitions of China half so well as looking down the tube of a microscope,"[51] he was unwittingly echoing the dead doctrines of the self-strengtheners. And when a Yale colleague declaimed that "if Yale can give to these boys an ideal of sportsmanship and fair play and high sense of honor and responsibility China can ask no greater gift,"[52] he was quite simply deceiving himself. The virtues he mentioned were not those most relevant to a war-torn, impoverished, humiliated, yet still defiant country.

Hume's first major crisis as president came in November 1924, when there was a riot after a football game which the Yale-in-China team had lost. Despite the fact that a faculty member who had slapped a student publicly apologized in the chapel, a massive student strike was called in December and over one hundred and forty students left the school. In a formal meeting with the Changsha city fathers, Hume agreed to modify the stricter sentences against some of the students. Thinking he had given in too easily, some teachers resigned. He was also criticized by senior members of the faculty. In face of this opposition in his own camp, Hume decided to ask for a vote of confidence. The vote was unanimous in his favor, but he saw the importance of what had occurred. "It is a serious thing in an institution like Yali when such a vote becomes necessary. The taking of it indicates how sharply the line will be drawn in days ahead between our Western training and instincts and our Oriental setting. We shall have to ask ourselves over and over again in the future as we have done during the past month — What is our essential contribution?" In another letter on the same day he added: "In 20 years I have never felt so humble, so utterly weak and so completely puzzled about the future."[53]

As the agitation in Changsha and on the Yale-in-China campus grew increasingly strident, bewildered and hurt school administrators found the explanation in Communist plotting. "Do not think that Chinese students are ungrateful," wrote the Yale-in-China executive secretary. "They are, just at present, the victims of insidious and subtle propaganda. Yali is helping them to see things in their true perspective."[54] Hume, however, was beginning to see that the problem lay far deeper than this and that Yali was not confronting just a few radicals, but rather the whole force of Chinese nationalism. He realized that the Westerners' role had changed and that "China will no longer submit to the ethics or attitude of the 'invader,' no matter what he comes to do."[55] He felt that many of his own colleagues were "men who are seldom close to the Chinese position of thought and action," and had "an attitude of strange non-cooperation."[56] He was even beginning to question the rationale for the existence of the institution of which he was now president, feeling that Yali was too small to function effectively where it was. He had enthusiastically backed a proposal of the China Educational Commission that Yali should merge with other Christian colleges to form a major new university in Wuhan, and he had also accepted the same commission's proposal that the Yale Medical College, which he had so painfully built up, should move location and be merged into a larger unit in Shanghai. Most of Hume's colleagues had flatly rejected these ideas.[57]

As Hume's concern grew, he poured out his thoughts in a series of letters to the Yale-in-China trustees in New Haven. He wrote in January 1925: "Unless a foreign institution or a foreign individual can become absorbed into the body of the organism as a graft is absorbed into a living tree, the thing dies. We have got to bend our energies now with renewed strength to the grafting of ourselves into the living tree of China."[58] He developed this idea in a letter to a Yale professor later the same month.

Here we are in China, whose national consciousness is rising by leaps, trying to bring a message from abroad. It is foreign, first of all. We who come from without ought to realize that we are the intruders, and seek to adjust ourselves to the character of the races we meet. . . . The Character of Races! What a subtle, intangible, elusive thing! Not to seek to understand, or, wording it otherwise, to live as if understanding were not fundamental, seems suicidal to an institution that comes from without.

What were needed were "foreigners who *love* the Chinese."[59]

The Chinese could not be blamed for their attitudes to Westerners, thought Hume: "It is as if a lot of Indians and other outsiders should come in to America and try to tell us how our education should be formed and developed. The Chinese are becoming fed up." And again: "No one can give effective service to China today, whom the Chinese do not welcome. We are guests here."[60] Therefore Yali must adapt. "Can we expect to make our work seem truly indigenous so long as it is clothed with so much of Western symbolism, of Western insistence on certain traditions, of a Western judgement on each passing phenomenon?" The Americans in China must become "more Chinese, more efficient, more Christian," and in that order Hume implies. "If there is one thing that has become clear throughout the winter it is this, that we foreigners only vaguely understand the Chinese attitude and the Chinese mind."[61]

While Hume mused about these problems, his campus was shaken by two more crises. The first was merely awkward, but is a good illustration of the kind of trouble student activists could make for Western educators. The Hunan Student Union suddenly declared that no students from Christian colleges should be allowed to compete in the big provincial athletic meeting at Hengchow in April 1925. Hume immediately saw the subtlety and efficacy of this boycott: "If our students go to the meet, they may be subjected to all kinds of indignity and the agitators may easily precipitate fighting. If we passively accept the adverse verdict, further domineering decisions are likely to be made."[62] As a compromise, Hume decided to send a delegation of six Yali students "selected on the basis of scholarship, athletic ability and self control." The student union countered by saying the delegation would only be admitted if they did not wear the badge or insignia of any Christian institution, and that they could only compete if they promised to leave the Christian institution where they were enrolled and never join another. The president of the meet and the governor of the province refused to take part in the squabble. Finally, the students went but did not compete. Although there was no violence, the whole experience was humiliating.[63]

The second crisis, however, was a nightmare. In early June 1925, the students of Changsha learned of the events of the "May 30th incident" in Shanghai, where British police of the International Settlement had fired on a demonstration of Chinese students and workers, killing ten and wounding fifty. The Yali students left their classrooms and took to the streets, joining crowds of students from other middle schools and colleges. Wild rumors spread through the city of Changsha, and the students "moved, seconded, and carried by acclamation that all foreigners in Changsha should be brought to the execution ground and shot at dawn on the following day."[64] In an "atmosphere electric with tension" Hume split his faculty into night watches to guard the campus. The lives of the American community were probably only saved by the Hunan governor's brief and dramatic declaration of martial law: "Anyone creating rumors will be beheaded. Anyone spreading Bolshevist propaganda will be beheaded. Anyone attempting to subvert the military will be beheaded. Anyone disturbing law and order will be beheaded."[65] In a formal note of thanks to the governor the Yali trustees declared that "they desire only the welfare of China and look for its establishment through the support of those principles of law and order which have been asserted and applied by His Excellency, the Governor of Hunan."[66]

The trustees' desires might be met, but it would no longer be through those principles that they publicly espoused. It was, for example, difficult to continue teaching the merits of the United States Constitution when the Changsha students could see the appalling effects of its implementation in their own city and province. Hunan, which had declared itself autonomous in 1916, had by 1922 finally written its own constitution (modeled on that of the California state constitution), with seventy-five electoral districts to vote for the provincial assembly, and an elective governor. But the provisions of the constitution were "openly and constantly violated," a Western observer noted, "especially in the matter of misappropriation of taxes and in elections which are ludicrous farces."[67] Candidates were elected thus: "The suffrage was nominally universal; but the voting papers were distributed in bundles of thousands amongst the responsible gentry of each sub-division of the counties. No one denies that from these gentry, the successful candidates bought bundles filled in with lists of names, at so much the thousand."[68]

Though the provincial leaders were willing to protect Westerners in times of major crisis in order to prevent international reprisals, by 1925 they were joining more and more openly with their own local populations in expressing their antiforeign feeling. There were frequent reports of police and soldiers ordering Americans out of their rickshas and making them walk. Chinese who carried Westerners' baggage were beaten up by students while the soldiers looked on, or even "handed over their pistols to the irresponsible boys who were stirred up to a frenzy."[69] Provincial troops fired on American priests, insulted the United States flag, and looted the mission. Travel, trade and property accumulation by Westerners all grew difficult, since the fact that these abuses went unpunished "entirely changed the attitude of the natives in the interior toward the white man." Hunan students boasted openly that the Boxers were their forerunners.[70] American women were spat on in the streets, and their children "reviled." Chinese boys naturally were scared to enroll in the Christian schools, and those who did, Hume wrote, "find it quite difficult to walk on the streets with foreign teachers. They are called 'Foreign Slaves' by bystanders."[71]

In such circumstances, it became increasingly difficult to run the Yale-in-China complex successfully. One of Hume's colleagues summarized the state student affairs had reached by 1926: "These middle school students wander through the streets, never attending classes. They are active propagandists of ideas which they have never scrutinized. They organize strikes in their schools, defy their masters,

and even at times go home and intimidate their parents into agreement with their subversive ideas. Deplore it as we may it is a fact
that law and order have practically disappeared in China. This is due
in many ways to student activity. There is a nasty inhospitable spirit
abroad on the streets today."[72]

Hume's position was enormously difficult. How could he possibly
placate everyone — his Yali students, the Changsha radicals, the
New Haven trustees? He took one major step in 1925, when he
handed over complete control of the medical college to a Chinese
board of managers under Dr. Yen, but the move only temporarily
deflected the growing opposition to the Yale-in-China operation, and
Hume's physician warned him that he was heading for a nervous
breakdown, adding that there was no treatment for his condition
"except elimination of expenditure of nervous energy and a long
period of recuperation."[73] The trustees offered Hume six months'
sick leave, but he turned it down since he "could not think of leaving
here during the impending time of stress in connection with the anti-
Christian movement, and during the time when we are uncertain as
to the future of our medical school."[74]

The recurrent crises with the Chinese students made Hume increasingly critical, not of the Chinese, but rather of the Yale-in-
China trustees and his own colleagues. It was as if every outbreak in
Changsha brought a new resentment of his own to the surface. He
felt that Yale was dragging its feet: "There has not been given to the
Chinese community a sense of active participation or a promise of
proprietorship which they have felt as likely to be realized within a
measurable period of time," he wrote, and the November 1924 riots
made him critical of his colleagues' self-deceptions: "You can see now
what an awakening has come to us all as to our real relationships
with the community, something far different from the air of confident fellowship which has been sometimes described to the trustees
by some who have returned from here. We have been asleep at the
switch and we are waking up."[75]

He began to realize that many of the American staff, appointed by
the trustees, were just not up to the job in hand. They were often

aloof and unadaptable to Chinese conditions, or poorly trained; and he urged that Chinese appointees should be given preference over Americans with parallel experience.[76] Then there were the "Yali Bachelors," members of the Yale senior class selected to spend one or two years in Changsha: the Chinese students found that these young Americans "neither brought anything in the way of teaching experience nor appreciated the culture and history of China. Against them there is great resentment." Let there be fewer of them, Hume urged, and let the trustees "call upon Mother Yale for less of her sons and more of her substance, so that more Chinese can be put in as teachers and administrators."[77]

And the nurses, too. "For let me say this very frankly and very sympathetically, unless our American nurses can show a spirit to the Chinese pupils and the Chinese patients different in many radical ways from what has been shown by some of the group during the past five years, we had better limit ourselves to the selection of Chinese, less well-trained perhaps, but far more able to understand the Chinese sick person's psychology and far more able to be genuinely gracious to them."[78] When the trustees went ahead and appointed another American nurse who was an expert in the "theory of nursing," without practical or Chinese experience, Hume was truly angry.[79]

He believed that the men in New Haven just didn't understand the issues and the severity of the situation, since, as he put it, "such things don't happen in America." He wrote to the secretary: "We shall have an important place to fill in Chinese education, in proportion as we meet the situation squarely and adjust ourselves to changing conditions. A good deal of modifying of attitudes and practices will probably be called for. This is inevitable."[80] When he was asked to approach Edward Harkness for more money to keep his medical school going, Hume refused. "My answer is that the issue seems to me a moral one. I could not approach Harkness for a large sum for the saving of the medical school in Changsha unless I were convinced that it would be the best thing for China so to do."[81] His thoughts dwelt increasingly on the merger solutions that had been suggested in

1922 and rejected by the trustees. Yale-in-China would cease to be Yale-in-China, but surely China would gain. A cable from the trustees put Hume in his place: "Board of trustees still decline relinquish either medical school arts college Changsha Hunan."[82] Accused of being pessimistic, Hume riposted that he had good cause, since "it is the very presence of the foreigner, stabilizing to be sure — but to the nationalistic mind, invading — that irritates and cause revulsion."[83] If one's mere presence was the irritation, surely there was little to do but leave.

In 1926 Hume returned to the United States, partly to take sick leave, partly to confront the trustees face-to-face. In June, after a series of meetings, he offered his resignation, because "it has become increasingly apparent to me that my position on many issues, educational and administrative, differs seriously from the position [of] the trustees." He hoped that his resignation would free the trustees for positive action and hasten the selection of a Chinese president for Yale-in-China.[84] The resignation was accepted. In January the following year he gave a final warning, writing to the secretary that the true test would lie "in finding whether or not Christian education can keep ahead of the national movements in a cooperative and constructive way."[85]

Student unrest had reached a peak in late 1926, as the Nationalist forces under Chiang Kai-shek advanced north in their attempt to unify the country, and Changsha became a stronghold of leftist sympathizers. Student demands became so impossible, threatening the whole integrity of the Yali educational structure, that the faculty voted for closure. In January 1927 the American vice-consul, John Carter Vincent, ordered the evacuation of all American personnel.[86] Hume, who had returned briefly, was promised a private railroad compartment by the governor but found the whole train full of troops; he and his family finally left Changsha in a baggage car curled up among the mailbags.[87]

It is unlikely that the Yali faculty and trustees regretted this mild humiliation of their former president. Hume had asked too many questions, questions that undermined the comfortable assumptions on which Yale-in-China had operated. In acknowledging the force of Chinese nationalism, and emphasizing the need for a more subservient role on the part of Americans, he denied China's helplessness, and hence her continuing need for moral uplift. Hume's programs, wrote a member of his faculty, were "conceived under the sway of emotions stimulated by an uncontrolled idealism."[88] Emotions and idealism, it was implied, led to a confusing of the issues. As a group of Yali faculty members wrote in a joint letter to the trustees in New Haven: "Dr. Hume, though boundless in energy and enthusiasm, and magnetic in personality, does not hew a straight line in his policies."[89] They could not understand that the concept of straightness might depend on the angle of vision; that the Chinese, in other words, still refused to see the Westerners as the Westerners saw themselves.

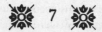

7

MIKHAIL BORODIN:

Life in the Sun

"When I asked him if he wanted to give me some facts — some of the 'Who's Who' sort of facts — he smiled his slow, expansive grin and shrugged. 'I was born in the snow,' he said, 'and I live in the sun — yes? What good are facts?' "[1] The reticence was not surprising. Mikhail Markovich Borodin, formerly Grusenberg, alias Berg, alternate alias Kirill, was a professional revolutionary.

Born into a Russian Jewish family in 1884 and raised in Latvia, in his mid-teens Borodin joined the Jewish Social Democratic Bund. By his late teens he had become a Bolshevik. He had achieved some prominence at the time of the Russian Revolution of 1905, but after the failure of that revolution a warrant was put out for his arrest and he made his way to the United States. He studied briefly at Valparaiso University in Indiana, married a Lithuanian immigrant, and made his home on the West Side of Chicago, where he founded a small school for emigré children. It was in the Chicago slums that Borodin developed his knowledge of the urban worker, and experimented with radical journalism. He returned to Russia after the success of the 1917 revolution, and in 1918 Lenin sent him to deliver a message to the workers of America. In the next few years Borodin was sent to Spain, to Scotland (where he was imprisoned for six months), to the Netherlands, and to Mexico — all this to carry out missions for the Comintern.[2]

The Comintern — the Third Communist International — was founded by Lenin in 1919, with the goal of hastening the world revolution. The enemies confronting the Comintern were seen to be both the forces of Capitalism and Imperialism, and also the gradualist non-Communist labor organizations which might blur the workers' revolutionary vision. Its means were the formation of Communist nuclei within existing trade unions, propaganda in the armed forces, agitation among the peasantry, and continuing support of all oppressed colonial peoples. By 1921, when hopes for the speedy onset of revolution throughout Europe had been crushed, the Comintern became an increasingly rigid, disciplinarian institution. At the same time, the disappointments and failures in Europe led the Soviet leaders to look more hopefully toward the Middle East and Asia: resolutions that the Soviet system might be established in precapitalist areas in the form of "the dictatorship of the poor peasantry" were adopted by the Comintern, and it was also agreed that Communist parties should support "national revolutionary movements" as long as they were anti-Imperialist.[3]

These Comintern decisions had immediate relevance to China where Sun Yat-sen, under constant warlord pressure, was barely managing to hold together his Nationalist party in the area around Canton. Though Lenin had derided Sun for his "inimitable — one might say — virginal naïveté," some of his advisers nevertheless shrewdly saw that Sun's party might one day become a potent anti-Imperialist and anti-feudal force. So Lenin decided to follow a three-pronged policy: Comintern agents were sent to organize a Chinese Communist Party, which was done in 1921; the Soviet government disowned many of the special privileges in China that had been won by the Tsarist regime, and sent diplomatic representatives to Peking; and lastly, both diplomats and Comintern agents approached Sun Yat-sen, urging him to admit Communists to the Nationalist party and to accept Soviet aid.[4]

As Lenin had hoped, Sun Yat-sen, who had desperately been seeking foreign aid for his beleaguered forces, responded warmly to Russian overtures. He agreed to admit individual Communists to his party, and in 1923 sent his young chief of staff, Chiang Kai-shek, to

Moscow, with letters of introduction to Lenin, Chicherin, and Trotsky. "I have dispatched him to Moscow," he told a Russian diplomat, "to discuss ways and means whereby our friends there can assist me in my work in this country." Chiang was well received, and carried out an intensive study of Soviet military techniques. The Russians, in turn, sent Borodin to Canton. His exact duties were not defined, but he was introduced to Sun as "one of the oldest members of our party, having worked for a great many years in the revolutionary movement," and described as "a permanent and responsible representative of the Soviet government" under whose guidance "things would be pushed ahead much more speedily."[5] The vagueness of these phrases was matched by official secrecy: to the outside world Borodin came to Canton in October 1923 as a correspondent for the Rosta News Agency.

Borodin and Sun Yat-sen got on well from the start, and within a few days they were seen strolling together, deep in conversation. Borodin figured that it would take at least five years to build up a revolutionary base in Kwangtung province, so he cooperated with Sun in reorganizing the Nationalist party, and set up regular arms shipments from Vladivostok to Canton. He urged Sun to follow a vigorously radical policy: declare an eight-hour day and a minimum wage for the workers, and redistribute land among the peasants. Sun balked at the latter suggestion, but agreed to encourage the formation of peasant unions. Sun showed his appreciation by naming Borodin as adviser to the committee which was reorganizing the Kuomintang — as Sun's Nationalist party was again to be called. The first national congress of the new Kuomintang, surely reflecting Borodin's influence, adopted in January 1924 the slogans "Down with Imperialism" and "Unite with Peasants and Workers."[6]

Borodin, while playing cleverly on Sun's egotism, and writing enormous powers for the Chinese leader into the new Kuomintang constitution, kept himself in the background. Sun in turn was confident that the new alliance would work to his advantage; Soviet skills and military aid were needed by the Kuomintang. He compared Borodin with Lafayette and confided to a friend that he was sure he would be able to use the best features of the Soviet system, while abandoning its evils.[7] So Sun adopted the principles of democratic centralism and strict party discipline, as Borodin had explained them, allowing the Kuomintang to be redesigned into a pyramid structure, rising from the district organizations at the base to a small Central Executive Committee at the summit; at the same time Sun retained his own political slogans of "Nationalism, Democracy, and People's Livelihood," the rather vague formulations for China's political development that he had been elaborating over the previous decade.[8]

Borodin's task was delicate and complex. He had to develop the Kuomintang to the point where it could become strong enough to reunite China and rout the Imperialist powers. At the same time (and the irony of this was to grow apparent later) he had to strengthen the Communist Party so that it might eventually transform a successful Kuomintang nationalist revolution into a socialist revolution. He had enemies on two flanks: certain Chinese Communists saw the dangers implicit in an alliance with a party dominated by the bourgeoisie; and conservative members of the Kuomintang felt that the Communists were dangerous allies, and should be crushed before they grew too strong. Borodin had to hold back Sun from making a precipitous march to the north that might wreck all their chances, and he had to restrain the more militant Communists from taking rash action that would irreparably alienate the Kuomintang. Through 1924 and 1925 he trod this tightrope successfully, and though his cover as a Rosta correspondent had been speedily broken, he was able to convince most observers of the sincerity of Soviet intentions. As a Canton newspaper editorialized about Borodin in September 1924: "If the distinguished gentleman who is today representing Soviet Russia in Canton were to suggest to President Sun the introduction of 'Bolshevism' here or anywhere else in China, his own government would recall him within twenty-four hours."[9]

One of Borodin's greatest assets in dealing with the Chinese was his personal charm, and his ability to convey an impression of sincerity and moderation. "He was a greater contrast to the type of person whom my fancy had depicted than I could possibly have imagined," wrote one journalist. "The man who stood before me was strong and well-proportioned, apparently in his late forties. All his motions were easy and graceful. He spoke slowly in a deep, sympathetic voice. His lined, thin face was animated by a pair of dark, impressive eyes that looked as if they belonged to a dreamer or inventor rather than to a desperate fanatic, an avenger and destroyer. His slow and rather heavy manner, his casual appearance, and his short English moustache reminded me of a British labor leader who had risen from the ranks but who also had a long career of political training behind him."[10] Another man remembered him as "a wholesome kindly individual with a needle-sharp mind and a memory like a filing cabinet," and felt that he seemed more like a big businessman or an engineer than a revolutionary.[11] Even the president of the Canton Christian College, Dr. James Henry, found Borodin "a very pleasing personality and received an impression of sincerity and deep earnestness. He puts one perfectly at ease. . . . I asked him if he liked the Chinese. He seemed surprised at my question and after some thought said that he had not given the matter any consideration." Borodin refused Dr. Henry's request that he come and address the students on Communism, explaining that he generally refused to speak on that particular topic: "Communism is a philosophy and ideal for which China is far from ready," Borodin told him. "China is 100 years behind the times, from a skyscraper to a rickshaw — what a contrast."[12]

Behind this courteous front Borodin was, of course, a tough and capable man, working carefully to consolidate his position. In July 1924 Sun had named him "Senior Adviser" to the Kuomintang political council. He had also been named as adviser to the agricultural section of the Kuomintang, many of whose members were Communists — among them Mao Tse-tung, at this time a strong supporter of the Kuomintang-Communist alliance, who became director of the Peasant Movement Training Institute.[13] With his passions for horseback riding and chess, Borodin rapidly became a well-known figure in Canton. He, his wife Fanny, and their two sons set up residence in a large and gloomy two-story house, backing onto the

Mikhail Borodin addresses a rally in Wuhan on the Yangtze, in 1927.

Canton parade grounds and facing the headquarters of the Central Executive Committee of the Kuomintang. The Borodins lived on the top floor in cold, poorly furnished rooms; below were his staff of secretaries and translators. They made a daily review of the Chinese and foreign press for him; the cuttings were kept in carefully classified archives, together with the proceedings of all Kuomintang executive meetings. Borodin also employed four Russian advisers to make studies of the worker and peasant movements in Kwangtung and Kwangsi provinces. These men formed Borodin's "braintrust," even though they were not all considered politically reliable; some of them had been sent to Canton because they had shown "an excessively critical spirit" in their native land, and were expected to redeem themselves through practical experience in a civil-war situation.[14]

To Borodin's house came a stream of visitors, including Chiang Kai-shek, Chou En-lai, and T'an Yen-k'ai (Hume's old friend, now a power in the Kuomintang). When Borodin was sick from his recurrent bouts of malaria, party conferences took place at his bedside. His wife acted as confidential secretary, scrambling around the old house to get necessary documents from Borodin's comprehensive files. But if he felt that a certain document might prove embarrassing, he made a secret sign to his wife, who would then ransack the files and declare the papers temporarily "lost." Besides his wife, Borodin had one other trusted aide. This was Chang T'ai-lei, an alternate member of the Central Committee of the Chinese Communist Party. "They never left each others' company," recalled Borodin's secretary, "they even lived in the same house. To him alone did Borodin trust the translation of his pronouncements, and with him he went to the meetings of the Kuomintang Politburo."[15]

It was a comfortable life in many ways, even though at times they had to modify their proletarian consciousness in the face of Chinese reality. "The occasional necessity of taking rickshaws always embarrassed us Soviet advisers in China," recalled a military officer on the mission. "At first we refused to take them at all; but after convincing ourselves that the rickshaw-men did not benefit in the least from our nobility, we would take them for short distances, though we did not let them run fast and paid them five times the usual fare." But to be borne aloft by palanquin was altogether delightful: though there was "a feeling of complete absurdity, archaism and abasement at this means of locomotion, that recalled Babylon and the Queen of Sheba, there was a magic feeling of movement in the air, without the slightest effort, jolt or noise."[16]

So, at times, must Borodin have traveled to another crucial center of his influence, the Whampoa Military Academy, just outside Canton. This Academy, founded in the spring of 1924, with Chiang Kai-shek as president, and Chou En-lai as deputy political director, was designed to train the young officers so desperately needed by the Kuomintang armies. The Soviet military advisers here were largely responsible for the technically brilliant training that brought the Whampoa cadets their first victory, against a local warlord, in 1925. Whampoa-officered armies were later to spearhead Chiang Kai-shek's northward march, and to preserve his power after he had broken with the Communists.

Chief of the Soviet military mission, Borodin's opposite number, was Vasili Blyukher, a thirty-five-year-old general who had led the Red armies to great victories in the Urals and in Siberia before being posted to China in 1924. He worked under the pseudonym of "Galin," heading a staff of forty Russian officers, all veterans and all party members, though some of them, like members of Borodin's staff, were being tested in China.[17] Galin's professional skill inevitably strengthened Borodin's position in the Kuomintang hierarchy and seemed to give proof of Russia's benevolent intentions. And Galin's enormous popularity strengthened the prestige of every Russian in Canton: the young, handsome, laconic, ex-factory worker, racing through the Canton streets in his touring car, guards with cocked revolvers swaying precariously on the running boards, was known to all. Chiang Kai-shek remembered him with an affection he gave to no other Westerner, calling him "an outstanding Russian general as well as a reasonable man and a good friend," and describing Galin's departure as "one of the most moving partings in my life."[18] On matters of training Galin was a martinet, a stickler for etiquette, a demanding teacher, who accompanied his cadets on their first campaigns and constantly emphasized the basic tactics he had developed in Russia: mobility, surprise, speed of march, and envelopment. Under his direction they became the best troops in southern China.[19]

The importance of the Soviet involvement in Canton slowly grew clear to all. Noting the numbers of Russian officers and civilians present in 1925, an observer reported that "everywhere, and into the minutest cog in the political and military machines, Soviet influence has peacefully penetrated." Borodin, he added, "the Soviet envoy extraordinary of the Third Internationale in Canton," was "the sinister figure in the background of this web of intrigue . . . distributing rifles and money with a lavish hand."[20] Conservative members of the Kuomintang agreed: "Nominally Borodin and Galin are advisers, but in reality they hold the supreme military and political command." They protested, urging that Borodin be discharged.[21]

But although Borodin's influence had grown rapidly, it was really Sun Yat-sen who had had the better part of the bargain. He had made good use of his advisers' political and military skills. The Kuomintang was now a tightly organized party, and its essential military base was expanding rapidly: 960 officers and men in the Whampoa-officered army in May 1924, 1,500 in January 1925, 9,000 in July, 30,000 in November. Sun was not indulging in idle rhetoric when, seriously ill with the cancer that killed him in 1925, he declared: "Now that we have Whampoa I may die peacefully."[22]

After Sun Yat-sen's death, Chiang Kai-shek advanced rapidly as the leading contender for control of the Kuomintang, but while he was consolidating his power in the area around Canton, Borodin was still of use to him. Chiang needed Soviet military aid, and accordingly silenced those who complained of Borodin's continuing presence with the reminder that it was Sun Yat-sen himself who had chosen Borodin as his political adviser: "[Sun] instructed me: 'The opinion of Borodin is my opinion; in matters pertaining to political problems, his opinions should be accepted.' . . . The Soviet comrades have cherished a sincere spirit towards our Party. . . . How can you speak of the 'one-man dictatorship of Borodin?' "[23] Borodin himself made the most of his former role, and worked willingly with Chiang to fix a radical image of the dead leader in the minds of the Chinese people. In death Sun was granted the status he had never obtained while alive: his works were widely circulated and praised, his body embalmed and a mighty mausoleum planned, his picture was hung in every Kuomintang government building, his slogans used in every speech. Sun's deathbed "Message to Soviet Russia," almost certainly drafted by Borodin, was given maximum publicity; in this message Sun praised "the immortal Lenin" and trusted that Russia and China would "go forward to victory hand in hand."[24] Borodin's policies seemed triumphantly vindicated by the great strike and boycott that the workers of Canton maintained against the British in Hong Kong from 1925 to 1926: this showed the strength of the new labor organizations and also the extent of anti-Imperialism among the Chinese.

Borodin, however, was unable to establish the close rapport with Chiang Kai-shek that he had formerly enjoyed with Sun Yat-sen. More ruthless and less visionary than Sun, Chiang was fully aware of the dangers that the Chinese Communists represented, and determined to keep them subservient. Ironically, it was Borodin who had put into his hands the means to control the Communists: with a disciplined Kuomintang hierarchy, and his crack Whampoa officers, Chiang was in a position that the Communists would find hard to challenge. Aware of the dangers, Borodin enforced Comintern directives as strictly as possible, continuing to dampen the revolutionary ardor of the Chinese Communists, and telling their secretary-general, Ch'en Tu-hsiu, that for the time being his party must "do coolie service for the Kuomintang."[25]

Waiting till Borodin was out of Canton in the spring of 1926 (Galin had recently returned to Russia), Chiang launched a lightning coup. Arresting a number of Chinese Communists and demoting them from their Kuomintang positions, he placed his Russian advisers under house arrest. Borodin's first, and natural, reaction was to undertake strongly offensive countermeasures, but caution prevailed; and when Chiang as a sop moved against some rightists and requested Borodin's return to Canton, Borodin acceded. That he was anxious to return was clear. As he euphemistically told an interviewer in Peking at this time: "In Canton may lie the future of all China. Certainly Canton is a great experiment. It is in the most elemental stage now. There is really nothing sensational about Canton, despite misrepresentation to the contrary. Canton is not communistic; there is a hard struggle for political, economic, and social progress, such as other countries have already gone through a hundred years ago. I feel it is a struggle worth while, with possibilities in store. So I stay and do what I can to help."[26]

Chiang and Borodin worked out a compromise: henceforth Communist Party members in the Kuomintang should be registered as such, they should have no secret organizations within the Kuomintang, they should not criticize Sun Yat-sen, and they should not have more than one third of the seats on any of the executive committees. In return for agreeing to these terms, Borodin was reinstated as adviser to the Kuomintang. Many Chinese Communists were alarmed at the new agreement, fearing that it would now be impossible for them to organize successfully. But Borodin was outwardly confident, and the official Soviet response was to deny that any coup had taken place, and to insist that conditions in China were more favorable than they had ever been.[27]

By the summer of 1926 Chiang Kai-shek, recently appointed commander in chief of the Kuomintang armies with virtually dictatorial powers, was ready to embark on the long-awaited Northern Expedition. Borodin and the other Russian advisers, fearing a military disaster that would wreck all their achievements to date, strenuously objected. They were overruled, and Borodin ostensibly yielded with a good grace, preparing for the expedition by embarking on an extensive study of the Taiping Rebellion. The Taipings, he concluded, had erred in tackling the Manchus, the Western Imperialists, and the bourgeoisie at the same time; if the Nationalists were to march on Shanghai, a stronghold of Western power and Chinese industry, they would be repeating the Taiping mistake. Instead, the

Nationalists should make for Wuhan, safely inland, an industrial complex with a strong urban proletariat.

But Chiang Kai-shek was a hard man to persuade, and the uneasiness that Borodin and the leading Chinese Communists felt at this time appears clearly in a report drawn up by a Soviet adviser in April:

> We consider Chiang Kai-shek a peculiar person with peculiar characteristics, most prominent of these being his lust for glory and power and craving to be the hero of China. He claims that he stands not only for the Chinese National Revolution but for the World Revolution. Needless to say, the degree of his actual understanding of revolution is quite another matter. . . . He acts entirely according to his individuality without depending on the masses. However, in order to obtain glory, which is his goal, he sometimes wants to utilize the masses, the Chinese Communist Party, and ourselves.[28]

The stunning successes of Chiang's armies in late 1926 temporarily stilled such criticisms. In a few months, thanks to good training and logistics, divided warlord opponents, and the skilled marshaling of peasant support, the Kuomintang had driven up to the Yangtze, capturing the cities of Changsha, Nanchang, and Wuhan. But these very successes brought new problems in their train: Kuomintang and Communist propaganda had assured widespread popular backing for the expedition, and as peasants and workers rose to help the new armies, what might have been a straightforward military campaign began to take on the overtones of the first phase of a revolution. The key question was what to do about the revolutionary forces now unleashed. Mao Tse-tung was one of many Communists fascinated and excited by the way the peasants struck out for themselves, turning on their old landlord enemies. "They raise their rough, blackened hands and lay them on the heads of the gentry," he wrote, "they tie the evil gentry with ropes, put tall paper hats on them, and lead them in a parade through the villages." Mao saw the inevitability of local terror and applauded it: "A revolution is not the same as inviting people to dinner or writing an essay or painting a picture or embroidering a flower. . . . A revolution is an uprising, an act of violence whereby one class overthrows the authority of another." The spontaneous actions of the peasantry were a challenge to the Chinese Communists, this Mao saw clearly. "All revolutionary parties and all revolutionary comrades will stand before them to be tested, to be accepted or rejected by them. To march at their head and lead them? To follow in the rear, gesticulating at them and criticizing them? To face them as opponents? Every Chinese is free to choose among the three, but circumstances demand that a quick choice be made."[29]

Mao's view was, however, a minority position, and Borodin made his own choice: his orders were to work within the Kuomintang, to help the Nationalists unify China and throw out the Imperialists. He felt that he could not achieve this goal if he supported rioting peasants who sought to overthrow the social structure from which many influential Nationalist supporters drew their incomes. He was adviser to the Kuomintang, not an agrarian Communist. It was safest to obey Stalin completely, to be orthodox at all costs, and this Borodin did, in a masterful statement that solved the problem by denying that any problem existed. "The land is not yet a problem," ran the Chinese Communist directive of December 1926, "because the peasant problem at the present consists of demands for the reduction of rent and interest, freedom of organization, armed self-defense, resistance against local bullies and the bad gentry, and opposition to excessive taxes and irregular levies. To lead the peasantry away from the actual struggle for these demands [so that they] devote themselves to the solution of the land issue alone, is to stop struggling."[30] In other words, moderation was struggle, but violence was not, and he accordingly disciplined those Communists who followed the violent path. It was a delicate line to tread.

At a conference in December 1926, Borodin and Chiang agreed on fine revolutionary slogans: "The peasant and worker masses are the main forces of the national revolution," they declared. "Wipe out all the counter-revolutionary groups."[31] But the implied harmony, and the very words themselves, were finally growing meaningless. Borodin, the leading Chinese Communists, and many of the Kuomintang radicals, were now ensconced in Wuhan, and wished to make this the base for the next phase of the Northern Expedition; Chiang and his confidantes were settled in Nanchang and wished to drive east down the Yangtze to capture Shanghai. Feelings ran high, and in January 1927 Borodin, in a rare loss of control, insulted Chiang publicly by calling him a mere militarist. He may have been prompted to this act of defiance by the fact that at the beginning of January a Chinese crowd had stormed into the British concession at Hankow and taken it over, thus proving that the proletariat were finally ready to assert themselves against the Imperialists. In February the Wuhan radicals voted to eliminate "all the old, confused, mediocre and rotten elements" from the Kuomintang, and started to reorganize the party hierarchy so as to undercut Chiang's power.[32]

Chiang, in turn, began to angle for the support of those Russians who did not get on with Borodin and, more importantly, to sound out the Western powers in an attempt to learn what their reactions would be if he ditched the Communists and set up an independent regime. One of Chiang's personal bodyguards, Morris Cohen — popularly known as "Two-gun Cohen" from the revolvers he always carried — visited the American consul general at Canton in February 1927, and reported that Chiang and Borodin had had "a serious disagreement" resulting in a "more or less permanent breach" between the two men. Cohen, noted the Consul General, told him that "if the Powers wanted to get the Russians out of China, they should now establish definite contact with General Chiang. He was sure Chiang hated the Russians and was only cooperating with Borodin because the Soviet government was supplying arms and ammunition which were absolutely essential for the success of the Cantonese forces."[33]

The Western powers would not commit themselves, and neither Chiang nor Borodin felt strong enough to force the final break, so through the spring of 1927 the uneasy alliance continued. When workers launched a great general strike in Shanghai, and took over the city from its controlling warlord, they delivered it to Chiang Kai-shek; they went even further, and obeyed the Comintern order that they should bury their arms and disband their pickets, lest Chiang be alienated in any way. With Shanghai in his possession, Chiang finally struck swiftly and decisively. On April 12 his troops rounded up the Communists and labor leaders in the city and had them shot.[34]

This Shanghai coup came as a shock to Stalin, who had declared only a few days before: "We are told that Chiang Kai-shek is making ready to turn against us again. I know that he is playing a cunning game with us, but it is he that will be crushed. We shall squeeze him like a lemon and then be rid of him."[35] But Stalin could not afford to admit that any mistake had been made, especially since Trotsky and other critics in Russia had been asking why the Chinese workers had not been organized into Soviets, and why the agrarian revolution had not been encouraged. To counter these criticisms, Stalin insisted that the events in Shanghai had, in fact, proved the correctness of the Comintern line for which he was responsible. All that had happened was that the right wing of the Kuomintang had now shown its true colors as the representative of feudal and comprador interests. But the first stage of the Nationalist and anti-Imperialist revolution was completed, said Stalin, and it was time for the Communists to forge a new alliance with the radical wing of the Kuomintang, which represented the petty bourgeoisie. "Only blind people," Stalin told Trotsky, "can deny the left Kuomintang the role of the organ of revolutionary struggle, the role of the organ of insurrection against feudal survivals and imperialism in China."[36] Instead of Chiang Kai-shek, the Chinese Communists should now ally with Wang Ching-wei, believed to be a left-leaning enemy of Chiang's, and with Feng Yü-hsiang, the powerful northern warlord who had visited Moscow, conferred with Borodin, and was known as the "Red General." So Borodin set about weaving a new alliance and new compromises, this time in Wuhan. And since the Wuhan members of the Kuomintang relied on the support of local warlords and financial interests, this meant that once again Borodin had to use his influence to hold the peasants and workers in check.

Initially Borodin gave no sign that the new assignment worried him. He set himself up in an imposing mansion, with enormous rooms, damask hangings, rich furniture, and central heating. His staff, including British and Americans as well as Russians, was large, competent, and energetic. He visited the representatives of the Western powers, who had been outraged by the seizure of their foreign concessions, to reassure them that he would restore the economic life of the city to normalcy. He continued to negotiate with Feng Yü-hsiang and other warlords in an attempt to get them to undertake the second phase of the Northern Expedition in alliance with the Communists. He was punctilious to Wang Ching-wei and other members of the "Left" Kuomintang in Wuhan, and continued to criticize peasant excesses, even after those same peasants were being rounded up and shot by his nominal "allies."[37] He read Sinclair Lewis's *Elmer Gantry* with approval, and played chess with his customary precision. His demeanor remained calm and philosophical. "Everything interests him," wrote a journalist in Wuhan; "to everything he applies the patient, humorous, thoughtful processes of his philosophy. In this he is totally unlike the typical revolutionary — the juiceless fanatic who sees everything from scenery to shoe-laces in the terms of class warfare. Borodin has, indeed, the detachment which Lenin is said to have preserved to the last, a recognition of the littleness of men and things in the vastness of their ultimate intention."[38] The man once known as "Emperor of Canton" seemed perfectly at home as the ruler of "Red Wuhan."

But Borodin knew that things were going badly. It was thanks to his policies that the workers' and peasants' organizations were being torn apart before his eyes, and executions of radicals took place daily. He himself was weak with malaria, and suffering from multiple fractures in his left arm after he had fallen from a horse; he felt unable to handle all the opposition in his own camp that had been aroused by his scrupulous obedience to Stalin's orders. Many Chinese Communists, and even some newly arrived Comintern agents, were disputing his authority. There were constant rumors that the radical Kuomintang were planning to junk the Communists and seek a rapprochement with Chiang Kai-shek. The Communists were being openly attacked in Wuhan, seat of their greatest strength. Some of the posters festooning the streets at this time were simply calculated to confuse and excite the business community. "Labor circles," ran one such announcement, "declared they would picket all foreign banks this morning and shut off all food supplies from the foreign staffs of all these institutions. Servants of the foreigners will be ordered to quit. Why is this being done? Ask M. Borodin!! He knows."[39] Others attacked him with a scurrilous levity that made the Communist cause a laughingstock. "The women's association suggests to have a naked body procession on the 1st of May, in promoting the principle of freedom," solemnly announced another poster, that was picked up by delighted newspaper editors across the country. "If any one wishes to enter into this naked body procession an examination of body is necessary. The choice will fall on the one who has a snow white body and a pair of swollen nipples."[40]

It was hard to guide a revolution in a city that rang both with mocking laughter and with the shots of firing squads, and by June Borodin was in an acute depression.[41] Things were not made any easier by Stalin's new orders, which had arrived by telegram at Wuhan on June 1. The Chinese Communists were told to confiscate the land of evil landlords but to leave intact the lands of their warlord allies; to destroy unreliable generals and to create a new army of fifty thousand workers and peasants; to put fresh radical blood in the Central Executive Committee of the Kuomintang; and to organize a revolutionary court to try reactionary military officers. Stalin's orders, designed to raise the revolution to a higher stage, might have been practicable if the Communists had possessed overwhelming military power and the unqualified support of the radical Kuomintang. But as things stood in Wuhan, the orders were meaningless. Obeying them was like "trying to take a bath in a urinal," the Chinese Communist leader Ch'en Tu-hsiu dourly commented.[42] Hoping to stimulate the left-wing Kuomintang leader Wang Ching-wei to radical action, the recently arrived Comintern agent M. N. Roy showed him a copy of Stalin's telegram. The effect was disastrous. Far from being inspired by the Communists' drive and vision, as Roy had hoped, Wang

Chiang Kai-shek (right) and the "Red General" Feng Yü-hsiang. Summer, 1927. *Courtesy P. & A. Photos.*

Ching-wei was alarmed and upset, accused the Communists of violating their agreements with his party, and set about seeking to heal the split in the Kuomintang by re-allying with Chiang Kai-shek. Borodin was furious, and asked Stalin to recall Roy, but the damage had been done.[43] Borodin's last hope vanished at the end of June, when the "Red General" Feng Yü-hsiang and Chiang Kai-shek reached an agreement to fight together.

A Danish journalist, who brought Borodin definite confirmation of this Chiang-Feng pact, was granted a late night interview. At its conclusion he asked the dejected revolutionary what had brought him to China in the first place, and what had made him stay on in China when his policies were so obviously failing.

Borodin leaned back in his deep armchair, and the lamp standing at his side shone upon his light, loose-hanging tropical suit, his pale face, heavily lined with shadows, especially beneath the jawbone, his dark eyes, and his thin black hair. For a long time he sat lost in thought, slowly stroking his little black moustache, but finally he said in a deep, muffled voice: "I came to China to fight for an idea. The dream of accomplishing world revolution by freeing the people of the East brought me here. But China itself, with its age-old history, its countless millions, its vast social problems, its infinite capacities, astounded and overwhelmed me, and my thoughts of world revolution gradually sank into the background. The revolution and the fight for freedom in China became an end in itself, and no longer a means to an end. My task was to grasp the situation, to start the great wheel moving, and as time has passed it has carried me along with it. I myself have become only a cog in the great machine."[44]

It was an honest statement showing real self-awareness. China had mastered Borodin and had made him aware that there were indeed things in this world that neither he nor Stalin could control. The

Chinese revolution was developing its own momentum, and though both Communists and Nationalists had benefited from Borodin's organizational expertise, both finally rejected him. The Nationalists had seen the dangers of subversion implicit in the Communist alliance, and the Chinese Communists had seen many of their best men killed as a result of continued obedience to Moscow's orders. Though Comintern agents were to continue active in China for a few more years, they were never again to exercise total control over the Chinese Communist Party.

Borodin's days in the sun were over. In early July he began to purchase and equip a convoy of motorcars to take him and his staff back across the Gobi desert to Russia. On July 27, 1927, Borodin left Wuhan. As he made his way north, he conferred with some more Chinese generals in a final search for an ally for the shattered Communists, but his heart wasn't really in the work. "When the next Chinese general comes to Moscow and shouts 'Hail to the World Revolution,'" he told one of his traveling companions, "better send at once for the G.P.U. [the secret police]. All that any of them want is rifles." Borodin's companion protested that the general they had just met seemed a friendly man, truly fond of Russia, "He's young," Borodin replied; "they are all good when they are young."[45]

The failure of his mission to China ended Borodin's career as a revolutionary. Upon his return to Russia he was given minor jobs as a teacher of English and as editor of an unimportant Moscow newspaper. It did not matter that in China Borodin had carried out his orders to the letter and that it had been Stalin's error to believe that Borodin could manipulate both the Kuomintang and the Chinese Communists in the interests of Russia. Stalin was not a man to admit his mistakes, so Borodin paid for them.

Borodin cannot have been too surprised at this turn of events. He had learned from his successive experiences with Chiang Kai-shek and Wang Ching-wei that there is an irony in the repetitive process of history. As Marx had written in his essay "The Eighteenth Brumaire of Louis Bonaparte": "Hegel remarks somewhere that all facts and personages of great importance in world history occur, as it were, twice. He forgot to add: the first time as tragedy, the second as farce. . . . Men make their own history, but they do not make it just as they please; they do not make it under circumstances chosen by themselves, but under circumstances directly encountered, given and transmitted from the past. The tradition of all the dead generations weighs like a nightmare on the brain of the living."[46]

It was obviously this somber quotation that was running through Borodin's mind shortly before he left Wuhan forever. When an insistent journalist asked him for a summary of his revolutionary experience in China, Borodin replied: "Four years of fighting and sacrifice in behalf of the revolution have been nullified. History repeats itself again. It begins as tragedy; the second time it is tragicomedy. The revolution extends to the Yangtze. If a diver were sent down to the bottom of this yellow stream he would rise again with an armful of shattered hopes."[47]

8

TODD *and* BETHUNE:

Overcome All Terrors

"The fierce and turbid stream carries our thoughts irresistibly to the future," exclaimed W. A. P. Martin in 1866, after gazing on the waters of the Yellow River in central China. "Spurning the feeble efforts of the natives, it waits to be subdued by the science of Western engineers."[1] Sixty-nine years later the river was still unsubdued, but O. J. Todd, an American engineer from Michigan, was giving the matter careful consideration: "China's need is clear," he wrote. "At present she must draw upon our resources for the engineering knowledge and skill sufficient to tame her two great unruly rivers. The problem of protecting human life against great catastrophes is so broad that it passes international boundaries."[2]

The immensity of the task delighted Todd, for he was a civil engineer with an almost mystical view of his vocation, who felt that "our profession is the one above all others that calls for the stamina, moral and physical as well as mental, that meets and overcomes all terrors and solves in the field the puzzles that present themselves."[3] After serving as a captain of engineers in France during the First World War, Oliver Todd had traveled to China in 1919 with John Ripley Freeman, who had been made a consultant on Yellow River flood problems by the Chinese government. Freeman was a famous engineer, a specialist in water storage and hydraulic power, who had made a careful study of historical Chinese writings on flood control and had grown convinced that there was "no part of the world where the science and arts of hydraulic engineering could do more for humanity than in China."[4] Freeman drew up plans for deepening and narrowing the channels of both the Yangtze and the Yellow Rivers to speed their flow to the sea, as well as an ambitious plan for land reclamation. Both plans fell through because of shortage of funds and the extreme conservatism of the local officials, and Freeman returned disappointed to the United States. But Todd stayed on, determined to tackle piecemeal some of the many problems that Freeman had hoped to solve through his grand design.

Flood and famine, the perennial twin scourges of the Chinese peasant, struck China repeatedly in the 1920's and 1930's. Untold millions died, and millions more were reduced to beggary, their houses burned for fuel and their few possessions sold to pay their debts. Though the Western governments, wary of China's political and economic instability, were unwilling to invest much money in relief work, Western missionaries, the International Red Cross, and a number of individuals like Todd were eager to face the challenge. The techniques they devised ranged from the simple distribution of grain or cash to the formation of rural cooperatives, experimental farms, mutual aid societies, and afforestation, irrigation and road-building projects. The China International Famine Relief Commission was formed in Shanghai in 1921 to coordinate such endeavors.[5]

Todd's first important work was in Shantung province, where he supervised some thirty-five thousand men on famine relief in the building of five hundred miles of earth road. While this work was in progress the Yellow River smashed a six thousand-foot gap in the dikes near Litsing and poured over the surrounding countryside, destroying five hundred villages and leaving a quarter of a million people destitute. The disaster gave Todd his first chance to battle with the river that for the rest of his life in China was to fascinate and appall him. That river — "China's Sorrow" — was almost human to Todd; he credited it with the "power to take over new terrain at will" and was determined to make it yield, to make it "follow the

wishes of man and remain in a definite channel delimited for its use."
He knew all about its 2,700-mile length, the fine silt with grains
under one-thousandth of an inch in diameter that swirled along in a
current of eight feet per second, each measure of water containing
10 percent of silt by weight, the silt falling imperceptibly but un-
ceasingly into the channel till the river rose above the dikes that man
had so painfully constructed and swept away his home and his
livelihood.[6]

It was the Western engineer who would master the Yellow River,
Todd believed, the Western engineer who would show this "patient,
plodding people" the reasons for their "so-called natural calamities."
New techniques must oust old superstitions. "I confess," wrote Todd,
"that as an engineer I wish all the rain gods could be dethroned and
forgotten, the bronze cows removed from the river banks, the drama
for appeasing the river dragons be abolished from construction work,
and instead the worship of the science of river hydraulics encouraged."[7]

Brushing aside the suggestion of a local Chinese general, who was
insisting that a giant iron claw should be dragged through the errant
river to stir up the mud and make it drift out to sea, Todd got down
to business in December 1922. The mighty river had to be forced
back through its original channel, which had to be redug at the base
of the ox bow it had scoured out of the rich farmland. Todd's description of this task must be read, not just as an engineering text, but as
an almost Promethean song of triumph:

The striking feature of this piece of river revision was the
construction of a rock-fill dam built from a timber trestle, put in
much as the Clarke dam was built across a break in the lower
Colorado River in 1907. Oregon pine timbers and round piling
were used for this work and an American pile-driver was
brought in for the job. The piles were driven to 25 or 30 feet
penetration in four-pile bents spaced ten feet on centers. This
dam was waterproofed by 300,000 bags of earth, 10,000 reed
mats, 5 feet by 8 feet, and the deposits of river silt that settled

in the pond just ahead of the dam. The trestle was driven in the low water period of spring and, at the same time, 400 river junks were transporting the 50,000 yards of rock a distance of 120 miles from the quarries located up-stream. In late April and early May, narrow gauge track was laid on the trestles so that coolies could push out and dump two lines of rock cars at once.[8]

Eight thousand men worked on the job; one million yards of earth were moved by hand, either on carrying poles or in wheelbarrows; new dikes, forty feet wide, were built and tamped with heavy stones. The work was completed on time, at a cost well under half that of the most hopeful Chinese estimates. Technology and the coolie had been united.

The engineer's role in China was now clear. As Todd put it, "He must adapt his plans and construction programs to the things available in China and of these the greatest is human labor — lots of it and of very good quality when in competent and experienced hands."[9] Among the most competent were the hands of O. J. Todd — "God-a-Mighty" Todd as his friends not-so-jokingly called him, in reference to his favorite expletive; "Todd Almighty" was the nickname more generally adopted by those who preferred a blunter parallel.[10]

His expertise proven, Todd was in rising demand. In 1925 he was called on to block the Yangtze River floods at Shihshow in southern Hupeh; in 1926 he was back on the Yellow River in western Shantung. It was here that he summarized for American readers the contributions that he felt a foreign engineer could make to the Chinese: firstly, judgment born of wide experience; secondly, promptness in carrying through work that has been carefully planned; thirdly, efficiency in handling men and funds "without permitting petty hold-ups or paying bribes." Todd went on to explain the peculiar advantages that a foreigner enjoyed. In a China torn by warring military factions "a foreign engineer attached to a non-political international organization is in a position to do much more in civil practice than could any of his Chinese contemporaries. It is almost impossible for them to work where there are military operations, and absolutely beyond their power to resist the order of requisition that may be placed on their equipment, men, and materials of construction, as well as upon their carts and boats. Foreign engineers under international commissions have certain immunities in this respect not enjoyed by the native."[11]

Todd had a chance to prove this point in 1927 when the Hupeh River Conservancy Board called him to Hankow to protect the city from the swollen Yangtze. Work on the dikes continued smoothly despite the growing tensions between Chiang Kai-shek and the Left Kuomintang, between the Left Kuomintang and the Communists, and between the Communists and the local warlords. Only in May did the forceful demands for higher wages, made by the newly organized "Dike Workers' Union," threaten Todd's project. He had with him only limited funds and could not afford to pay more than the previously standard wage. His solution was to ask Borodin's cooperation, and through an intermediary an appointment with Borodin was made for May 24. As Todd recalled the meeting, "I at once launched into the matter of our dike work and trouble with the local labor and asked what he could do to restrain these workers who were threatening stoppage of important work supported by the Govt. He said of course wages depend on living costs and if prices of food went up wages must follow. I assured him that our funds were limited and our estimates were made on a basis of wages as they existed when the work was started two months earlier and said a time agreement was necessary to protect the engineers, reminding him of term agreements by most unions in the USA. He said he would consider that angle and realized the work must go forward and would look into the matter. He left the impression that for this emergency work he would see that there was no work stoppage."[12] There was no work stoppage, and three weeks later the work was completed.

Todd's war with China's rivers continued, without respect to Chinese politics. Occasionally he faltered, as in 1935 when he noted darkly that "civil war and maneuvers for political control have tended to assume far greater importance in the minds of men than works of seeming drudgery such as putting a great river under human control,"[13] yet he undertook new projects in 1936 and 1937. Todd was forced by the advancing Japanese to leave China in 1938, and that same year Chiang Kai-shek blasted the dikes of the Yellow River in a desperate attempt to stem the Japanese advance. It was natural that at the war's end Todd should be summoned back to China, on the staff of the United Nations Relief and Rehabilitation Administration (UNRRA), to repair the damage that man had done to the river. "So in December, 1945, I reached Shanghai to begin one of the most hazardous undertakings of my career," wrote Todd. "Based on many years of close contact with the Yellow River as an engineer I had no hesitation in tackling the problem. . . . It was the outstanding project of the UNRRA program in many ways because of its size, its importance, its color and its risks."[14]

Directing a labor force of two hundred thousand coolies, Todd worked with the support of Chinese Nationalists to divert the Yellow River near Kaifeng and restore it to its northern channel, which the Communists had agreed to deepen. It was an uneasy alliance, and scattered fighting between the two forces constantly threatened to halt the project. The Communists resented the work because they had to dispossess the squatters who had settled in the old riverbed; Nationalists resented it because it was interfering with the movement of troops to Manchuria; equipment was blown up, the weather was bad, and there were constant delays and frustrations. Yet the project was completed in 1947. Todd explained his success laconically: "I slept with one eye open and took from both coat pockets all the tricks I had learned over a period of nearly twenty years working with the Chinese on many projects in many parts of the country."[15]

These projects had not all been flood-control work. Since arriving in China in 1919 Todd had traveled "approximately 25,000 miles annually by train, coastal or river steamer, automobile, ricksha, Peking cart, mule litter, muleback, mountain chair, junk, bicycle and on foot."[16] Much of this travel was in connection with his second dream — the construction of an efficient road network in China. This road construction — often tightly linked to relief work as it employed laborers who would otherwise have starved — was an integral part of Todd's conception of a better China. "All this work is in line with a program that is necessary before China will be the neighbor we hope she will be — one with living standards sufficiently high so that she may partake in a large way of all our own country has to offer to the rest of the world. To bring up these living standards measurably through the 'interior' of China is no small task."[17]

The task took him from the borders of Mongolia to the borders of Vietnam. In pursuit of his goal that one day there would be a million men at work grading modern motor roads he conferred with many of the most powerful warlords: Wu P'ei-fu in the area around Peking, Feng Yü-hsiang in Suiyan, Yen Hsi-shan in Shansi.

It was backbreaking work, even with the support of an international organization, capable Western colleagues, and young and dedicated Chinese assistants. "Why should people live in these hard places of earth?" Todd asked himself, as he toiled through a three-week journey in mountainous southwest China from Yunnan to Kweichow province in late 1927. The major part of the journey was along narrow earth or stone paths, which became steep flights of stone steps as they plunged down the hillsides, over swift-flowing rivers, and clambered up the opposite ridge. And if they had to live in such places, why couldn't they better their lot? "I am often amazed in China," Todd wrote on this same journey, "at the opportunities missed by the Chinese. Is it possible that the routine of centuries has deadened perception, even where new food supplies are concerned?"[18] Yet one could not say there was no progress. A few miles outside the Kweichow capital city of Kweiyang, Todd was met by a seven-passenger American automobile, the first in the province. Chinese engineers had completed the plans Todd had drawn up the previous year, and a new macadamized road now ran through the city. Admittedly the road didn't lead anywhere, it had been built by drafting schoolchildren and troops, and the car had been carried in pieces over the mountains — a fifty-day journey, by bamboo litter and the backs of men. But it was a triumphal entry all the same, with Governor Chou Chi-tsun in white uniform and gold-ornamented sword, an honor guard of ten thousand troops, and the bandmaster leading his brass in spirited renderings of "The Red, White and Blue" and "Swanee River."[19]

Little by little some roads got built. They were not much by Western standards, but they were firm, well drained, with grades restricted wherever possible to seven percent or less. As they were for motor vehicles, the old heavy carts, with their giant wooden wheels, lumbered along on the shoulders, so that the precious surface should not be torn up. Though scarcely used then, Todd hoped that one day trucks would roar down them, carrying grain and rice to stricken areas, while the private cars of officials and merchants would speed by with the promises of fairer administration and wider trade. Todd knew that this would only be achieved by intelligent overall planning: "To increase the general prosperity of the country requires concerted action of a constructive nature and the prosecution of a program that will conserve the natural resources as well as the manpower of the nation. Conflicts at arms will not do this. China's manpower, translated into constructive service along well-developed lines of civil endeavor, is her great strength and hope."[20] When civil strife grew so disruptive that even Todd could not work on roads or rivers he would retire to his Peking home and work on the machinery that he was developing to extract high-grade oils from spearmint plants: "I adopted this as a hobby in China instead of bridge or golf, for we need diversified occupations."[21]

Todd spent twenty-one years of his life in China, and he did not regret it: "What lasting value did this work have? It was all beneficial. The roads we built were not paved but had good grades and were later macadamized in places. . . . Most of the irrigation work we did was lasting. Near the Mongolian border during a period of lawlessness bandits destroyed some of the structures, but this was an isolated case. Our minor projects were part of a more extensive plan to be carried out when government became more stable. The work of the Famine Commission started a movement that has grown in more recent years until more foot-hill lands have come under irrigation.

O. J. Todd on the Yellow River Project, 1923.
Courtesy O. J. Todd.

Governor Chou Chi-tsun of Kweichow Province in southwest China stands beside his new motor car. Mrs. Todd smiles to the Governor's left. *Courtesy O. J. Todd.*

. . . The Yellow River Project of 1946–47 was definitely a success and has stood all flood tests since its completion."[22]

Moreover Todd prided himself on his independence: "My work was that of a *civil* engineer and I kept out of military matters, following a completely neutral course so far as political ties were concerned." The same, he felt, was true of his colleagues. "My Western co-workers in the engineering profession were not greatly interested in reforming China aside from setting examples of good technical performance. They were not social or political reformers and they were few in number." Most of his staff were Chinese, who had studied modern American engineering textbooks in Chinese universities. Though Todd conducted his work with them in English and kept his supervisory role in all major projects, he took satisfaction from knowing that he had "influenced these men in branching out in their profession. They have become bolder and more international minded."[23] To a contemporary, Todd was "a reassuring figure, the representative of the solid workers of this world, who keeps the wheels turning over, the necessary business moving. . . . This ruddy-skinned, clear-eyed engineer from America puts a man's mind at rest."[24]

Todd's work is not easy to evaluate. Certainly his achievements were staggering — his roads, often placed in the middle of nowhere against overwhelming odds, were amazing individual feats, as were the flood and irrigation works. Yet at the same time he failed to win wide support from the Chinese he was so anxious to help, he was unable to develop a rudimentary network of modern communications, or to introduce Western engineering science on a massive scale. The reasons for this were various. Part of the trouble was that he lacked funds and manpower. In 1935, for example, Todd yearned for a group of twenty Western and one hundred Chinese engineers, and a grant of $500,000 to make a preliminary survey of China's general flood problems. Such a sum was simply not available for use in China. Partly his work was hampered because China was divided between warring factions all the time that he was there, and political animosities often precluded cooperation even on matters affecting

China's vital needs. Partly, too, his work could be seen as a threat to those who were entrenched in their own domains: better communications would mean stronger central control, roads and rails could carry food but they could also carry invading armies.

Yet the major impediment to his success was surely his status as the representative of foreign powers, however strenuous his own disclaimers. For as long as the West still played so great a part in Chinese affairs there could be no true neutrality for a Westerner. Hume had learned this the hard way. Todd never had it thrust at him, but as early as 1924 he was writing of "trying to understand what this great nation has been and what it is capable of becoming under the tutelage and with the assistance of Western nations."[25] Assistance might be welcomed by the Chinese, but foreign *tutelage* was not. For tutelage had teeth. The same month that Todd was working, with Borodin's cooperation, to stop the floods near Hankow, another Comintern agent was writing: "The seat of the Nationalist government, Hankow, is practically a beleaguered city. A formidable array of cruisers, destroyers, and gunboats arrogantly challenges the right of the Chinese people to govern this country in their own way. English, American, French marines crowd the streets of the Nationalist capital. The Nationalist government smarts under this indignity." Though this may have been anti-Imperialist rhetoric, there was truth in it; and Nationalists, Communists and warlords were all using anti-imperialism as a unifying propaganda device.[26] Whether he needed them or not, Todd was working under the shadow of Western guns.

Todd believed that his work would "make both China and America prosper in the long run."[27] The ideal was for a program of truly mutual benefit. But the Chinese were skeptical, and in 1936 a reporter noted that "insistence by China upon 'working out its own salvation,' even if that means being saved slowly, has marked recent relations of the Nanking Government and Occidental experts."[28] Strongly nationalistic Chinese could not but be wary as Americans pushed car sales in Sian and explored the market in Tibet, and as Detroit showed strong interest in founding a "Michigan in China" to train Chinese engineers. Todd himself wrote that "American autos are being brought in to be used on these roads. American mining machinery will follow as will a hundred other things American."[29] This was not what the Chinese were struggling for.

*   *   *

In December 1938 the Canadian doctor Norman Bethune was serving with elements of the Communist Chinese Army behind the Japanese lines in north China. In the cold clear hours of early morning, after working all day and all night, he marshaled his thoughts on disease and death:

> Gangrene is a cunning, creeping fellow. Is this one alive? Yes, he lives. Technically speaking, he is alive. Give him saline intravenously. Perhaps the innumerable, tiny cells of his body will remember. They may remember the hot, salty sea, their ancestral home, their first food. With the memory of a million years, they may remember other tides, other oceans and life being born of the sea and sun. It may make them raise their tired little heads, drink deep and struggle back into life again. It may do that.
>
> And this one. Will he run along the road beside his mule at another harvest, with cries of pleasure and happiness? No, that one will never run again. How can you run with one leg? What will he do? Why, he'll sit and watch other boys run. What will he think? He'll think what you and I would think. What's the good of pity? Don't pity him! Pity would diminish his sacrifice. He did this for the defense of China. Help him. Lift him off the table. Carry him in your arms. Why, he's light as a child! Yes, your child, my child.[30]

At this time, Norman Bethune was forty-eight-years-old, and intimately acquainted with death. He had served with the Canadian Army in the First World War as a stretcher-bearer, and been seriously wounded. After studying medicine in Canada and Europe, and leading a flamboyant and extravagant life, he finally set up in private practice in Detroit, only to find that he had contracted virulent tuberculosis. He was not expected to live; on the walls of his sanatorium room he painted himself clasped in the arms of the Angel of Death, with the legend: "My little act is over, and the tiresome play is done."[31] If he did nothing, he estimated, having carefully followed the track of his disease, he would be dead in 1932. "Contemplation," he wrote to his ex-wife, "becomes one's special form of action, and no one here can escape the changes, the discoveries, the greater self-knowledge that are inevitably the product of such enforced contemplation."[32] For Bethune, self-knowledge brought desire to live. He insisted that he be used as a guinea pig in the newly developing compression treatment for tubercular patients known as "artificial pneumothorax." The treatment was successful, and on recovery Bethune joined the faculty of medicine at McGill University as a specialist in thoracic surgery.

His self-knowledge had brought him renewed life; the intellectual discoveries that he had made profoundly altered the content of that life. He began to question the ethics of the medical profession, where doctors grew rich while the myriad poor died of disease and undernourishment in the slums that the Depression had spawned. "There is a rich man's tuberculosis and a poor man's tuberculosis," he reflected. "The rich man recovers and the poor man dies. This succinctly expresses the close embrace of economics and pathology."[33] He treated the poor free, began to examine systems of socialized medicine and to argue for them in public, learned to admire the achievements of the Russian Revolution: "Creation is not and never has been a genteel gesture. It is rude, violent and revolutionary."[34] In 1936 he was invited by the Committee to Aid Spanish Democracy to lead a Canadian medical unit to Madrid, to help the Loyalists in their fight with Franco. The invitation confused and excited him. "Go to Spain? Last week I had to decide whether to operate on my child. Now I have to decide whether I go to Spain. I am surprised, honored — and perplexed. Am I the right person? Am I ready? Yesterday's answers seem to prepare new questions for today. And tomorrow — what? The times impose cruel and irreversible decisions on us!"[35]

Bethune reached Madrid in November 1936. He stayed there several months, developing mobile blood transfusion units that could operate near the front line, and establishing the necessary blood banks to back them up. He saw, once again, hundreds of men dying in action and the civilian refugees dying on the roadside. His anger with the Western democracies that stood aside while the Fascist armies triumphed grew ever stronger. In the summer of 1937 he returned to Canada on a fund-raising mission and joined the Communist Party. The newspapers were full of China. He could not ignore it. "I refuse to live in a world that spawns murder and corruption without raising my hand against them. I refuse to condone, by passivity, or by default, the wars which greedy men make against others. . . . Spain and China are part of the same battle. I am going to China because I feel that is where the need is greatest; that is where I can be most useful."[36] In January of 1938 he was in Hankow, on the Yangtze, conferring with Nationalist Chinese officials; by early March he was at Hotsin in western Shansi province, treating the demoralized troops of the warlord Yen Hsi-shan: he found no serious cases, and was informed that this was because all the seriously wounded men had died. By the end of March he had crossed the Yellow River with a small Communist supply team and arrived in Yenan.

Yenan was Mao Tse-tung's base, the center of the Chinese Communist movement. After the disasters of 1927, the Communists had either gone underground in the cities, or retreated to poverty-stricken areas of the countryside, where they had established provisional "Soviet" governments. In the early thirties Mao had created such a government in the southeastern province of Kiangsi, but the unremitting attacks of Chiang Kai-shek, directed by German military advisers, had finally forced the Communists to retreat on the Long March to the northwest. It was on this march, in early 1935, that Mao had gained control of the party, and it was in Yenan that Mao had regrouped the scattered and dispirited Communist forces.[37]

As his rallying cry, Mao had adopted the potent slogan of "Unify China to resist the Japanese." Chiang Kai-shek had found it increasingly difficult to group his followers round the anti-Communist cause while the Japanese were threatening China's very existence, and by mid-1937 he and the Communists had once again formed a United Front. The Front was little more united than it had been in the early twenties, but at least a semblance of harmony was maintained. De facto recognition was given by Chiang to the Communists' Border Area government in the provinces of Shensi, Kansu and Ninghsia, and they were encouraged to conduct guerrilla operations against the Japanese in the northeastern area of Shansi, Chahar and Hopei. For their part the Communists, still shaky from their near defeat, and anxious to maintain good relations with the wealthier peasants in their base areas, had adopted a moderate program of rent reduction instead of pushing for land redistribution, and had established the structure for a democratic government. This was the "Yenan Communism" that so appealed to the few Western observers who were able to get through to Shensi. They found the Communists tolerant, cheerful, courageous and pragmatic, and they reported their findings to an absorbed Western readership.[38]

Bethune was as delighted as anyone, and noted the contrasts between the Communist and the Nationalist areas that he had seen: "In Hankow I found confusion, indecision, depressing signs of bureaucracy and inefficiency. In Yenan there is a sense of confidence and purpose in administrative circles. In the towns and cities I passed through on my way here I became accustomed to the sights of semi-feudalism — filthy dwellings, polluted streets, people in rags. Here, among the ancient structures, the streets are clean, teeming with people who seem to know where they're going."[39] He had a lengthy interview with Mao, who impressed him by his knowledge of the Loyalist political and military leaders in the Spanish Civil War, and was enthusiastic about Bethune's plan for setting up mobile base hospitals. He found Mao convinced of the Chinese people's will to resist, and of the inevitability of their final victory, however long that might take. "The man is a giant!" wrote Bethune after the interview was over. "He is one of the great men of our world."[40]

Bethune lingered only three weeks in Yenan, to assemble supplies and a small staff, before moving out to join General Nieh Jung-chen's troops who were ensconced in the mountains between Shansi and Hopei. Here he was formally named "Medical Adviser to the Chin-Cha-Chi Military District," and treated his first Communist patients: "The wounded are crawling with lice. They all have only one uniform, and that they have on. It is filthy with the accumulated dirt of nine months' fighting. Their bandages have been washed so often they are now nothing but dirty rags. Three men, one with the loss of both feet through frost-bite gangrene, have no clothes at all to wear. There is only a coverlet for them. Their food is boiled millet — that's all. All are anaemic and underfed. Most of them are slowly dying of sepsis and starvation. Many have tuberculosis."[41] It was worse even than Spain, but Bethune felt a definite sense of exaltation, for this was his true destination. "I am in the centre of the centre of the war. Now I can truly taste the strange, exalted flavor of this stupendous struggle."[42]

This was guerrilla war: small groups of Communist troops, co-operating with local peasant partisans, to harass the Japanese all over north China. They filled in the defensive ditches dug by the Japanese, cut telephone and power lines, derailed trains, blew bridges. Isolated detachments of Japanese troops would be surrounded and killed, their captured weapons going to arm fresh guerrillas; occasionally a Japanese convoy or blockhouse might be attacked by Communist forces of battalion strength or greater. Before Japanese reinforcements could be brought up, the guerrillas would retreat back to the mountains, the partisans return to their villages. Under these villages were networks of tunnels, growing in length and complexity each year of the war, where food, weapons, and the soldiers themselves could be hidden. At first the Japanese responded sluggishly; but as the guerrilla attacks grew in intensity — in some areas the Japanese needed eighty soldiers to guard a single mile of rail line — they resorted to violent countermeasures: burning whole villages, and

Mao Tse-tung (right) in Yenan, 1942.

either shooting the inhabitants or transporting them to "safer" areas. But this policy backfired; the Communists, who had always used their regular forces also as an educational vanguard, setting up schools and politically indoctrinating the villagers, found that Japanese atrocities made the peasants more, not less, responsive to their message.[43]

It was in this shifting, bitter, violent war that Bethune had to develop some kind of a hospital system. He had a staff of five Chinese doctors, and no other skilled assistance at all, to serve several hundred square miles of mountainous country and over one hundred thousand regular and irregular troops. His solution was to attack all problems simultaneously: he cleaned up and reorganized the existing base "hospitals" (which were usually long-abandoned temples with no facilities of any kind); he taught orderlies the basic principles of hospital hygiene and application of field dressings; showed villagers how to make splints, stretchers and bandages; wrote a textbook to be used in nursing and medical schools; and by patient and reiterated example persuaded the local people first to give their blood for emergency operations and then to form volunteer blood donor corps. The exaltation passed, to be replaced by a deep and simple satisfaction: "I am tired, but I don't think I have been so happy for a long time. I am content. I am doing what I want to do. And see what my riches consist of! I have vital work that occupies every moment of my time. I am needed. More than that — to satisfy my bourgeois vanity — the need for me is expressed."[44]

As soon as the base hospital was in reasonable running order Bethune was off to the battle zones, to implement his plan for mobile field-hospitals. For the last year of his life, from October 1938 until November 1939, he was to follow the ever-mobile Communist armies as they jabbed at the Japanese strongpoints and communications, then retreated before the inevitable Japanese counterattacks.

Bethune's new watchword was "Doctors: Go to the wounded. Don't wait for the wounded to come to you."[45] To accomplish this goal, he developed a miniature unit in which everything was planned to the last detail. Bethune and his orderlies traveled on horseback, and two mules carried all the necessities for handling one hundred patients at a time and equipping an operating room, a dressing station and a drug room: splints, bandages, surgical instruments, disinfectants and chloroform. The operating theater was any weatherproof building near the battle zone — often within three miles of the firing line; naturally the setup was crude, but it was better than anything that had existed previously. When anesthetic ran out, as it frequently did, operations and amputations were carried on without it. If the Japanese approached the mobile station and could not be stopped by local troops, Bethune and his staff were ready to move everything at ten minutes' notice and ride to safety. The non-walking wounded had to be left hidden in the villages.[46]

The work was unceasing. Bethune himself regularly put in an eighteen-hour day, and drove his staff ruthlessly, insisting the while on the highest technical standards conceivable in the circumstances. When the 359th Brigade of the Eighth Route Army attacked a Japanese column on the road from Kwangling to Lingkiu in the mountainous northeastern corner of Shansi, Bethune, who had ridden seventy-five miles to the scene, performed seventy-one minor and major operations in forty hours. In early March 1939, he treated 115 casualties in a sixty-nine-hour stretch.[47] When he had spare moments, he wrote of his experiences in a savage, lyrical prose:

Old filthy bandages stuck to the skin with blood-glue. Careful. Better moisten first. Through the thigh. Pick the leg up. Why, it's like a bag, a long, loose, red stocking. What kind of stocking? A Christmas stocking. Where's that fine, strong rod of bone now? In a dozen pieces. Pick them out with your fingers; white as dog's teeth, sharp and jagged. Now feel. Any more left? Yes, here. All? Yes, no, here's another piece. Is this muscle dead? Pinch it. Yes, it's dead. Cut it out. How can that heal? How can those muscles, once so strong, now so torn, so devastated, so ruined, resume their proud tension? Pull, relax. Pull, relax. What fun it was! Now that is finished. Now that's done. Now we are destroyed. Now what will we do with ourselves?[48]

In the course of the year 1939 Norman Bethune systematically worked himself to death. The legends around his name multiplied in the villages and mountains of northeast China; his name was invoked as a battle cry; as the Communist government in Yenan strengthened its organizational structure in Shensi and extended its control over the newly mobilized peasantry, Bethune received ever stronger backing and popular support, but his work increased proportionately. At the age of forty-nine he looked seventy: white-haired, flesh sunken, teeth ruined. He had spells of dizziness. He became deaf in one ear. But if depression was there, he masked it totally. Only occasionally did he even express nostalgia for his past life, his former friends. "Are books still being written?" he asked in a letter to Canada. "Is music still being played? Do you dance, drink beer, look at pictures? What do clean sheets feel like in a soft bed? Do women still love to be loved?"[49]

In October he was given the chance to go back to the United States and Canada on a fund-raising trip, to buy desperately needed medical supplies. He passed the opportunity by and went instead to Laiyuan in west Hopei, where the Japanese had mounted a strong new attack. In early November he slashed his finger during a hurried operation while the Japanese were moving in on his unit. His unit escaped, but in the harried days that followed he neglected to treat the finger, which grew seriously infected. He insisted on continuing to operate on Chinese troops, as his own health weakened. His arm swelled, and he drily diagnosed septicemia. "I am fatally ill. I am going to die," he told General Nieh in a brief letter that was also his last will and testament. He bequeathed his two cots and his English shoes to the General; his riding boots and trousers were willed to the local divisional commander. His surgical instruments were carefully shared between the Chinese doctors with whom he had worked. His aides received a blanket each. "The last two years," he concluded, "have been the most significant, the most meaningful years of my life. Sometimes it has been lonely, but I have found my highest fulfilment here among my beloved comrades. I have no strength now

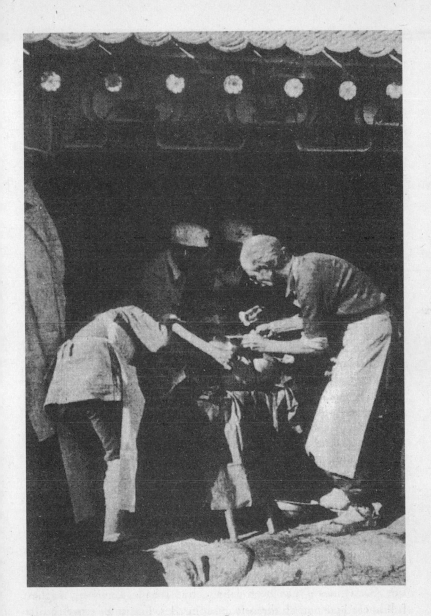

Norman Bethune operates on a Chinese Communist soldier, 1939, in a guerrilla base area in northeast China.

to write more. . . . To you and to all my comrades, a thousand thanks."[50] On November 13, at dawn, Bethune died,

Bethune was an emotional, irascible, talented man. He had incredible self-discipline, but did not submit to discipline imposed by others. He had drawn strength from the comradeship of communism but it is unlikely that he would have made a good Communist, even though he had a clear enough view of the capitalist enemy, as can be seen from the questions he asked himself in the Chinese winter, amid the smells of blood and chloroform:

> What do these enemies of the human race look like? Do they wear on their foreheads a sign so that they may be told, shunned and condemned as criminals? No. On the contrary, they are the respectable ones. They are honored. They call, and are called, gentlemen. What a travesty on the name! Gentlemen! They are the pillars of the State, of the church, of society. They support private and public charity out of the excess of their wealth. They endow institutions. In their private lives they are kind and considerate. They obey the law, their law, the law of property. But there is one sign by which these gentle gunmen can be told. Threaten a reduction on the profit of their money and the beast in them awakes with a snarl. They become as ruthless as savages, brutal as madmen, remorseless as executioners. Such men as these must perish if the human race is to continue. There can be no permanent peace in the world while they live. Such an organization of human society as permits them to exist must be abolished. These men make the wounds.[51]

Bethune's experiences had given him the right to dream of a world without wounds, though he was not concerned with the details of how such a world would be attained. The Chinese might have an answer and that was sufficient. In the meantime there were more than enough wounds to keep a thousand Bethunes occupied, and an endless succession of children waiting in the wings to be wounded in their turn. Certainly he had no expectation of seeing that world himself; he wooed death tenaciously, although his work was barely begun. The patterns of his life, and the manner of his leaving it, show that Bethune did not simply go to China to save wounded soldiers who would otherwise have died, nor even to be in the forefront of the world struggle against fascism or capitalism. He went to China to expiate the sins of his generation, to purge himself of the apathy and callousness and pursuit of profit which he believed had rotted his civilization. His technical brilliance was the entry card into a society that would otherwise have rejected him. No less than other Western advisers he used the Chinese for his own ends and was in turn used by them. He differed from all others, however, in that he used the Chinese to attain a meaningful death.

In the same hut in Shansi, where he cried out at those who made wounds, he also wrote: "How beautiful the body is; how perfect its parts; with what precision it moves; how obedient; proud and strong. How terrible when torn. The little flame of life sinks lower and lower, and with a flicker goes out. It goes out like a candle goes out. Quietly and gently. It makes its protest at extinction, then submits. It has its say, then is silent."[52]

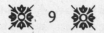

9

CHENNAULT, STILWELL, WEDEMEYER:

A Compass for Shangri-La

Claire Lee Chennault had a passion for planes: "I loved them from the start — the way the horizon spins around your nose in a roll, the kaleidoscope of sky and earth in a loop, the feeling of hanging tight against the safety belt in inverted flight, and the precise co-ordination of hands and feet on stick, rudder, and throttle that merges man and machine into a single instrument seeking mastery of an element."[1] Only alone in the air or fishing and hunting in the oak woods and cypress swamps around his Louisiana home did he feel at ease. A self-styled loner and adventurer, short-tempered, lacking advanced education, and consistently insubordinate, by the spring of 1937 he had made a shambles of his chosen career in the United States Army Air Corps. His superiors were wearied by his insistence on the importance of fighter planes and his criticisms of their unescorted bomber tactics. His hearing was impaired, and his brilliance at close-formation flying and aerial acrobatics no longer impressed them. He was slated for retirement. So when the Chinese Aeronautical Commission offered him a three-month contract to make a survey of the Chinese Air Force, at $1,000 a month plus expenses, he gladly accepted the offer and retired from the U. S. Army at the age of forty-seven.

The preliminary results of his survey were discouraging. He found that the Chinese Air Force, largely trained by Italian advisers in the 1930's, was short of planes and pilots, and the standards of flying were abysmally low. Under one-fifth of the five hundred planes nominally ready for action were fully operational. Chennault might well have completed his survey and returned home, but for a momentous meeting with the acting head of the aeronautical commission "the Generalissimo's wife, looking twenty years younger than I had expected and speaking English in a rich Southern drawl. This was an encounter from which I never recovered. To this day I remain completely captivated. That night I wrote in my diary, 'She will always be a princess to me.' "[2] This was the beginning of a loyalty to Mme. Chiang which was soon carried over to her family and her husband, the de facto rulers of Nationalist China; this loyalty was to be rewarded with money and influence such as he had never obtained in his homeland.

Chennault's survey mission was still uncompleted when Japanese and Chinese troops clashed at the Marco Polo Bridge, near Peking, on July 7, 1937. There had been many such clashes before, but this time the fighting spread. Japanese troops captured Peking, and in mid-August they attacked Shanghai. The United States, pursuing a policy of "morality and neutrality" in Asia, continued to express sympathy for the Chinese and to sell scrap iron and oil to the Japanese. Chennault, however, reacted violently: "I immediately wired the Generalissimo, offering my services in any capacity he could use them." Chiang Kai-shek accepted the offer, and ordered Chennault to Nanchang to direct the training of fighter groups.[3]

Chennault had finally found someone who could use him, and renewed Japanese successes brought him further prominence. As he described the shift in his role, "Madame Chiang suddenly discovered that there wasn't a single Chinese air officer who knew how to plan and organize a combat mission of any size. She asked me to take over."[4] But there was little that Chennault could do with the material at his disposal. The Chinese pilots were so inexperienced that they completely miscalculated their bombing runs, often hitting

Chinese troops or civilians instead of the Japanese. Their mistakes were agony to watch. "Flying weather was perfect as they circled to land," wrote Chennault of a squadron returning from an attack on Shanghai. "The first pilot overshot and cracked up in a rice paddy. The next ground-looped and burst into flame. The third landed safely, but the fourth smashed into the fire truck speeding toward the burning plane. Five out of eleven planes were wrecked landing and four pilots killed." By October 1937 Chennault concluded that the Chinese Air Force was at "the end of its rope," its pilots "an endless chain of moving ducks in a shooting gallery."[5]

At the end of 1937 Chiang Kai-shek's position was desperate. His best troops had been lost in a tenacious but futile defense of Shanghai and Nanking, and he was forced to transfer his capital to Chungking. Here, in the backward province of Szechwan, Chiang was cut off from his former sources of wealth and power, the great cities and seaports of eastern China. For support, he was dependent on conservative local warlords; militarily he was head of a coalition rather than supreme commander. The Japanese, through their puppet governments, controlled the major concentrations of heavy industry in Manchuria and in north and central China. Cut off from the coast, Chiang was dependent for supplies that could come by air, or overland from Burma. To his north, the Chinese Communists were entrenched in Yenan, still nominally joined with him in the United Front, but uncooperative allies at best. Chennault was not to be put off by this dark picture. He had hitched his wagon to the Generalissimo's star, and shrugging off an official U.S. warning that American nationals should not get involved in the Sino-Japanese War with the remark "Guess I am Chinese," he followed Chiang to western China.

Chennault set up his base at Kunming, in Yunnan, and here he labored for two years at what he called "the seemingly hopeless task of forging a new Chinese Air Force from an American mold." His staff were reserve officers from the American Air Corps. "Excellent airmen, vociferous gripers, and dangerous men around a poker table," Chennault called them, adding that the training school was far from peaceful: "With mechanically minded Americans teaching classically educated Chinese to fly, there was ample opportunity for all the clashing elements of the two conflicting civilizations to rub raw against each other in nerve-racking discord."[6] Chennault made the Chinese pilots retake their basic flying training, instructed them in fighter tactics, supervised the building of adequate airstrips, and linked the airstrips by an air-raid warning system.

The Chinese still could not muster enough planes and pilots, either to defend Chungking from Japanese bombing or to retaliate against Japanese airfields and troop concentrations. Accordingly Chiang Kai-shek sent Chennault back to the United States to recruit volunteer pilots and purchase modern fighter planes. Opinion in the United States was beginning to harden against Japan, and Chennault was well received by both Secretary of the Treasury Morgenthau and by Secretary of State Hull. A fifty-million-dollar loan to China was confirmed in April 1941, a lend-lease agreement similar to that with Britain was signed in May, and one hundred P-40 fighters were made available. American officers who contracted to serve with the "American Volunteer Group" in China were assured that they would be placed on "inactive status" without loss of seniority.[7]

In all, one hundred and one men from the Army and Navy Air Forces agreed to serve under Chennault in China; they were offered salaries up to $750 per month, full travel expenses, one month's paid leave, and a bonus of $500 for every Japanese plane they shot down. Their contracts were to run for one year. There had been no such band of Westerners, fighting for the Chinese under Western officers, since Ward had recruited his mercenaries from the Shanghai waterfronts in a similarly desperate situation nearly a century before. Such men, the Chinese feared, might be hard to control, and Chennault carefully wrote into their contracts that they would be "subject to summary dismissal by written notice for insubordination, habitual use of drugs or alcohol, illness not incurred in line of duty, malingering, and revealing confidential information."[8]

These, then, were the "Flying Tigers," and as American adventurers in a strange land they inevitably developed their own mystique. They looked on the Chinese as children who came "to see these brave strangers from beyond the seas and their marvellous wagons that travelled through the sky." They were sure no ordinary resentments were harbored by these children. The Chinese "loved those tall, round-eyed wild men," thought a Flying Tiger squadron commander. "They loved them in spite of their flair for driving their jeeps into the sidewalk shops of Kunming and running over pushcarts and rickshas, and they even loved them when they laughingly upset the coolies carrying honey buckets balanced on gin poles."[9] Chennault was their hero; the middle-aged failure, suffering from deafness, had become "a leather-faced, steel-eyed, wiry man of fifty-one, with the aura of adventure and hardship unmistakably upon him." The pilots — "tall, drawling men" — were, so the mystique went, "great American adventurers who would have fought just as hard for peanuts or Confederate money — as long as they were fighting for General Chennault and were flying those beloved P-40s." To them "this was the grand old story of David versus Goliath, in modern dress. Here they were, a few American boys, novices in war and in life as well," and they were dying for China in "their patched and bullet-ridden fighting planes."[10]

But, for the time being this naïveté brought results. When the Japanese bombed Pearl Harbor on December 7, 1941, the Flying Tigers had barely begun training together. Yet in the next six months, flying their increasingly battered P-40's, and hunting in two-plane elements as Chennault had taught them, they destroyed nearly three hundred Japanese planes over Burma and South China, for a loss of fifty planes and nine pilots.[11]

This was Chennault's war. He was doing what he knew how to do, and doing it well. The issues were clear-cut. There was a minimum of red tape — he was tactician, coordinator, commander. It all seemed so simple. With a few planes and a few pilots he had wrought great havoc on the Japanese; with more planes and more pilots he would wreak greater havoc. China would be saved from the air. For Chiang Kai-shek, confronting the virtually insuperable problems of economic disintegration and military defeat, the argument could not but be appealing.

The tragedy of Chennault was that the simplicity of a pilot's vision bore little relation to the complexity of China's situation. Though he held to the view that the war could be won by a few brave men under his direction, already the war was changing around him. In March 1942 General Joseph Stilwell, assigned by President Roosevelt to be chief of staff to the Generalissimo, and commander of all U.S. forces in the China-Burma-India theater, arrived in Chungking. Chennault became Stilwell's subordinate. In April the Japanese cut the Burma Road to China, so that henceforth Chennault was to be dependent on Stilwell for the few supplies and spare parts that could be flown to China from India. In July the American Volunteer Group was replaced by the "China Air Task Force," still commanded by Chennault who had been recalled to active duty as a brigadier general, but subordinated to the United States 10th Air Force, based in India. Only five of Chennault's original Flying Tigers agreed to undergo induction into the new force — the remainder returned home on leave, or rejoined their original units.[12]

Despite the fact that the Japanese had routed the British and Chinese armies in Burma, overrun most of Southeast Asia, and severed all China's land communications with the Western allies, Chennault continued to push the claims of his air force as single-mindedly as ever. With just one hundred new fighters, he told Stilwell, and thirty B-25 medium bombers, he would take responsibility for achieving the following: destruction of large numbers of Japanese aircraft, military and naval establishments, Japanese shipping on the sea and China's inland waterways, and destruction of Japanese air force morale.[13] Stilwell was not averse to air force activities, but felt that Chennault was oversimplifying the logistical problems implicit in his planned operations. He also felt that top priority should go to defending the mountainous airlift route from India known as "the Hump." Stilwell's main interest was in assuring that the British and the Chinese should agree to launch a major allied counterattack against the Japanese in the spring of 1943, to open once again the Burma Road supply routes to China. Chennault's and Stilwell's plans were not compatible: if Chennault was to take the Hump supplies to build up his air force, Stilwell could not build up the Chinese army for the Burma counterattack; if Stilwell concentrated on developing the Chinese army, he could not allocate much fuel, spares or ammunition to Chennault.

Chiang Kai-shek's reaction to the Pearl Harbor bombing had been immediate. On the day of the attack, he presented his ideas for a grand coalition of the United States, China, Britain and the Commonwealth nations, the Netherlands, and the Soviet Union, to defend the Pacific against Japan. But his plans for joint action failed. The men needed to make decisions of this magnitude were not in Chungking, they were in London and Washington. And, not surprisingly, London and Washington did not share the Generalissimo's scale of priorities. For Churchill, Europe was the center of the stage, and he did his best to ensure that Roosevelt should have the same sense of priorities: "I told the President how much I felt American opinion overestimated the contribution which China could make to the general war. . . . I said I would of course always be helpful and polite to the Chinese, whom I admired and liked as a race and pitied for their endless misgovernment, but that he must not expect me to adopt what I felt was a wholly unreal standard of values." It was decided that there would still be no large-scale involvement of British or American troops in the China area.[14]

Nonetheless, Chiang, expecting the eventual defeat of Japan, felt his role in the implementation of the allied war effort to be at an end. He turned to the task of consolidating his own power and preparing for an expected postwar confrontation with the Communists in the North — the United Front was over. In the intervening years he planned on employing the hallowed Chinese tradition of "using the barbarians to fight the barbarians" — in this case, the Americans to fight the Japanese — while squandering as few of his own resources as possible.

This concept ran head-on into that of Stilwell, who was at best a cantankerous chief of staff; he was asking embarrassing questions about the Chinese high command, demanding radical reorganization of the ground forces that would upset Chiang's careful system of alliances, and hinting that the Communists might make useful allies;

and he was known to have made sarcastic references to the Generalissimo himself. Fortunately, Chiang was able to "play off one barbarian against the other." Chennault made no secret of his admiration for the Generalissimo, was offering to win the war for China speedily, at almost no cost to the Chinese, and in a way that would not force the Generalissimo to undertake a single reform.

Chiang Kai-shek made it clear that he liked Chennault's ideas, and in response Chennault began to make even broader claims. In a letter to President Roosevelt in late 1942, Chennault stated that with 105 fighters and 42 bombers he could "destroy the effectiveness of the Japanese Air Force" and "accomplish the downfall of Japan." He would move in sequence: first destroy the Japanese air force in China, then break their southwest Pacific supply lines, then destroy Japan's heavy industry with bombing raids launched from eastern China. "The road is then open," he concluded triumphantly, "for the Chinese Army in China, for the American Navy in the Pacific and for MacArthur to advance from his Australian stronghold — all with comparatively slight cost . . . My entire above plan is simple. It has been long thought out. I have spent five years developing an air warning net and radio command service to fight this way. I have no doubt of my success."[15] Roosevelt, like Chiang, unwilling to commit massive resources for the China theater, grew increasingly intrigued by Chennault's predictions, as did Wendell Willkie, Harry Hopkins and Lauchlin Currie, the President's close personal advisers, and Clarence Gauss, U.S. Ambassador to China. Among his backers, Stilwell could now only count on Secretary of War Stimson, and General George Marshall, head of the Joint Chiefs of Staff.[16]

The pressures on Stilwell piled up. In early January 1943, Chiang announced that he would not, after all, agree to a spring offensive in Burma. "What a break for the Limeys [British]," observed Stilwell. "Just what they wanted. Now they will quit, and the Chinese will quit, and the god-dam Americans can go ahead and fight. Chennault's blatting has put us in a spot; he's talked so much about what he can do that now they're going to let him do it."[17] When told by Marshall that pressures from the popular press, and the President's own feelings, meant that Chennault must be given a chance to fulfill his claims, Stilwell grudgingly acceded to being "benched," as he put it. In February Stilwell was directed to set up a separate air force — the 14th — under Chennault's command. Bad feeling between the two men continued and in late April, President Roosevelt summoned both Chennault and Stilwell to Washington, to restate their cases.

Chennault made a fine impression. After he had presented his plan, he recalled, President Roosevelt "banged his fist on the desk and chortled, 'If you can sink a million tons, we'll break their back.' "[18] Stilwell commented dourly that "nobody was interested in the humdrum work of building a ground force but me. Chennault promised to drive the Japs right out of China in six months, so why not give him the stuff to do it? It was the short cut to victory."[19]

Stilwell in turn did not give an effective presentation of his own case though he repeated his warnings that "any attempt to bomb Japan is going to bring a prompt and violent reaction on the ground. . . . If that is done, we will have to fold up out there."[20] Politicians and generals alike were shocked by the bluntness of Stilwell's descriptions. General Albert Wedemeyer, who sat in on some of the meetings, was surprised to learn that Stilwell "didn't think Chennault was loyal to him. He accused Chennault of deliberately disobeying his instructions and carrying on intrigue with various Chinese officials, generals, or provincial warlords." Stilwell also "castigated the Chinese President as coolie class, arrogant, untrustworthy, and absolutely impossible to get along with."[21] Chennault was more restful to the ears of those used to being respected and obeyed. He described one of the meetings at which Stilwell was declaiming on the poor quality of Chinese leadership. The President broke in on Stilwell:

" 'What do you think of the Generalissimo?' he asked.

" 'He's a vacillating, tricky, undependable old scoundrel, who never keeps his word —' Stilwell growled.

" 'Chennault, what do you think?' the President interrupted, turning to me in the corner.

" 'Sir, I think the Generalissimo is one of the two or three greatest military and political leaders in the world today. He has never broken a commitment or promise made to me,' I replied."[22] Nobody had changed anybody's mind, but Chennault had been given his head and Stilwell put in his place.

Ever since the Flying Tiger days Chennault had waited for this opportunity. He was now chief of staff of the Chinese Air Force and enjoyed direct access to the Generalissimo; he was free to follow up his theories, and Stilwell could not interfere, although he still grumbled: "The development of the Chinese Army will be a secondary consideration. The air will get all the supplies and we'll be left to struggle along in the mud unaided. But they'll expect us to damn well produce a force that can protect the fancy boys while they do their spectacular stuff."[23] Chennault's problem was that he had made so many claims along such simplistic lines that he now had to produce the impossible. Joseph Alsop, who was on Chennault's staff, informed Hopkins that the Chinese leaders were "downright terrified of what may happen if there is not some sort of immediate, fairly spectacular action to revive the spirits of the Chinese people and troops," and warned of a possible Chinese collapse.[24] Instead of scoring stunning successes Chennault's force was for the first time outmaneuvered by the Japanese pilots, who had learned to waste Chennault's precious fuel by luring his planes into the air on false alarms, to feint, to strike and run, to close in on a lone plane — all the tricks he had once used against them. In the summer of 1943 the 14th suffered heavy losses. Chennault's response was to blame Stilwell for withholding supplies and to request more planes from the United States, more fuel, and more ammunition.[25]

It was not in Chennault's character to reflect that Chiang Kai-shek might be using him to drag as much free aid as possible out of the U.S. government while conserving his own resources. He did not see the air war as a Chinese way of marking time; he saw it as *the* war, and himself as a key adviser. Chennault was sure that he was leading the Chinese: "rolling with their punches," as he put it, and "yielding on many minor, unimportant matters and always facing them down with a determined, stubborn stand on every major issue. It took a tremendous amount of time and energy, which many Americans were unwilling to expend on the Chinese, but in the end I felt it was worth it because it worked and enabled me to accomplish the things I wanted to do."[26] He had never lost his view of the Chinese as shrewd children of nature. "The Chinese may not understand the workings of an internal combustion engine," he wrote, "but they can see through a man and tell what makes him tick in an instant. They have been evaluating human nature for thousands of years and are experts."[27]

Chiang Kai-shek finally pushed his luck too far by requesting, in December 1943, a one-billion-dollar loan from the United States, vastly increased Hump tonnage, and American payment in full for the new B-29 airfields that were to be built in China. "They are just a bunch of crooks," Secretary of the Treasury Morgenthau protested, "holding a pistol to our heads." After extensive conversations between Roosevelt, Stimson, Marshall and Morgenthau, the loan request was turned down.[28]

The Joint Chiefs of Staff began to look at Chennault more quizzically. General Marshall had already noted that though he might be a tactical genius "Chennault knows nothing about logistics . . . was, for many years, a paid employee of the Chinese Government and, hence, under the undue influence of the Generalissimo."[29] In February 1944, when Chennault requested a unified command over all Air Forces and supporting services in China, General Arnold wrote curtly that "this looks like another one of Chennault's independent thoughts and ideas, with no coordination with [Headquarters]."[30] Secretary of War Stimson felt that Chennault was "failing abjectly to stop the Japanese,"[31] and things grew worse as 1944 progressed and the Japanese attacks grew in strength.

Anxiously Chennault wrote to President Roosevelt that his pilots were operating on a shoe string, and that he could "honestly say that my men in the East have worked miracles with the force at their disposal."[32] But the miracles were no longer apparent to Washington. Chennault's air bases were suffering terrible supply problems.

While heavy inflation continued to whittle away at the Nationalist government's resources, many of the available supplies were lost through corruption. The roads east were operating at only a tiny percent of capacity, with not more than 10 percent of the trucks operational. Moreover the damage that the 14th Air Force's new offensive was inflicting on the Japanese produced the results predicted by Stilwell. For the first time since 1938 Japanese troops launched a massive coordinated counterattack on the Chinese, to win control of the Hunan-Kwangsi and the Canton-Hankow-Peiping railroads, and to "destroy Chennault's bases of operation from the ground." The bitterness between Stilwell and Chennault flared into open hostility as the 14th Air Force failed to check the Japanese advance or to live up to Chennault's exaggerated claims. As the exchanges grew bitterer, Stilwell concluded that Chennault was insubordinate and should be relieved.[33]

For Roosevelt, Churchill, Stalin, and their chiefs of staff, China had always been a peripheral theater. Events in mid-1944 made it seem even more of a backwater. As allied forces under General Dwight D. Eisenhower landed on the Normandy coast of France, and the U.S. forces met with increasing success in their Pacific "island-hopping" campaign, Marshall told Stilwell: "The decision has been made . . . that operations in China and Southeast Asia should be conducted in support of the main operation in the Central and Southwest Pacific. Japan should be defeated without undertaking a major campaign against her on the mainland of Asia if her defeat can be accomplished in this manner."[34] Moreover, in a special memorandum to Roosevelt, the U.S. Joint Chiefs of Staff stated: "Our experience against both the Germans and the Japanese in theaters where we have had immensely superior air power has demonstrated the inability of air forces alone to prevent the movement of trained and determined ground armies."[35]

This effectively ended Chennault's reign, though ironically it was Stilwell who was recalled first, in October 1944. Chennault, after all, still had the confidence of the Generalissimo, was in personal communication with President Roosevelt, who responded cordially to his letters, and had an active and imaginative staff whose public relations skills kept alive the image of the bold innovator.[36] It was generals, not politicians, who found him an obstruction. As General Arnold bluntly stated to Stilwell's successor, General Wedemeyer:

> General Chennault has been in China for a long period of time fighting a defensive air war with minimum resources. The meagerness of supplies and the resulting guerilla type of war-fare must change to a modern type of striking, offensive air power. I firmly believe that the quickest and most effective way to change air warfare in your Theater, employing modern offensive thought, tactics and techniques, is to change com-manders. I would appreciate your concurrence in General Chennault's early withdrawal from the China Theater. He should take advantage of the retirement privileges now avail-able to physically disqualified officers that make their pay not subject to income tax.[37]

Chennault's boys had been all right in their battered P-40's, was the implication, but these individual heroics were of no importance in the new world. The new world was General Curtis LeMay, with his low level night attacks, in which massed fleets of B-29's dropped their fragmentation and incendiary bombs on the crowded cities of Japan; the new world was the March 1944 attack in which 334 B-29's from Guam and Saipan burned out 15.8 square miles of Tokyo, and killed 83,793 people in "an outstanding show," as the public relations officer for the 20th Air Force described it. Returning from this attack, B-29 tail gunners noted that the flames of the burning city could be seen for 150 miles.[38] Chennault was not in this league. A cool efficient planner, someone like General Stratemeyer, would be better.

China had given Chennault a fresh chance, and he had done his best. His emotional involvement with China had been intense and personal. But for the Chinese, as well as for the Americans, it had been a business arrangement, a contract sealed, performed, and forgotten. Chennault was no longer useful. "I flew back to Kunming with a bitter, bitter taste in my mouth," wrote Chennault after hearing the news. "I thought of all the grim years behind me and the first bright glimmerings of victory now visible on the horizon. I thought of all the thousands of American airmen who would now have to sit in China and India in boredom and idleness so that a general could wear three stars on his shoulders. I thought of Stratemeyer's staff putting in their promotions all down the line, and it made me sick."[39]

*   *   *

Joseph Stilwell had not wanted to go to China in 1942. He knew the country too well. As a junior officer he had studied Chinese from 1920 to 1923, been stationed in Tientsin from 1926 to 1929, and been a military attaché in Peking from 1935 to 1939. Watching the performance of the Nationalist Chinese armies in the late thirties, he had grown skeptical of the Chinese claims that they had been beaten by the Japanese simply because they lacked modern arms. On the contrary, Stilwell believed, the Chinese had "committed basic military errors: neglect of fundamental principles of strategy and tactics; improper use of supporting weapons; indifference to military intelligence; inability to adopt sound command and staff procedures; failure to establish a communications net; and failure to keep vehicles and weapons in operating conditions."[40]

When the Japanese attacked Pearl Harbor, Stilwell was a fifty-eight-year-old major general, commanding an Army Corps in Monterey, California, and looking forward to retirement after a successful but unspectacular military career. After the attack, of course, retirement was out of the question, but when he was summoned to Washington he assumed it was to help plan the projected allied campaign in North Africa. When the question of a possible posting to China as chief of Chiang Kai-shek's Allied Staff came up, Stilwell noted in his diary: "Me? No, thank you. They remember me as a small-fry colonel that they kicked around. They saw me on foot in the mud, consorting with coolies, riding soldier trains."[41]

The Chinese had made a curious qualification in their request for a senior American officer: "This officer need not be an expert on the Far East; on the contrary, he [the Generalissimo] thinks that military men who have knowledge of Chinese armies when China was under warlords, operate at a disadvantage when they think of the present Chinese national armies in terms of the armies of the warlords."[42] This rather suggested that the Chinese wanted a yes-man who would not be qualified to ask embarrassing questions. Both the U.S. War and Treasury Departments were wary of this proviso. The Chinese had already requested heavy trucks that would have torn up Chinese roads, semiautomatic rifles that they were not trained to use, thirteen-ton tanks that would have fallen through Chinese bridges, and a third of all the U.S. Navy's dive-bombers, which they did not know how to fly. To American experts all this seemed to point to a Chinese desire to have the biggest and best equipment on principle, and to prove that the Chinese had no knowledge of the true complexities of armored warfare.[43] Their importunate demands that promised U.S. loans in 1941 should be paid immediately and in full had provoked Secretary of the Treasury Morgenthau to the wish that they "go jump in the Yangtze."[44]

Certainly the Chinese had cause to be worried about the genuineness of an American commitment to China: it was only in the 1940 election campaign, after all, that President Roosevelt had said, "While I am talking to you mothers and fathers, I give you one more assurance. I have said this before, but I shall say it again and again: Your boys are not going to be sent into any foreign wars."[45] The American loans and diplomatic assistance that had been given were grudging at best.

After Pearl Harbor the United States needed China as an ally against Japan, but also wanted to keep a close eye on her. Ironically, therefore, it was just for the reasons Stilwell used against himself — that he had lived in China as a junior officer and consorted with the common man — that government officials began to favor Stilwell for the China appointment. To them, this experience made Stilwell a China expert. In the middle of January 1942 Stilwell was ordered out to a meeting at Secretary of War Henry Stimson's house. "When

I got there, found I was the only guest. Henry and I talked for an hour and a half on China. . . . Has been looking all over for the right man to go out and run the show. Thinks the Chinese will accept an American commander. Told him I doubted it, but he had that distinct impression. Asked me how I felt, and I told him I'd go where I was sent. He said, 'More and more, the finger of destiny is pointing at you.' "[46]

Stimson was impressed by Stilwell, whom he found "very quick-witted and alert-minded," and recommended his appointment. Summoned to another meeting with General Marshall, Stilwell gathered that if he went to China his duties would be to "co-ordinate and smooth out and run the [Burma] road, and get the various factions together and grab command and in general give 'em the works. Money no object."[47] By late January it was definite, and Stilwell received orders from the War Department to "increase the effectiveness of United States assistance to the Chinese Government for the prosecution of the war and to assist in improving the combat efficiency of the Chinese Army."[48]

Stilwell was neither pleased nor impressed by his assignment, noting that "the old gag about 'they shall offer up a goat for a burnt sacrifice' is about to apply to my own case." A visit to the White House followed. Roosevelt found Stilwell "an immensely capable and resourceful individual, [who] is thoroughly acquainted with the Chinese people, speaks their language fluently, and is distinctly not a self-seeker." The sentiments were not reciprocated. "F. D. R. very pleasant, and very unimpressive," wrote Stilwell in his diary after the meeting. "Just a lot of wind. After I had enough, I broke in and asked him if he had a message for Chiang K'ai-shek. He very obviously had not and talked for five minutes hunting around for something world-shaking to say. Finally he had it — 'Tell him we are in this thing for keeps, and we intend to keep at it until China gets back *all* her lost territory.' " Roosevelt's adviser, Harry Hopkins, barely clarified the issue by telling Stilwell, "You are going to command trooops, I believe. In fact, I shouldn't be surprised if Chiang K'ai-shek offered you the command of the Chinese Army."[49]

Nobody, indeed, seemed to know very clearly what Stilwell's duties were, or how far his authority extended. When Stilwell, with a hastily assembled staff, reached Chungking in March 1942, he was chief of the Generalissimo's Joint Staff, commanding general of U.S. forces in India, Burma and China, President Roosevelt's military representative in China, and dispenser of lend-lease materiel. As Chennault observed, "Stilwell's mission to China was certainly the toughest diplomatic job thrust on a professional soldier during the war." It was not a good omen that when Stilwell's impending arrival was announced by an American officer in a secret interview with the Generalissimo's secretary, no less than four Chinese servants were found eavesdropping behind a curtain.[50]

At first, things seemed to go well enough. Stilwell received a cordial welcome from Chiang Kai-shek and met Chennault: "Had a talk. He'll be O.K. Met a group of the pilots, they look damn good."[51] At the first conferences at Chungking, the Generalissimo gave Stilwell command of the Chinese Fifth and Sixth Armies in order to stem the Japanese advances in Burma. Stilwell was appreciative, summarizing Chiang's conversation: "He had a lot of good sense in his talk. Importance of making good — first foreigner to handle Chinese troops. Impression made on these troops will make or break me. Must look to future."[52] Chennault wrote how "Madame Chiang was bubbling over with good spirits after the initial conferences with Stilwell. She took Stilwell and myself by the arm and led us out onto a terrace outside the conference room. As we paced up and down the terrace arm in arm, she told us how happy she was that at last China had the help of two American military leaders, how Stilwell and I must work smoothly together, and what high hopes she had for the joint Sino-American war effort under our direction."[53]

This harmony was short-lived. Arriving in Burma in March, shortly after the Japanese had captured Rangoon, Stilwell found that his command over the Fifth and Sixth Chinese Armies did not include the power to make them obey his orders: "I can't shoot them," he wrote in his diary; "I can't relieve them; and just talking to them does no good. So the upshot of it is that I am the stooge who does the dirty work and takes the rap." He was convinced that Chiang Kaishek was countermanding his orders behind his back: "He can't keep his hands off: 1600 miles from the front, he writes endless instructions to do this and that, based on fragmentary information and a cockeyed conception of tactics. He thinks he knows psychology; in fact, he thinks he knows everything, and he wobbles this way and that, changing his mind at every change in the action."

Angry and frustrated, Stilwell flew back to Chungking, and on April 1 had an interview with the Generalissimo in which he asked to be relieved of his command. "It was a very frank interview," he noted, "and the bombs burst rather loudly. In plain words, the army and division commanders had failed to obey, and I had insufficient authority to force them to obey." Chiang Kai-shek expressed concern, and agreed to make it plain to the senior Chinese officers in the Fifth and Sixth Armies that Stilwell was their commander and enjoyed his confidence. Stilwell was mollified, concluding that his blunt approach had won the day: "My only concern is to tell him the truth and go about my business," Stilwell reflected, echoing the conclusion that Chennault had come to five years earlier. But he added, "if I can't get by that way, the hell with it: it is patently impossible for me to compete with the swarms of parasites and sycophants that surround him." Stilwell also acknowledged that "in justice to all of them, however, it is expecting a great deal to have them turn over a couple of armies in a vital area to a goddam foreigner that they don't know and in whom they can't have much confidence."[54]

Back in Burma, Stilwell soon learned how little his tough stance had achieved. Not only was there still no coordinated allied policy — the British wanted to retreat, the Chinese to hold firm, and Stilwell to counterattack — there was constant muddle in the Chinese high command, and continued and flagrant disobedience to Stilwell's orders. His demands that one Chinese general be reprimanded, and another removed from his command, were not met by the Generalissimo. In mid-April the Chinese division guarding the approaches to the key Burma Road city of Lashio disintegrated and fled to the hills.

Reinforcements sent to its aid turned back without orders. While Stilwell planned a massive stand at Lashio, the Chinese Sixth Army commander ordered one of his best divisions back to China; Stilwell was not informed of this withdrawal. A few days later the Fifth Army also began withdrawing, again without Stilwell's knowledge. Lashio fell to a Japanese regiment on April 29. Stilwell still hoped to make a last stand at Myitkyina in northern Burma, but that city also fell on May 8, and Stilwell had to march out through the jungle, reaching India on May 15. Officially he was not blamed for what had happened. Madame Chiang stated that her husband still had "entire confidence" in him, and Roosevelt expressed "great satisfaction over Stilwell's handling of the whole situation."[55]

Stilwell, living up to his growing image as "Vinegar Joe," made no excuses for the disaster: "We got a hell of a beating. It was as humiliating as hell. We ought to find out why it happened and go back!" In his diary, scribbled on the march out, was an even harsher statement, which showed that Stilwell already had a clear enough picture of why it had happened: "Hostile population; no air service; Jap initiative; inferior equipment . . . inadequate ammunition . . . inadequate transport . . . no supply set-up; improvised medical service; stupid, gutless command; interferences by CKS [Chiang Kai-shek]; Br[itish] mess on R.R. [railroads]; rotten communications; Br. defeatist attitude; vulnerable tactical situation; knew it was hopeless."[56]

After the Burma disaster, Stilwell's attitude to the Chinese hardened. As single-mindedly as Chennault had ever pushed for expanded air power, Stilwell insisted on three basic points. Firstly, there must be an immediate counterattack in Burma, to reopen the Burma Road supply route into China. Secondly, aid should not be given to China unless there was a quid pro quo policy by which the Chinese undertook to fight hard in return for that aid. Thirdly, the Chinese armies must be completely overhauled.

Each of these points found echoes in current American thinking: Churchill had early noted, with astonishment, the fact that the American Chiefs of Staff considered the "opening of the Burma

Road indispensable to world victory." Morgenthau had reflected on a massive loan to China that "I would like to do this thing in the way that we could sort of kind of feed it out to them if they keep fighting, but I would hate to put $300 million on the line and say, 'Here, boys, that is yours.' " The American ambassador echoed this sentiment more tersely, reporting that Stilwell "lacks trading cards to elicit Chinese offensive effort."[57] And reports by American officers had shown that the Chinese army was enormous, unwieldy, and incompetent. In the spring of 1942 there were 3,819,000 men under arms, divided into 316 divisions. Of these troops (who had between them an estimated one million rifles), about thirty divisions were considered personally loyal to the Generalissimo; the rest were divided among twelve war-area commanders, who were virtually autonomous rulers, tied to the Generalissimo in a military coalition. Since their personal strength depended on their armies, few commanders were willing to risk losing troops by fighting lengthy engagements with the Japanese forces.

Stilwell failed to see that his plans to slash back the number of divisions in the Chinese army, to redistribute arms and equipment among a select number, and to purge inefficient high commanders was not a simple matter of military reform; it would cut at the heart of the Generalissimo's power structure, and might well lead to his downfall, since Chiang's position depended on a delicate balance of personal loyalties and alliances. Convinced that he must be right, and the Generalissimo wrong, Stilwell grew increasingly irritated. "With the U.S. on his side and backing him, the stupid little ass fails to grasp the big opportunity of his life," he noted in his diary. "The Chinese government is a structure based on fear and favor, in the hands of an ignorant, arbitrary, stubborn man . . . Only outside influence can do anything for China — either enemy action will smash her or some regenerative idea must be formed and put into effect at once."[58]

The increasingly derogatory references to the Generalissimo reflected Stilwell's frustrations, as through the summer and fall of 1942 he sent memo after memo on various ways to "improve the combat efficiency of the Chinese army"; the Generalissimo did not bother to acknowledge receipt of these memos, let alone act on them. In July Stilwell was reflecting: "Sympathy here for the Nazis. Same type of government, same outlook, same gangsterism." By August he was analyzing Chiang as a man who "jumps to a conclusion in keeping with a fancied resemblance to some former experience; and in his obstinacy refuses discussion. He has lost all habit of discussion, in fact, because everybody around him is a Yes-man. No one dares tell him an unpleasant truth, because he gets mad." And in September he began to refer to the Generalissimo regularly as "Peanut," the code name for the Generalissimo used in radio messages. "The Peanut is out of town," he wrote to his wife in California, "and of course the machinery of government has shut down. A one-man dog is a grand institution but a one-man government is something else. If I last through this job, and get back to Carmel, it will be as an old man of eighty and you'll have to push me around in a wheelbarrow." Stilwell ended a private paper headed "Troubles of a Peanut dictator" with a simple question: "Why doesn't the little dummy realize that his only hope is the 30-division plan, and the creation of a separate, efficient, well-equipped, and well-trained force?"[59]

While Stilwell's estimation of China's leader steadily dropped, Chiang's attitude to the United States was hardening. He was furious when all available U.S. aircraft in India, and other aircraft en route to China, were diverted to Africa in the summer of 1942 to help the British in their fight against Rommel. He was further angered by the allies' refusal to include Chinese officers in their Combined Chiefs of Staff. His bitterness increased after the United States repossessed certain crucial military supplies that could not be delivered to China now that Burma was lost and the Burma Road blocked off. And he was distressed by the savage reprisals that the Japanese were taking in the province of Chekiang against the Chinese who had helped Doolittle's flyers, forced to land there after their Tokyo raid. At the end of June, Chiang handed Stilwell, for transmittal to Roosevelt, a list of the three minimum requirements essential for the maintenance of the China theater of war. The three, which came to be known as the Three Demands, were: "1. Three American divisions should arrive in India between August and September to cooperate with the Chinese Forces in restoring the line of communication through Burma. 2. Beginning from August the Air Force in the China Theater of War should consist of 500 planes continuously fighting at the front. . . . 3. Beginning from August, the monthly aerial transportation [over the Hump Route] should be 5,000 tons." The purpose of listing these requirements was, as Mme. Chiang bluntly put it, to get "a yes or no answer to whether the Allies consider this theater necessary and will support it."[60]

By further hinting that pro-Japanese sentiment was strong in the Nationalist areas, the Generalissimo made his point clear: without intensive aid, China would make a separate peace, and leave the United States virtually alone in the Pacific War. This was the other side of the argument that Stilwell and Marshall had urged: unless the Chinese gave some graphic signs of cooperation, some quid pro quo, the United States should not continue giving massive financial and material aid. The result in this instance was a compromise: instead of three U.S. divisions, there should be one division, and no deadline would be set on the delivery of the 500 planes or the 5,000 tons per month. Roosevelt was clearly impressed by Chiang's strong stand, and felt Stilwell was going about things in the wrong way. Thus Roosevelt, already committed to the idea that China should be a "great power" after the war, refused to accept the principle that Chiang must pay for help. Stilwell noted: "Well, well. This has angles. Our fool publicity 'heroic resistance — five years' struggle' etc., etc. have set it up for Chiang K'ai-shek — he can say to us 'Sorry, we've reached the limit: without help we can't go on.' "[61]

Stilwell was certainly peeved, but he continued to train the Chinese troops (who might one day form his elite thirty divisions) at Ramgarh in India, and in Yunnan province. He also tried to cooperate with Chennault who, as head of the newly formed China Air Task Force, was ever more aggressively pushing the claims of air power in China. In March 1943, however, Roosevelt sent Marshall a strong letter, in which he declared his opinion that "Stilwell has exactly the wrong approach in dealing with Generalissimo Chiang who, after all, cannot be expected, as a Chinese, to use the same methods that we do. . . . He is the Chief Executive as well as the Commander-in-Chief, and one cannot speak sternly to a man like that or exact commitments from him the way we might do from the Sultan of Morocco."[62] Passages of this letter were sent to Stilwell, who understood that the President was personally rebuking him.

Stilwell was no longer confining his feelings about the Chinese to his diaries; in a radio message, which Marshall passed on to the President, Stilwell claimed:

Chungking cannot or will not enforce its orders in this area [Yunnan province]. Our presence threatens to affect the enormous smuggling racket here, and you may expect a campaign of vilification against me personally. I have already been accused of bad faith for keeping military supplies from racketeers. The continued publication of Chungking propaganda in the United States is an increasing handicap to my work. Utterly false impression has been created in United States public opinion. Army is generally in desperate condition, underfed, unpaid, untrained, neglected, and rotten with corruption. We can pull them out of this cesspool, but continued concessions have made the Generalissimo believe he has only to insist and we will yield.[63]

It was Stilwell's belief that Chennault's stepped-up air attacks would lead the Japanese to retaliate with their armies against the Chinese airfields in Nationalist territory; an army such as the one Stilwell described would inevitably be defeated.

The impasse continued. Stilwell and Chennault each wanted five-eighths of the available Hump airlift supplies. While Chennault began an ambitious program of airfield building, Stilwell tried to stockpile stores for his army training program. He declined to guarantee even a firm 1,500 tons per month for Chennault, though his advisers warned him that failure to help Chennault would lead to increasingly heavy anti-Stilwell political pressures in Chungking. Chennault believed that Stilwell was deliberately hampering him, since "ridicule for the new weapon [of air power] was the fashion for Stilwell's military contemporaries, and it is not surprising that he shared this view. Stilwell was an even more violent partisan of the infantry than I was of airpower. His acceptance of the airplane was limited to using it as a method of personal transport and later as a means of emergency supply to rescue his forces from the results of too casual logistical planning."[64]

The issue was further complicated by the fact that the Chinese government itself took a good deal of the Hump tonnage: over an eight-month period in 1942–1943, for example, 9 percent of all Hump supplies was Chinese paper currency, engraved in the United States on lend-lease allotments, and then flown out to bolster China's sagging economy. Chennault's pilots occasionally would dump this money — together with nonessential items such as office supplies for Stilwell's staff — into the jungle, and load up instead with ammunition and spare parts, cigarettes and whiskey.[65]

Tempers ran increasingly high. On his sixtieth birthday, in March 1943, Stilwell serenaded his absent wife with a "Lyric to Spring":

> I welcomed the Spring in romantic Chungking,
> I walked in her beautiful bowers.
> In the light of the moon, in the sunshine at noon,
> I savored the fragrance of flowers.
>
> (Not to speak of the slush, or the muck and the mush
> That covers the streets and alleys.
> Or the reek of the swill, as it seeps down the hill,—
> Or the odor of pig in the valleys.)[66]

It was in this spirit that he flew to the U.S. in April, to argue his case with Chennault. Chennault's argument won out, and an even angrier Stilwell returned to China in the summer of 1943. "Back again on the manure pile," he told his wife. "Chiang same as ever — a grasping, bigoted, ungrateful little rattlesnake."[67]

Through much of the summer and fall of 1943, however, Stilwell was forced to concede that "the rattlesnake was affable as hell."[68] Mme. Chiang called Stilwell "Uncle Joe." Some of his memoranda were read and discussed, and plans were again under way for the second Burma campaign. Lord Louis Mountbatten had been named to the new post of Supreme Allied Commander for the Southeast Asian Theater, removing some of the onus from Stilwell. There were clashes, of course: Stilwell's suggestion that Communists in northwest China be used to make a diversionary attack on the Japanese, forestalling them from striking at Chennault's increasingly active airfields, was coldly received and led to Chiang's telling one of Roosevelt's emissaries that he would like Stilwell recalled.[69] There were wild rumors in the air that Stilwell was planning to oust Chiang and take over the Chinese army in person, but they were satisfactorily quashed. Much of the time there was an air of weary harmony. Stilwell felt that he had done what he could; the rest was up to the Chinese. As he told Marshall and Stimson: "Everything concerned with the 1st 30 [divisions] is under way. I cannot hurry the preparations already en route. Training teams are with armies in Yunnan, and training has started in some units. The President's orders for the first 4,700 tons over the Hump each month to go to air force has resulted in depriving Y-force of weapons and ammunition urgently needed for the campaign. . . . The agreement to mold units has not been kept. Result will be reduced strength divisions. . . . Road repair going well. Truck situation deplorable, etc. What more can I do?"[70]

This rather muted Stilwell was, to his surprise, invited to accompany Chiang Kai-shek to the November 1943 conference in Cairo, where the British, Americans and Chinese would settle the final details of the forthcoming Burma campaign. The meetings were cordial: it was agreed that all Chinese lands in Japanese hands would definitely be returned to China, and that the allies would launch an amphibious operation across the Bay of Bengal to aid China in the Burma campaign. In the postwar world, Chiang's China would be one of the "Big Four." As the Generalissimo left for China on

November 26, his wife sent a note to Roosevelt: "The Generalissimo wishes me to tell you again how much he appreciates what you have done and are doing for China. When he said goodbye to you this afternoon, he could not find words adequately expressive to convey his emotions and feelings nor to thank you sufficiently for your friendship."[71]

Roosevelt, however, was not as committed to China as Chiang thought. When the President and Churchill traveled on to Teheran, to meet Stalin, the talk swung naturally to the war against Germany. Stalin and Churchill were skeptical about China's power, and wanted full allied cooperation on the massive cross-channel invasion of German-occupied France. Burma could wait, thought Churchill; "going into swampy jungles to fight the Japanese is like going into the water to fight a shark."[72] If the Chinese were a great power, let them prove it on their own. After Germany was defeated, Stalin added, the Russians would attack Japan in the East. Roosevelt, who had not consulted with his Secretary of State, Cordell Hull, before coming to Cairo, and who had been impressed by military reports which showed that Japan could be beaten in the Pacific rather than in China, was persuaded to downgrade China's priorities. There would be no joint allied operations in the Burma area for at least a year. Roosevelt requested Stilwell to tell the Generalissimo of this change of plan.

Understandably puzzled, Stilwell tried to find out in an interview what exactly Roosevelt's plans for China were. Should it be U.S. policy "to build China up"? he asked. "Yes. Build her up," replied the President. And if the Japanese beat Chiang Kai-shek? "Well, then, we should look for some other man or group of men, to carry on." As forcefully as he could, Stilwell put the question a last time: "We need guidance on political policy on China." "Yes. As I was saying," came the President's reply, "the Chinese will want a lot of help from us — a *lot* of it."[73] So, at least, Stilwell recorded the conversation.

General Marshall, knowing how difficult Stilwell's position would now be, offered him a high post in another war theater. Stilwell, always tenacious (and perhaps eager to witness Chiang's discomfiture), declined the offer. He returned to Chungking, to find that Chiang had come back with a "squeeze play," as he described Chiang Kai-shek's request for a loan of a billion dollars. This was the loan request that Roosevelt finally turned down. After two years of what Stilwell and others had thought to be weakness in the face of Chinese pressures, Roosevelt had finally swung the other way. Chiang had gone too far, insisting that the billion-dollar loan was to be at a rate of 20 to 1, though the Americans knew that the black market rate was around 240 to 1 and rising. Also, Chiang expected the United States to assume the entire cost of building new airfields in China.[74]

The vacillations, intrigue, deceit, and outright robbery were finally too much for Stilwell. Cairo and its aftermath left him exhausted; in his words, "a brief experience with international politics confirms me in my preference for driving a garbage truck. . . . It is very confusing to a deck-hand to be pitchforked in among this class of people, especially if he is a military deck-hand."[75] His solution was to retire into the jungles of Burma, to lead the Chinese troops trained in India, and some U.S. forces, in alliance with the British, on a limited land offensive against the Japanese.

In the jungle, with his troops, Stilwell found peace from both the Chinese and the Allied General Staffs. "The jungle is a refuge," he wrote to his wife in January 1944, "and I am leaving the shoveling of manure to a couple of my boys. . . . We eat straight rations or Chinese chow and we live where we have to and the trails are tough, and we get wet and muddy, but we sleep soundly and the food tastes good because we are usually hungry."[76] Wearing his old campaign hat, G.I. shoes, canvas leggings and a rumpled uniform, Lieutenant General Stilwell could almost believe he was a private soldier. "With his unruly eyebrows, his glasses, and his funny, loping walk," wrote one observer, "he looked like some itinerant vegetable peddler a little down on his luck."[77] The British general, William Slim, "was struck, as I always was when I visited Stilwell's headquarters, how unnecessarily primitive all its arrangements were. . . . He delighted

General Albert Wedemeyer (left) decorates Claire Lee Chennault in Chungking, spring 1945. Chennault was recalled soon afterwards. *U.S. Army Signal Corps photograph.*

General Joseph Stilwell, spring 1944, on foot in the Burmese jungle. "The jungle is a refuge," he wrote to his wife, "and I am leaving the shoveling of manure to a couple of my boys." *United Press International.*

in an exhibition of rough living which, like his omission of rank badges and the rest, was designed to foster the idea of the tough, hardbitten, plain, fighting general."[78] There Stilwell stayed, while crucial decisions in India and China clamored for his attention and spring dragged into summer, on foot in the Burmese mud.

Why did he stay? "Because it was the simplest military venture in his theater of operations," answered one of Chennault's flyers, because Stilwell "was a brave man, all right, but he was fighting the wrong war."[79] Chennault concurred: "As a devout student of infantry tactics, Stilwell's view was always concentrated on the simple objective of blasting out the enemy immediately ahead and then advancing. This was an ideal temperament for a division commander but hardly the viewpoint of a competent theater commander. There was considerable truth, along with the malice, in the oft-repeated description of Stilwell as 'the best four-star battalion commander in the Army.' "[80]

But there was more to it than that. Stilwell's job, regardless of his formal titles, was to advise the Generalissimo on the conduct of the war. He had early decided that China could only emerge from the war successfully if the Burma Road was reopened and certain radical changes in staff, organization, and training of the ground forces were pushed through. When both Chiang and Roosevelt adopted Chennault's marvelously cheap and apparently successful policies instead of Stilwell's, he was angry. He was also convinced that Chennault's plan would fail, and its failure would take his own cherished plans down with it. Stilwell's response, after Cairo, was quite simply to let Chiang and Chennault stew in their own juice. It was not sophisticated action for a senior general to take, but once embarked on it Stilwell stuck it through. "Over in China things look very black," he wrote to his wife in July, 1944. "It would be a pleasure to go to Washington and scream, 'I told you so,' but I think they get the point. This was my thesis in May last year, but I was all alone and the air boys were so sure they could run the Japs out of China with planes that I was put in the garbage pail. They have had their way and now the beans are spilled, but what can anyone do about it? It's just one of those sad might-have-beens. The people who are principally to blame will duck all criticism and responsibility. If this crisis were just sufficient to get rid of the Peanut, without entirely wrecking the ship, it would be worth it. But that's too much to hope."[81]

The crisis was many-sided. First, in Burma itself, the Generalissimo was personally giving orders which countermanded Stilwell's, exactly as he had done in the 1942 Burma campaign. When Stilwell expostulated, Chiang told him blandly, "I hope we will not cause unexpected damage and failure to our friends and units" — in other words that he did not want troops and commanders personally loyal to him to suffer in action. Second, Roosevelt was getting increasingly tough with the Generalissimo, pushing for the sending of a U.S. observer mission to the Communist areas around Yenan, and asking why the Generalissimo refused to send his Yunnan army across the Salween into Burma to help Stilwell's forces pushing down from the north. In April 1944 the Americans sent an ultimatum: either the Yunnan force moved into action, or it would receive no more lend-lease supplies. Finally, new evidence came to suggest that in China itself Chiang Kai-shek was keeping desperately needed supplies from his own Army commanders who were trying to halt Japanese advances, and that other commanders were abandoning key positions to the Japanese without attempting to fight.[82]

If all this brought a sour satisfaction to Stilwell, it must have been compounded by the fighting along the Salween in May. Here the Yunnan armies, so carefully trained by American advisers under Stilwell's direction for over a year, completely rejected all the advice they had received — and paid the penalties. "In view of the enemy's defensive attitude and our superior strength," reported an American colonel observing the opening Salween battles, "American liaison officers urged the use of a small continuing force and a strong encircling movement to cut the trail . . . behind the Japs. Nevertheless orders were received for direct attacks on the prepared positions. . . . Several days were wasted and heavy losses incurred . . . in suicidal charges by a succession of squads against enemy pillboxes. Teamwork in use of weapons and supporting fire and the use of cover were conspicuously lacking. . . . Most casualties resulted from attempts to walk or rather climb up through interlocking bands of machine gun fire. As a demonstration of sheer bravery the attacks were magnificent but sickeningly wasteful. . . . Adjoining or supporting units would idly watch some single squad or platoon get mowed down in a lone advance then try it on their own front."[83] The only positive result was that many Chinese officers now saw the value of the advice they had refused to follow: "The fact that American and Chinese officers stood side by side and watched excessive casualties pile up day after day, chiefly as a result of violations of proper tactical and technical procedure, furnishes a common ground of ideas for improved training," another U.S. colonel reported. "These same Chinese officers saw important objectives taken and held, at comparatively small cost, by troops following American training doctrines. There can be no doubt but that the American Liaison Team concept has been justified."[84] It had still been an expensive lesson, and there was no reason to suppose that its message would reach those who had not been on the spot.

In the light of these various developments Marshall sent Stilwell a radio message on July 1, 1944, asking him if he would consider undertaking "the rehabilitation and in effect the direction of the leadership of the Chinese forces in China proper." Stilwell replied unenthusiastically that there was "still a faint chance to salvage something in China but action must be quick and radical and the G-Mo must give one commander full powers." This answer was sent on July 3, and on July 4 the Joint Chiefs of Staff, under Admiral Leahy's signature, made the following recommendation to President Roosevelt: "The time has come, in our opinion, when all the power and resources remaining to China must be entrusted to one individual capable of directing that effort in a fruitful way against the Japanese. There is no one in the Chinese government or armed forces capable of coordinating the Chinese military effort in such a way as to meet the Japanese threat. During this war, there has been only one man who has been able to get Chinese forces to fight against the Japanese in an effective way. That man is General Stilwell." The Joint Chiefs then asked Roosevelt to "dispatch to the Generalissimo the attached message, urging him to place General Stilwell in command of all Chinese armed forces," and to "promote General Stilwell to the temporary grade of General, not only in recognition of his having conducted a brilliant campaign with a force, which he himself made, in spite of continued opposition from within and without and tremendous obstacles of terrain and weather, but in order to give him the necessary prestige for the new position proposed for him in China."[85]

On July 8, Stilwell noted in his diary: "Radio from F. D. R. to Chiang K'ai-shek and from George Marshall to me. They have been pouring it into him about me. F. D. R. told Chiang K'ai-shek to give me full authority to run the show, promotion to full general."[86] The following day he sent his acceptance to Marshall, though even at this point he could not resist a sarcastic jibe: "If this new assignment materializes, I will tackle it to the best of my ability. I am keenly aware of the honor of the President's confidence and of yours, and I pledge my word to him and to you that I will 'consistently and continuously avoid unnecessary irritations' and get on with the war. I fully realize that I will have to justify that confidence, and I find it even in prospect a heavy load for a country boy."[87] Stilwell was duly made full general, the only other officers of that rank at the time being Marshall, MacArthur, Eisenhower, and Arnold.

Thus was the stage set for the most ambitious and the most arrogant of all attempts by Western advisers in China to gain power. The idea was not just Stilwell's; he shared it with his President and the senior military officers in his country. For anyone with any knowledge of Chinese history and politics it should have been clearly inconceivable that the Chinese would voluntarily put a Westerner in command of all their armed forces on their own soil, and obvious that doing so would bring about the fall of Chiang Kai-shek. But to Stilwell, flushed with pleasure at the discomfiture of Chennault and the fine performance of his Chinese troops in Burma, and to the Joint Chiefs, proud of their performances in Europe and the Pacific, it seemed a simple and logical step.

Chiang Kai-shek, not surprisingly, stalled. He acknowledged Roosevelt's "effective suggestion" with "much pleasure," but pointed out that "Chinese troops and their internal political conditions are not as simple as those in other countries. Furthermore, they're not as easily directed as the limited number of Chinese troops who are now fighting in north Burma." The project should be embarked on slowly, and "there must be a preparatory period in order to enable General Stilwell to have absolute command of the Chinese troops without any hindrance."[88] Roosevelt expressed satisfaction at the Generalissimo's attitude, and agreed to his request that "an influential personal representative" be dispatched to China. It took some time, however, to find the right man, and Roosevelt was also involved with planning his trip to Honolulu where he discussed Pacific strategy with General MacArthur and Admiral Nimitz; so it was not till late August that General Patrick Hurley was agreed on as the best presidential emissary, and sent to Chungking.

Pending Hurley's arrival, Stilwell stayed on in Burma, directing the siege of Myitkyina which the Japanese were defending with great stubbornness. The Japanese counterattack in China continued unabated, and Hengyang fell to them on August 8. The following day Stilwell learned that certain Chinese generals were apparently planning a coup against Chiang Kai-shek and jotted "Hooray for crime!" in his diary. But he continued to forbid his subordinates to meddle in internal Chinese politics, and when Chennault sought permission to drop supplies to a Chinese general not in the Generalissimo's favor, Stilwell cautioned: "The time for half-way measures has passed. Any more free gifts such as this will surely delay the major decision and play into the hands of the gang. The cards have been put on the table and the answer has not been given. Until it is given, let them stew."[89] The Generalissimo, for his part, drafted three "conditions" for Stilwell's appointment: he should not have direct control over Communist troops unless they agreed to obey orders from Chungking; Stilwell's functions and authority should be clearly defined; and Chiang himself should have control over the distribution of lend-lease supplies. The last of these would obviously be unacceptable to the Americans, and more time would pass while the issue was negotiated.

Hurley arrived in Chungking on September 6, and on September 7 he and Stilwell met with Chiang Kai-shek. Chinese armies were falling back on the Salween and the Hengyang fronts, and the Generalissimo seemed to be in a conciliatory mood. He told Hurley that he was "prepared to give General Stilwell actual command of all forces in the field in China and that with this command he is also giving him his complete confidence."[90]

Stilwell did not, apparently, doubt Chiang's sincerity, and retired to his office to work out the details of his new status as the most powerful Western adviser in Chinese history. His title, he told Hurley in a memo, should be "Field Commander of the Chinese Army." It should be clearly announced by the Generalissimo that "all the Chinese Armed Forces, air as well as ground, are included in General Stilwell's command"; furthermore "General Stilwell must have the authority to support his responsibility. This must include the right to reward and punish, to relieve and appoint officers, all in conformity with Chinese law." Stilwell also drafted the circular telegram he would send to all Chinese war area and group army commanders once the Generalissimo had announced his new command:

I am asking for your full support in this endeavor. There may be some of you who say: "What is the foreigner doing here?" I ask you not to think of me in that way. I have spent many years in China. I have travelled all over the country, I respect the Chinese people and their character, I have seen the Chinese soldier fight, and I have always stood up for him and the Chinese people. I hope that you will believe I am China's true friend. Now the G-mo has honored me by appointing me to command the Field Forces. This great honor makes me very conscious of my shortcomings. The responsibility is great and my ability small. To accomplish anything I must have the support and cooperation of you all.[91]

Caught up in the same dream world, General Hurley drafted the directive that the Generalissimo would give to Stilwell:

> You will proceed at once, with the reorganization and reloca-
> tion of Ground and Air Forces of the Republic of China and
> with the preparation of plans for a counter-offensive, by the
> Allied Forces in the China Theater, to regain the areas of
> China now occupied by the Japanese. In carrying out this mis-
> sion, you are authorized to activate and equip new units; to
> disband old units; to transfer personnel from one unit to an-
> other and to transfer units from one command to another and
> from one locality to another without regard to the jurisdiction
> of commanders or of provincial and war area boundaries. . . .
> You will initiate at once plans to improve the livelihood (living
> conditions) of the officers and soldiers of the Ground and Air
> Forces of the Republic of China so that it will be at least equal
> to that of the people in the rear areas.[92]

There was no immediate response from the Generalissimo, and Stilwell grew impatient. A trip to Kweilin in mid-September con-vinced him that the city was about to fall, leaving the route to Kunming open to the Japanese, who would thus sever China's last supply line. Returning to Chungking on the fifteenth, he had "one and a half hours of crap and nonsense" with Chiang Kai-shek. "Usual cock-eyed reasons and idiotic tactical and strategical concep-tions. He is impossible."[93] That evening Stilwell sent off a long and despondent report to Marshall, stating that the Generalissimo was planning to pull his troops back across the Salween. "I am now convinced that he regards the South China catastrophe as of little moment, believing that the Japs will not bother him further in that area, and that he imagines he can get behind the Salween and there wait in safety for the U.S. to finish the war."[94] On the sixteenth, Stilwell had some "plain talk" with T. V. Soong. His notes for the talk show that he himself did not want the command post unless he could have freedom of action; if he didn't get that freedom, then someone else could have the job: "Who this is to be is immaterial, but whoever it is has my full sympathy, since he will have to gather up the broken and dispirited remnants of a beaten army, and with antiquated machinery and inefficient personnel, organize a force to oppose a first-class military power. I hope that the Generalissimo will realize that I do not seek the job; I have been delayed, ignored, double-crossed, and kicked around for 2½ years in my attempt to show the Chinese how they can hold up their heads and regain their self respect."[95]

Stilwell's letter to Marshall was relayed to Roosevelt at Quebec, where he was conferring with Churchill. A tough reply to the Generalissimo was quickly drawn up. Roosevelt told Chiang: "I have urged time and again in recent months that you take drastic action to resist the disaster which has been moving closer to China and to you . . . I am certain that the only thing you can now do in an attempt to prevent the Jap from achieving his objective in China is to reinforce your Salween armies immediately and press their offensive, while at once placing General Stilwell in unrestricted command of all your forces. The action I am asking you to take will fortify us in our decision and in the continued efforts the United States proposes to take to maintain and increase our aid to you."[96] It was an ultimatum, the clearest that Roosevelt had ever sent to Chiang Kai-shek: either he must push the Salween campaign and install Stilwell, or American aid would cease.

Stilwell received this message on September 19, and took it to the Generalissimo's house to deliver it in person. As he wrote that evening in his diary:

Mark this day in red on the calendar of life. At long, at very long last, F. D. R. has finally spoken plain words, and plenty of them, with a firecracker in every sentence. "Get busy or else." A hot firecracker. I handed this bundle of paprika to the Peanut and then sank back with a sigh. The harpoon hit the little bugger right in the solar plexus, and went right through him. It was a clean hit, but beyond turning green and losing the power of speech, he did not bat an eye. He just said to me, "I understand." And sat in silence jiggling one foot. . . .

I came home. Pretty sight crossing the river: lights all on in Chungking.[97]

Chiang could not forgive Stilwell for handing him such a message in such a way. In a return message to Roosevelt he stated that he would accept an American officer as commander in chief, but not Stilwell. Stilwell had to go because he "had no intention of cooperating with me, but believed that he was in fact being appointed to command me." Roosevelt replied that "the ground situation in China has so deteriorated since my original proposal that I now am inclined to feel that the United States Government should not assume the responsibility involved in placing an American officer in command of your ground forces throughout China."

This reply was meant to be part compromise and part warning, but it had no effect on the Generalissimo since he had just heard from his brother-in-law in Washington that Harry Hopkins believed Roosevelt was going to recall Stilwell. On this tenuous evidence the Generalissimo took his stand. In a long letter to Roosevelt he blamed Stilwell for all China's military failures of the last year and insisted on his right as "Head of State and Supreme Commander in China . . . to request the recall of an officer in whom I can no longer repose confidence." Roosevelt replied coldly that the major Burma decisions had been made by himself, Churchill, and the Combined Chiefs, not by Stilwell. But he agreed to recall Stilwell. The China-Burma-India theater would be split in two. As commander of U.S. troops in China he would appoint General Wedemeyer, if Chiang agreed to have him as his chief of staff. No American officer "should in the present situation assume responsibility in a command position for the operations of Chinese forces in China."[98]

The recall order reached Stilwell on October 19. He had known it was coming. As he told his wife: "It looks very much as though they had gotten me at last. The Peanut has gone off his rocker and Roosevelt has apparently let me down completely. If old softy gives in on this, as he apparently has, the Peanut will be out of control from now on. A proper fizzle. My conscience is clear. I have carried out my orders. I have no regrets. Except to see the U.S.A. sold down the river."[99] These words were too brave. Stilwell did have regrets, and he was anxious to clear his name which had been muddied in the struggle. "Will a statement be made to explain the relief?" he wrote in some notes, scrawled as he was leaving Chungking. "Will I be allowed to make a statement?"[100] The War Department forbade him to discuss Chinese matters with the press, so Stilwell started his own personal account. When he died in 1946 the beginnings of several drafts were found among his papers, but all of them broke off after brief introductions. Joseph Stilwell, never at a loss for words, had for once not known how to begin.

*   *   *

After meeting Albert Wedemeyer in 1943, Stilwell had noted that "the young man sure does appreciate himself."[101] The "young man" had a right to. Born in 1897, in Omaha, Nebraska, Wedemeyer had graduated from West Point in 1918. The Second World War brought his outstanding talents as a staff officer to the fore: still a major in December 1941, he was a major general by the fall of 1943, a phenomenal promotion record even in a war in which fast promotions were commonplace.[102]

His most "professionally remunerative assignment" in the peacetime army, Wedemeyer felt, had been his years in the German War College (the Kriegsakademie) where he had been posted from 1936 to 1938. It was here, he wrote in his autobiography, that he had been

exposed to constant propaganda about the Bolshevik menace. Beneath the propaganda I discerned a great deal of truth about Communist aims, practices, and methods unknown or ignored in America until recently. I had also come to see Germany in a different light from most of my contemporaries. Not that I approved of the Nazi regime or condoned its brutalities, but I

realized that Hitler had come to power as a result of the treatment of Germany after the First World War, and that his hold
over the German people was due to their desperate search for a
way out of the economic chaos and misery which had been
their lot during the last years of the Weimar Republic. However much one disapproved of Hitler's methods, the feeling of
the German people that he had raised them out of the abyss
was real.[103]

On returning to the U.S. he had, by his own account, been
closely questioned by the F. B. I. about his pro-Nazi leanings, but
the investigation had been dropped.

Wedemeyer had made his reputation as a planner, and was a man
who understood the value of precision. But he was also a man who
liked to have a clear view of the overall objectives of a particular
assignment. To this end he had formulated — taking off from earlier
theorists and also from what he had seen of Nazi Germany in
action — his own theory of "Grand Strategy." This he defined as "the
art and science of employing all of a nation's resources to accomplish
objectives defined by national policy."[104] The absence of such
strategy, it appeared to Wedemeyer, meant that the U.S. was "traveling on uncharted seas without a compass toward a fatal Shangri-la,
and with only the stars to guide us."[105]

Both as planner and as grand strategist Wedemeyer found the
prospects of the China command, offered to him in October 1944
after Stilwell's recall, distasteful. "A year or so back," he wrote, "I
would have welcomed the opportunity to try to solve the problems of
the China Theater, but by now the difficulties seemed practically
insurmountable. I had heard many times over that China was a
graveyard for American officials, military and diplomatic; that you
couldn't do anything with the Chinese, they just wouldn't co-operate,
they led you into difficulties with your own government as well as
with theirs, and so on. Many a good officer had had his career ruined
in China." An aide tried to cheer him by mentioning previously
successful military advisers such as "Chinese" Gordon, the Russian

Galin, and the German Von Falkenhausen, but Wedemeyer was not convinced.[106]

The instructions that Wedemeyer had received from the Joint Chiefs of Staff were ostensibly clear: "a. Your primary mission with respect to Chinese Forces is to advise and assist the Generalissimo in the conduct of military operations against the Japanese. b. Your primary mission as to U.S. combat forces under your command is to carry out air operations from China. In addition you will continue to assist the Chinese Air and Ground Forces in operations, training and in logistical support. c. You will not employ United States resources for suppression of civil strife except in so far as necessary to protect United States lives and property."[107] The Generalissimo's fight with the Communists, in other words, was his own affair; there was no more talk of "improving the combat efficiency of the Chinese Army"; and no mention of a command position from which Wedemeyer might control Chinese troops.

But as adviser to the Generalissimo he could not ignore these delicate issues and do his job properly. The Japanese must be stopped before they captured the crucial supply depot of Kunming; Japan's overall military intentions must be estimated and the Chinese army itself strengthened. "The disorganization and muddled planning of the Chinese," Wedemeyer told Marshall, "is beyond comprehension."[108] Some coherence must also be brought to the allied command structure, where Wedemeyer was appalled to find that army, air force, supply units, British and other clandestine intelligence operations, were either partially independent or subject to overlapping controls. The work was not easy. As Wedemeyer told Marshall in December 1944: "In previous radios I have suggested that the Chinese attitude was apathetic. This remains true; however, I have now concluded that the Generalissimo and his adherents realize seriousness of situation but they are impotent and confounded. They are not organized, equipped, and trained for modern war. Psychologically they are not prepared to cope with the situation because of political intrigue, false pride, and mistrust of leaders' honesty and motives."[109]

Learning his lesson from Stilwell, Wedemeyer did not let these sentiments appear in public. From the first he was cautious and conciliatory, punctilious to Chiang Kai-shek and courteous to Chennault. Wedemeyer did not harp on corruption or incompetence as the reason for the armies' incapacity; instead he pointed to the proliferation of local agencies, inadequate storage and transport, faulty planning, and the system that gave exemptions from military service to those with advanced education — the very men who would make the best junior officers. Reviewing Chinese troop strengths, and the unwillingness of commanders to order their troops on long marches, Wedemeyer found that many of the Chinese troops were in a state of semi-starvation, and their commanders knew that a long march would kill them. These semi-starving armies were incapable of sustained military action, and the measures taken to conscript more troops to fill the faltering ranks were not conducive to boosting morale. To remedy the defects, Wedemeyer suggested American know-how and personnel: American Service of Supply officers should be given control of nonessential trucks and aircraft to help with food distribution, and there should be a government-directed pool of motor transport with an American enlisted man at each control to tabulate traffic.[110]

Like Chennault and Stilwell before him, Wedemeyer had found his answer. Like their answers, it was simple. And like their answers, it was wrong because it did not pay enough attention to the complexities of the Chinese situation. Wedemeyer's answer — the practical application of Western expertise to the problems of logistics and training — would have been correct in the United States or in Germany. But in China he could not avoid politics, nor did he understand that almost every move he made as ranking U.S. officer in China had political overtones. He could not know — no one had taught him to know — that the kind of efficiency he wanted might work against Chiang Kai-shek, undermining his castle of compromises, bringing new men to the fore, ousting favored supporters. And he was unable to see that Chiang Kai-shek did not want to commit his forces until the United States had won the war against Japan. Wedemeyer's faith in his own expertise was so profound that he could not believe that it was inadequate. When the expertise failed in Chinese conditions he had to believe that China had been "lost" by Americans undermining his own efforts, since he could not believe that it had been lost by the Chinese themselves.[111] But that was when the war was over. As long as the war continued, he would advise to the limits of his capacity and his comprehension.

The war was not going well, that much was clear. As the Japanese attacks grew in intensity, and even Chungking appeared threatened, senior members of the Chinese government began to sound out Wedemeyer on the possibilities of their getting plane rides to America and safety. It was "amusing and also tragic," Wedemeyer told Marshall, that two Chinese generals were among those seeking sanctuary.[112] In January 1945 the Japanese launched an attack on the 14th Air Force base at Suichuan. General Hsüeh Yüeh, an independent-minded militarist to whom Chiang Kai-shek had jealously refused to give arms or munitions, was defeated and the airfield was taken. Yet at the same time the Japanese attacks on Kunming and the Generalissimo's main power bases slowed down. Could there be, Wedemeyer wondered, some truth in the rumors that Chiang had reached some "understanding" with the Japanese? He asked Chiang straight out, and received an unencouraging response: "To this the Generalissimo was absolutely noncommittal. There was no indication, emotional or otherwise, that he either denied or admitted it. His spontaneous reaction was a dry cackle."[113]

Like Stilwell, Wedemeyer learned that his plans could be foiled by simple noncooperation. Thus after the successful conclusion of the Salween campaign in January 1945, Wedemeyer smoothly airlifted two divisions of Chinese troops back to China, and then requested that the Fifty-third Army on the Salween, the Fifth Army in Yunnan, and the Fifty-seventh Army in Sian be transferred to accord with his overall strategy for the defense of Kunming. None of the armies moved. Wedemeyer's minutes of a private meeting with Chiang that followed this crisis show his agitation: "I feel it is impossible for me as you [sic] chief of staff to serve well. I feel badly and concerned about this. Therefore I ask for privacy to talk to you.

Time is short, and unless firm decision is made so that we don't have so many changes [of plan made by Chiang], I don't know how to cope with the situation. I do want to serve China."[114]

So Wedemeyer determined to concentrate his resources on "supervision" of the armies in the area around Kunming. The supervision was to be far-reaching, covering "(1) combat, in which the Americans would come very close to having operational control; (2) training, which they would completely supervise; (3) supply, where Americans would be present at every level."[115] Such plans were easier to draw up than to implement. One of Wedemeyer's earliest suggestions was that the U.S. government might pay each Chinese soldier in the elite divisions one U.S. dollar per month; Chiang replied that it would be better if the United States gave this money directly to him, whereupon he would ensure that each Chinese soldier received 100 Chinese dollars for each American dollar. Since the current exchange rate was about 500 to 1, and rising daily, this alternative was not acceptable. Wedemeyer was not put off by such frustrations; he had made up his mind to modernize the Chinese army and he would do so. "My approach to the Generalissimo has been friendly, direct, and firm," he told Marshall. "I believe that he likes and respects me now." In his memoirs, Wedemeyer recalled that Chiang "was very sensitive and almost as intuitive as a woman. . . . It was my feeling that he was not too well equipped, either in training or experience, to cope with the multitude of problems confronting him."[116]

Since he saw this "multitude of problems" as being military rather than Chinese political ones, Wedemeyer had no doubts at all that the Americans were "well equipped," and could accordingly remedy the Generalissimo's deficiencies. What was needed, he felt, was better liaison at the staff level, and an American adviser with every Chinese regiment. A start should be made by building up thirty-six "well-trained, well-fed, and well-led divisions." And the Chinese must learn to take their advisers' advice. As Wedemeyer put it in an operational directive of February 15, 1945: "Any Chinese commander who continually fails to follow the well considered advice of his U.S. advisor will be replaced or have U.S. assistance withdrawn from his unit."[117] About four thousand Americans would be involved, split into "combat sections" of twenty-five officers and fifty enlisted men. U.S. liaison teams would endeavor to supply accurate statistics on the local situation, training, and personnel to the higher levels of Chinese command and the China theater headquarters. By March the Americans had managed to set up both a general staff and an infantry school, but no Chinese students appeared. When asked the reason for this absence, Chinese generals politely replied that they were so busy reorganizing in other areas that they could not spare the officers who would be the students in the new schools. They hoped, however, to have some by April. There was clearly no great rush to partake of U.S. expertise.[118]

Pending recruits for the advanced officer training program, the Americans tried to improve the lot of the common Chinese soldiers, who were "suffering from every sort of disease and are just able to walk," in the words of a team of American observers. "Occasional stretchers carry those too weak to make even an attempt to walk. It is not unusual to see the occupants of the litters dumped by the road either dead or soon to die. . . . The seriously sick replacements had to cook for themselves in kitchens which were immediately adjacent to latrines. About one blanket was provided for each three men. The dead were lying next to the barely living and left there at times for several days."[119] Obviously the giving of advice could not be restricted to combat operations, since this problem preceded combat. The answer was multivitamin capsules for each man, and a rounded diet. The trouble was that the multivitamin pills supplied by the Americans were often declared "poisonous" and condemned by the Chinese officers. So Wedemeyer established a "Food Service Program" with American liaison officers and supervision down to the battalion level. The Generalissimo completely approved of the American-planned diet for his troops, which would cost Chinese $2,000 per man per month. Since the Generalissimo, however, continued to provide only Chinese $600 per man, the extra food could not be obtained. So the Americans went ahead and established six "Ration

Purchasing Commissions," which by the summer of 1945 were sup-plementing the diets of 185,000 Chinese soldiers.[120]

This reflected a general pattern: as supply routes opened up, and new tasks were undertaken, the American role grew greater and the number of U.S. personnel in China naturally increased. By January 1945 there were about thirty-three thousand Americans in China; by June the number had risen to fifty-nine thousand and more were needed. At the same time the problems of finance increased. The exchange rate between Chinese and American dollars, still around 500 to 1 in April, was 750 to 1 by June and over 3000 to 1 by the late summer. Speculation and dishonest use of funds were common, and Wedemeyer declined the Generalissimo's request that he should issue a public statement to refute charges that U.S. supplies were being mishandled and misappropriated. Instead, Wedemeyer set up a special department to deal with lend-lease allocations.[121]

In accordance with the broad goals of his anti-Communist grand strategy, Wedemeyer directed his activities almost exclusively to help-ing the Chinese Nationalists. Though on assuming command in late 1944, he had presented to the Generalissimo various proposals drawn up by the American staff for helping the Communists play a greater part in the war against Japan — such as arming and organizing three Communist regiments under the command of an American officer, or sending several thousand U.S. technicians to Yenan to increase the Communists' fighting capabilities — he had not encouraged such proposals nor helped to activate them. And when in early 1945 a colonel in the Office of Strategic Services (OSS) negotiated directly with the Communists to arm and equip twenty-five thousand Com-munist guerrillas, to set up demolitions and communications schools, to give one hundred thousand pistols to the People's Militia, and "to receive complete co-operation of their army of six hundred fifty thousand and People's Militia of two and one half million when strategic use required by Wedemeyer," Wedemeyer himself took vigorous counteraction. He ordered that "officers in China Theater will not assist, negotiate, or collaborate in any way with Chinese political parties, activities, or persons not specifically authorized by

Commanding General, U.S. Forces, China Theater [i.e., Wede-meyer]. This includes discussing hypothetical aid or employment of U.S. resources to assist any effort of an unapproved political party, activity, or persons. This also forbids rendering local assistance."[122]

This order was aimed not only at those negotiating with the Communists, but also at those like Chennault who liked to work independently with warlords who he felt could help the war effort, even if they did not have the Generalissimo's backing. Wedemeyer had abandoned the options (however abused) that Chennault and Stilwell had always kept open. "In China," wrote Wedemeyer, "I no longer needed to be overly cautious or equivocal in recommending constructive measures in the political, economic, social, and psychological fields, since Chiang Kai-shek and his government were as well, or better, aware of the reality of the Communist menace. America was on the front line in the battle against communism in this remote but important area. It was of vital importance that the Communists, who were even greater enemies of liberty than the Nazis, should not win out in China."[123] But this was in his memoirs, long after the Communists had come to power in China. At the time he phrased his goals somewhat less dramatically. "All I am doing," he told a friend in July 1945, "and I am sure you would do the same, is trying to conduct this show in a straightforward manner."[124]

But it was hard to be straightforward when no one else was. Meeting at the Crimean town of Yalta in February 1945, Roosevelt and Churchill had made important secret concessions to Stalin, offering leases to Port Arthur and Dairen, restoration of Russian "rights" to the Manchurian railroads, and possession of southern Sakhalin and the Kurile Islands, in return for Stalin's promise to enter the war against Japan on the side of the allies two or three months after Germany had surrendered. In China, both Nationalists and Communists were clearly preparing more for postwar hostilities than for the coalition that Hurley (now U.S. ambassador) was trying to arrange. American Foreign Service officers were emphasizing Kuomintang weakness and corruption, contrasting it with the strength and verve of the Chinese Communists. They did not agree with Wedemeyer, who had "a low estimate of the future military capabilities of the Chinese Communists," and believed that "the rebellion in China could be put down by comparatively small assistance to Chiang's central government."[125]

Wedemeyer planned to forge the Nationalist armies in combat, by means of a massive drive across southern China which would culminate in an attack on Canton and Hong Kong in early 1946. After the fall of Germany, which Wedemeyer projected for May 1945, he hoped to have the services of Generals Patton, Simpson and Truscott: Patton would be assigned north China and would push to Peking, Truscott would move down the Yangtze valley to Shanghai, and Simpson would be Wedemeyer's deputy commander.[126] Such ambitious plans demanded top-level consultation, and Wedemeyer flew to Washington to present his case to the Joint Chiefs of Staff and the President. Though the Joint Chiefs were sympathetic, the meeting with the President was most unsettling. Later Wedemeyer was to describe the sick President as having been obviously incapable of understanding the Communist menace:

I had luncheon alone with Mr. Roosevelt in his office, and endeavored to discuss the many problems of the China area with him. I had not seen the President for several months and was shocked at his physical appearance. His color was ashen, his face drawn, and his jaw drooping. I had difficulty in conveying information to him because he seemed in a daze. Several times I repeated the same idea because his mind did not seem to retain or register. . . . I told the President that the Communists were not of immediate concern but I felt certain that they would cause trouble as soon as the war ended. He did not seem to understand what I was talking about.[127]

The instructions that Wedemeyer received were not very helpful. He was told that the short-term goals of the United States were to unify China's resources for war against Japan, the long-term goal was

to help establish "a united, democratically progressive, and cooperative China." The Communists should not presently be armed, but if
the United States were to undertake operations on the China coast,
then steps would be taken to arm the Communists. The "united"
China for which the U.S. hoped, he was told, would not necessarily
have to be under the leadership of Chiang Kai-shek.[128]

Wedemeyer returned to China to continue work on his long-range
plans for the assault on Canton. The situation appeared promising:
renewed Japanese attacks in April had been beaten back by Chinese
troops using some of the lessons on supporting fire, signals and
transport that the American advisers had taught them; the skies were
controlled by the 14th Air Force; on the first of April, also, U.S.
forces landed on Okinawa. But the China theater was still peripheral
to the allied leaders, and Wedemeyer could not know that Marshall,
Stimson and the new President, Harry Truman, were all stalling on
crucial Far Eastern decisions pending the results of the first atomic
bomb tests and that Stalin was also awaiting the test results with
interest, having learned of them from Soviet agents in the United
States.[129] It was not until July 30 that Marshall told Wedemeyer
what Wedemeyer had been urging for some time — "that co-ordination of plans to be followed in event of Japanese surrender was a
pressing necessity." But Marshall's message added that "the Joint
Chiefs of Staff do not desire to become involved in the campaign in
China on the mainland other than by air, [though] it is considered
highly desirable to seize the ports in order better to facilitate the
reoccupation of the country by Chinese forces."[130] Though this was
an indication that the war might soon end, this message gave
Wedemeyer no precise information on which he could base future
plans. He accordingly continued to concentrate on the Chinese drive
for Canton, and to bolster the flagging morale of American personnel
who were beginning to feel that their efforts were "futile."

In July and early August Chinese troops moved steadily toward
phase one of the operation, the capture of Fort Bayard, on the
Luichow peninsula near Hainan Island. The campaign was not
dramatic: "Having decided to withdraw, the Japanese forces did

withdraw in a leisurely and ordered manner. Chinese forces, unwilling to engage in, and unable to see any reason for, costly combat
operations, followed closely but carefully. What fighting did occur
was largely a matter of rear-guard patrol action. There were cases of
Japanese platoons holding up Chinese regiments or divisions for
several days or longer."[131] By August 3 the Chinese armies were
only twenty miles from Fort Bayard, prepared to open a major port
and reestablish supply routes by sea for the first time in seven years.
But before the final thrust could be made, the war was over. On
August 6 an atomic bomb was dropped on Hiroshima. On August 8
the Soviet Union declared war on Japan, and the Russian armies
moved into Manchuria. On August 9 an atomic bomb was dropped
on Nagasaki. On August 10 Japan made a tentative offer of surrender. On August 14 General Arnold launched, as a final grand
gesture, a thousand-plane raid on the Japanese mainland. The planes
were still in the air when the Japanese Emperor announced his
country's unconditional surrender.[132]

There were no adequate plans, on either the American or the
Chinese side, to deal with this situation. On August 1 Wedemeyer
had warned Marshall that "if peace should come within the next few
weeks we will be woefully unprepared in China. On the American
side we could handle our own unilateral personnel and property
interests but many of our activities are inextricably tied in with the
Chinese, and if peace comes suddenly, it is reasonable to expect
widespread confusion and disorder. The Chinese have no plan for
rehabilitation, prevention of epidemics, restoration of utilities, establishment of balanced economy and redisposition of millions of refugees." He felt that Americans "may be unavoidably drawn in as
advisers to Chinese officials in a status analogous to that of Americans
at present with Chinese military forces. I am sure that you will agree
that we should assist the Chinese in that manner to reestablish a
modicum of order and normalcy."[133]

But what was "a modicum of order and normalcy," and could it be
gained by the employment of more Western experts, civilian this
time as well as military? The Russians did not agree: they syste-

matically occupied Manchuria and started to ship all heavy industrial equipment back to the Soviet Union. The Chinese Communists did not agree: they moved out of their northern bases, coordinated their scattered guerrilla forces, and began to accumulate the arms and munitions of the surrendering Japanese troops. Chiang Kai-shek did not agree: he raced with the aid of airlifting U.S. planes to try to reestablish control over all China, ruinously overextending his lines of communications despite the warnings of Wedemeyer. The American people did not agree: they urged the demobilization of their armies that had fought overseas for four bitter years. And Marshall himself did not agree: he opposed military involvement in China and strove to achieve a workable Nationalist-Communist coalition.

And, curiously enough, perhaps Wedemeyer himself didn't really agree. One of the Flying Tigers wrote later that "it would have been so simple to have halted the Reds."[134] Senator Joseph McCarthy was to write that in late 1945 "Chiang Kai-shek was in a position to deal with the situation. He had thirty-nine American-trained divisions, he had equipment, he had a high morale among his troops. . . . The situation was not difficult. . . . The government at Chungking was our ally. We had come through a long, hard war together."[135] Yet on August 5, 1945, Wedemeyer had forwarded an extremely strongly worded report to the Generalissimo, telling him that it contained "information that should reach you. It has been carefully verified and I believe contains much factual data that will assist you and myself in our many intricate problems." The tactic was a Stilwellian one that Wedemeyer had hitherto avoided: jolt the Generalissimo into action. The report described Chinese conscription patterns as a "ravaging disease," a corrupt and vicious human cattle market whose victims — "their skin [the] shabby cover of an emaciated body which has no other value than to turn rice into dung" — were nevertheless "fulfilling the most important function of a citizen of Free China! to be a source of income for officials." The Chinese Army hospitals where the sickest conscripts ended up were compared to the German extermination camps at Buchenwald. The report ended by pointing out that "every military observer who came to this country" had recommended slashing back the numbers in the Chinese army, and developing a few elite divisions. "But as soldiers are primarily a source of income for officials and a source of political power and influence for generals, which general will allow himself to be robbed of his army? . . . Armies are instruments to win wars. Does the Chinese Government not want to win the war? The answer is: Not unconditionally. Not at the price of entrusting Chinese concerns to the American army. Not at the price of introducing democracy which might control the government and officials. Not at the price of collaborating with the Communists, with their exaggerated ideas of how to carry on a war of resistance, who wouldn't approve of the tactic of 'waiting for victory.' "[136]

The Generalissimo's response is not recorded, but in any case that response had become irrelevant. Had he chosen to heed the Americans' varying advice, and to take the consequences, the American advisory role might have been continued. The war in Vietnam gives some indication of what that might have entailed for both parties. But Chiang chose not to. China was not America, and the battle for China would be fought according to Chinese ground rules, rules which he hoped to call. If that was wishful thinking it was still his decision, and he had had plenty of time to arrive at it. The Americans were not to find their Shangri-la in China, with or without a compass.

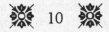

10

THE LAST ROUNDS:

U.S.A. and U.S.S.R.

The end of the Second World War did not immediately mean the end of United States involvement in China. With American assistance, nearly half a million Kuomintang troops were moved to key positions in east and north China, and American marines occupied Peking, Tientsin, and important mining and railway centers. To further thwart the Communists, the American command also tried to enforce the ruling that Japanese troops in China should surrender only to Chiang Kai-shek or his representatives, and in many areas the Japanese held out against Communist forces until the Nationalists arrived. But at the same time the training of Nationalist troops by American advisers was stopped, and American officers were forbidden to furnish direct military aid to the Nationalist forces. Top priority had to go to the occupation and pacification of Japan, and the United States government did not intend to get involved in a Chinese civil war.[1]

In November 1945 Wedemeyer, having sized up Chinese Communist strength in north China, the presence of Russian armies in Manchuria, and the continuing corruption, demoralization and absence of logistical sophistication in the Nationalist forces, made a fresh analysis: "1. The Generalissimo will be able to stabilize the situation in south China provided he accepts the assistance of foreign administrators and technicians and engages in political, economic and social reforms through honest, competent civilian officials. 2. He will be unable to stabilize the situation in north China for months or perhaps even years unless a satisfactory settlement with the Chinese Communists is achieved and followed up realistically by the kind of action suggested in paragraph 1."² President Truman echoed these sentiments. He reiterated the need for "a strong, united and democratic China," urged the cessation of hostilities between Nationalists and Communists, and suggested that Chiang modify his "one-party government" to include "other political elements." Then he held out the carrot: "As China moves toward peace and unity along the lines described above, the United States would be prepared to assist the National Government in every reasonable way to rehabilitate the country, improve the agrarian and industrial economy, and establish a military organization capable of discharging China's national and international responsibilities for the maintenance of peace and order."³

The granting of American aid and advice followed these general guidelines. General George Marshall was sent to China as Truman's special representative, to negotiate a truce between the contending forces prior to the formation of a coalition government. Wedemeyer went to China after Marshall's failure in 1947, and tried to induce Chiang Kai-shek to reform his administration and move away from reliance on purely military solutions. A Military Advisory Group in China (MAGIC) of about one thousand American officers and men was sent to China under the direction of General McClure. Between V–J Day and early 1948, the United States gave nearly one and a half billion dollars of aid to China, of which almost half was military. This figure did not include enormous amounts of matériel that had been sold cheaply as "army surplus."⁴ A further half billion dollars was authorized by Congress in the China Aid Act of 1948. In addition, the United Nations Relief and Rehabilitation Administration (UNRRA) and its successor, the Board of Trustees for Rehabilitation Affairs (BOTRA), dispensed over half a billion dollars on irrigation, fisheries, rural industrialization, pharmaceutical production, mechanization of agriculture, and other projects.

Sino-Soviet harmony in 1955. Above, a Russian expert instructs a worker in the Taiyuan steel mill. Below, young Russian and Chinese soldiers fraternize in Manchuria. "We'll never forget you!" and "We'll remember you as long as we do our own families!" run the original Chinese captions.

But the rot in the Nationalist army, disaffection in the country-side, and the spiraling inflation could not be cured from outside. The Communists were ebullient, united, well led by seasoned commanders, and well equipped with captured Japanese, Nationalist (and American) arms. In late 1948 Lin Piao routed the Nationalists in Manchuria. Peking, with a garrison of one hundred thousand troops, surrendered in January 1949. As Chiang Kai-shek resigned the presidency and shipped the Nationalist gold reserves, many of his best troops, and the Imperial Palace collection of priceless paintings to Taiwan, the Communists continued their race south: they occupied Nanking in April, Shanghai in May, Canton in October, and Chungking in November. China was theirs.

It was time for the Soviet Russian advisers to come in, to make up for their failures in the nineteen-twenties and do for the Chinese Communists what the Americans had been unable to do for the Nationalists. They came in large numbers — some eleven thousand of them between 1950 and 1960 — and they worked in the same fields as their Western predecessors: in science and engineering, in higher education and medicine, and in the army.[5]

After Mao Tse-tung visited Moscow in early 1950, Stalin pledged economic and technical aid for fifty major Chinese industrial projects; in 1952 the number was increased to 141, and these projects formed an integral part of China's first Five Year Plan (1953–1957). Three hundred Soviet specialists worked on the Anshan steel complex in southern Manchuria; five hundred worked to develop Sinkiang's oil fields; hundreds more worked to reorganize China's northern railway network, designed automobile and tractor factories, developed oil refineries and hydroelectric power plants. In 1955 Soviet specialists were sent to construct an atomic reactor and a cyclotron, and twenty top Chinese nuclear physicists were sent to the Joint Institute of Nuclear Research at Dubna, near Moscow. Soviet advisers also participated in geological surveys, bridge building, state farm planning, and the management of the Peking hospital.[6]

Soviet specialists were equally active in the field of education. In the early 1950's, 1,393 textbooks were translated from the Russian and used to replace out-of-date texts in China's schools. Hundreds of thousands of books and periodicals were sent to Chinese university libraries. At least one thousand Chinese scientists received advanced training in the Soviet Union in the 1950's, and some thirty-seven thousand undergraduates, graduate students and technical personnel also received instruction there. Soviet experts overhauled curricula in Chinese universities, reorganized departments, and developed research institutes. To take just one example, the director of the Chinese Institute of Mathematics reported major Soviet influence in "theory of the structure of functions, application of electronic-computer techniques in engineering and scientific problems, research on partial differential equations relating to aerodynamics, elliptic partial differential equations generated from capillary, and partial differential equations relating to thin-shell theories." There were also major changes in the study of nuclear physics, chemistry, engineering, biology, and medicine.[7]

Though the numbers of Soviet military advisers are not known, their influence was profound. The loosely structured Chinese Communist army of around five million men, without efficient air or naval arms; and with obsolete equipment, that had defeated the Nationalists in 1949, was completely overhauled after the Korean war. A military science institute and other specialized training schools were developed, senior Chinese officers were sent to the staff school at Kiev, equipment was standardized, and the Chinese were assisted in forming engineer, air defense, signals and armored corps. Finally in early 1955 the old revolutionary informality and egalitarianism of the Chinese army — a holdover from the guerrilla warfare days — was ended. In its stead, the Chinese adopted fourteen officer ranks, distinction according to specialization, sharply graded pay scales, and the full panoply of military insignia and decorations. Corresponding developments took place in the navy and air force.[8]

These advances were not, however, made without friction. It was not just that the Chinese expectations were too high, that they expected "every Soviet specialist to be a sort of magician," as a Russian research chemist in Peking put it, "capable of giving them the one correct answer to all sorts of complex problems."[9] Nor was it simply that the Russians drove a hard bargain, insisting on payment for all technical services rendered, prompt repayment of credits, and over-pricing some exports to China.[10] The trouble lay, as it had so often in the past, in China's fear of what lay behind this Western technical expertise, in the fact that the advisers brought ideological demands along with their mastery.

Mao Tse-tung had fought for over twenty years to reestablish a strong and unified China. Now that the country had been finally reunited he was not willing to see it slide slowly under Russian influence. Nor was he willing to abandon the revolutionary momentum that had been so carefully generated in the first years of Chinese Communist rule. By 1955 it was clear that many Chinese were becoming overreliant on Soviet technology. Then, in 1956, Khrushchev attacked Stalin's memory, and in doing so seemed to be attacking Mao, who had just publicly praised Stalin. Open Soviet deprecation of China's new communes in the Great Leap Forward of 1958 brought one of Mao's cherished policies into question. Khrushchev's direct approach to President Eisenhower at Camp David in 1959 hinted at a new era of Soviet-American peaceful coexistence. The importance of Soviet technical assistance was not great enough to transcend such slights. As early as the summer of 1957, leading Chinese Communist spokesmen were declaring that "we should rely on our own strength as much as possible" and reduce "reliance upon foreign countries."[11] Setbacks in the Great Leap Forward led Mao-ists to fear that discontented members of the army and administration might seek closer ties with Russia and that Russia would not be unreceptive to such overtures. In late 1959, accordingly, the Chinese Minister of Defense and the Army Chief of Staff, who were believed to want more massive Soviet aid, were both dismissed. The loyal Lin Piao was brought in to reorganize the army, to extend political control over the armed forces, and to continue mass participation at the militia level.

In the summer of 1960 proponents of the Soviet and the Chinese viewpoints clashed openly at Communist Party meetings and congresses in Bucharest, Peking, and Hanoi. In an apparent attempt to cow the Chinese, the Russians abruptly withdrew all technical advisers from China, leaving a number of major projects unfinished. The Chinese responded by recalling most of their students from the Soviet Union. These actions, the Chinese later admitted, "caused heavy losses in China's construction work and dislocated its original plan for the development of the national economy, greatly aggravating our difficulties."[12] But neither side would make major concessions, and the Sino-Soviet rift gradually widened: from the ambiguities of the October 1960 conference of eighty-one Communist Parties in Moscow, through Khruschev's attack on Albania in 1961, to China's claims to be the champion of "true revolutionary Marxist-Leninists" in 1964, and the violent attacks on Russian revisionism in the Great Proletarian Cultural Revolution of 1966–1968.

The ten years of Soviet advice had been of great benefit to China. It had helped them in the programs of crash industrialization and military reorganization so desperately needed if they were to first rebuild and then protect their shattered country. When the advisers withdrew in 1960, however, one major task was still unfinished: the development of an atomic bomb for China.

China wanted and needed the Bomb — this was the terrible legacy of the Western technological civilizations, their high point and their nadir, the most ambiguous and the most challenging of all scientific breakthroughs. Arguments over the atomic bomb were at the heart of the growing Sino-Soviet friction. By 1955 Chinese Communist leaders were fully aware of the importance of nuclear weapons; they knew that the Soviet role would inevitably be important in this area, whether nuclear weapons were to be developed in China or whether China contented itself with sheltering under the Soviet nuclear "umbrella." The Russians were in an awkward situation: they did not want to deny their Chinese allies this supreme technical assistance, but on the other hand they were far from sure that they wanted a nuclear neighbor. The policy decided upon was a compromise that ended up by satisfying neither party.

By an agreement of October 1957, the U.S.S.R. pledged that it would help China with the "new technology for national defense"; the Chinese understood this to mean that the U.S.S.R. would supply them with a sample atomic bomb, and with the technical information needed for its subsequent manufacture within China. By 1959, however, it had become clear to the Chinese that they were not going to get this kind of substantive and immediate nuclear assistance. The Russians contented themselves with helping the Chinese to build nuclear reactors and a gaseous diffusion plant for the production of fissionable material. Though these were the two main routes for developing nuclear weapons, the Russians seem to have believed that the Chinese would still be unable to make the final leap to atomic bomb manufacture without continuing advice. The price of this advice, they told the Chinese, would be Chinese acceptance of Soviet leadership in a joint Far Eastern command structure. The Chinese were to claim later that they suspected this to be a plan "to bring China under Soviet military control."[13]

After Soviet technical personnel were withdrawn from China in 1960, the Chinese determined to press ahead on their own. Their friendship with the U.S.S.R., they insisted in 1961, was still "as firm and indissoluble as the Himalayan mountains, as deep as the Pacific Ocean and as boundless as the Yangtze and the Volga."[14] Though this of course was not true, the Chinese were nevertheless aware that the Russians had put into their hands the means to achieve their nuclear goal. There was no way that the Russians could withdraw the advice they had already given, no way that they could dismantle the nuclear reactors and the gaseous diffusion plants without committing an act of war.

The Chinese detonated their first atomic bomb in the Sungkiang testing grounds on October 16, 1964. It was "a crude nuclear device," noted President Johnson, "which can only increase the sense of insecurity of the Chinese people." On the contrary, said the Chinese, their first atomic bomb was "a major contribution made by the Chinese people to the cause of the defence of world peace."[15]

The bomb tested had been about twenty kilotons, comparable to the bomb dropped on Hiroshima in 1945 by the United States. Of itself, this Chinese bomb did not make China a nuclear power; the world watched to see if China could follow it up with a sophisticated development program. A second bomb, of about the same size, was tested in May 1965. A third, tested in May 1966, was ten times larger and employed some thermonuclear material. In October 1966 there was a fourth test, of a smaller bomb, but one that for the first time in China was carried on a missile. A fifth bomb was detonated two months later, yielding over three hundred kilotons. Then on June 17, 1967, the Chinese detonated a thermonuclear (or "hydrogen") bomb, of at least three megatons — one hundred times as powerful as the bomb that had destroyed Hiroshima.[16]

As elated Chinese crowds cheered in the streets, beating drums and gongs, and letting off firecrackers, Western analysts pondered the surprising performance. It was possible, they explained, that Chinese scientists had perfected the "gas centrifuge process for uranium separation," a technique that had been attempted but then dropped in the United States, several years before.[17] In their official communiqué, the Chinese volunteered no technical information. The triumph, they noted simply, had been made possible by the officers and men of the People's Liberation Army, by the workers, and by the scientists, who had jointly "given play to their collective wisdom and sttength, cooperated closely with each other, surmounted all difficulties in the revolutionary spirit of 'seize the day, seize the hour,' and, opening up a path of their own, have ensured the smooth success of this hydrogen bomb test."[18]

The purpose of the test, the Chinese reiterated — as they had after each test since 1964 — was purely defensive, and their ultimate goal remained the attainment of world peace through a worldwide prohibition of nuclear weapons. But at the same time they pointed out what a severe blow they had inflicted on both the U.S.A. and the U.S.S.R., and how great an encouragement China's achievement must give to the Vietnamese, the Arabs, and those peoples throughout the world who were resisting imperialism and aggression. Nuclear power, and nuclear disarmament, they were saying, was no longer a Western preserve. If final decisions were to be made, then

China must be in on them; China had her own chosen policies, and the proven power with which to advance them. The Chinese had shown, to their satisfaction at least, that the Western adviser was no longer needed.

CONCLUSION

The simultaneity of China's hydrogen-bomb test and the most dramatic phases of the Great Proletarian Cultural Revolution was not, of course, a total coincidence. In the document of August 8, 1966, often taken as the charter of the Cultural Revolution, China's leaders had emphasized that responsible personnel "who have made contributions" were to be treated with "special care" and were not to be disturbed by the Red Guards or other groups. Nevertheless, the dramatic nature of this technological achievement—combined with China's strident foreign policy, eruptions on university campuses around the world often partly in the name of "Maoist" principles, and the absence of any reliable agricultural or industrial production figures from China—made China's decision to reject any further Western advances seem totally plausible. In the virulence of China's anti-Western pronouncements lay a paradoxical combination of hostility and relief. If China had caught up with the West in certain areas, it was still true that she had been almost destroyed in the attempt, and that she was still threatened.

In the past, however, as we have seen, China's aloofness had not negated China's receptivity. Every technique that Western advisers had brought had eventually been assimilated: heliocentric theories and calendrical science, sophisticated medical surgery, economic planning, engineering, interdisciplinary universities, long-distance communications, mechanized warfare, nuclear physics. The Westerners had presented their expertise as the wrapping round an ideological package, however, and had tried to force the Chinese to accept both together. It was this that the Chinese had refused to tolerate; even at their weakest, they sensed that acceptance of a foreign ideology on foreign terms must be a form of submission. This common pride and common wariness linked men as disparate as the pioneer anti-Christians Shen Ch'üeh and Yang Kuang-hsien, the nineteenth-century statesmen Lin Tse-hsü and Tseng Kuo-fan, and the bitter rivals Chiang Kai-shek and Mao Tse-tung.

As we look back across the cycle from 1620 to 1960, we can observe the standpoint of superiority from which the Western advisers approached China. This superiority sprang from two elements: the possession of advanced technical skills and a sense of moral rightness. Convinced that their goals were good and that their advice was sorely needed, the Westerners adopted a proprietary air toward China; Chinese refusal to accept the validity of their goals, and Chinese rejection of their advice, were met with Western bewilderment or anger. Driven on by their varying visions, most Western advisers developed some degree of emotional involvement with China; they demanded more from the Chinese than payment for services rendered. They did not see that the Chinese had a contractual view of the relationship and maintained, as nominal employers, the right to terminate the agreements when they saw fit. The repercussions of this misunderstanding could be serious, and among Americans, for instance, once so active as advisers during the late Ch'ing and the Republican periods, there emerged theories of betrayal and of the "loss" of China. Americans had not been betrayed, however; they had failed no more than others had failed in the past, and they had lost no more than others had lost—money, life's work, hopes. China had not been America's to lose, any more than it had been Roman Catholic Europe's or Great Britain's or would be Soviet Russia's. Fryer, Gordon, and Hart, for example, are historical briefs for Hume, Stilwell, and Todd.

The advisers' lives serve us as examples and as warnings at a time when Westerners are still complacent about their civilization, convinced of their moral rightness, and eager to "develop" those whom they consider lower than themselves on the ladder of human progress. Let us by all means applaud those attributes that reflect a measure of credit on the West: the tenacity of Fryer and Martin; the energy of Schall, Lay, and Todd; the sensitivity of Hume and Borodin; the shrewdness of Gordon and Stilwell; the organizational ability of Hart and Wedemeyer; the ingenuity of Verbiest and Parker; the personal courage of Ward and Chennault; the dedication of Bethune. Each gave a significant part of his life to China.

On balance, though, the story of these men is more a cautionary tale than an inspirational tract. It is not just that negative personal attributes offset the positive ones—such as the arrogance, impatience, intolerance, tactlessness, or stupidity that at different times turned the Chinese against the advisers. There are also broader problems that should be explored, problems relevant not only to the advisers who worked in China but also to those who are still trying to carry out similar work in other parts of the world.

What were the basic motives of these men, and what did they hope to achieve? What was the personal cost of their type of service? By what right did they go?

One motive, certainly, was to help to bring either spiritual or material improvement to China. This seems to have been true of all the advisers I have considered here—those who went of their own volition, those who were invited, and those who were ordered there by superiors. Help meant making China more like the West, bringing change that by definition was understood to be constructive. It therefore did not matter to the Westerners that they were initiating a series of events whose outcome they would be unable to determine. But implicit in most of their actions was a more complex motive, a desire not so much to help China as to help themselves. Most advisers had a character that thrived on risk and yearned for radical solutions, a pattern generally exacerbated by feared or experienced frustrations at home. China seemed to offer them freedom of maneuver, a chance to influence history by the force of personality, and thus to prove their own significance.

Many of the advisers did indeed find a measure of psychological fulfillment, but the cost of the experience was, not surprisingly, high. Even if some Chinese received them warmly, there were always more who met them with indifference, deception, or hostility. Each adviser had sought to control China's destiny in some fashion; the dawning realization that such would not be the case was a serious disappointment. Sensing that they were being used by the Chinese rather than using the Chinese, that they were being swallowed by their own technique, they took one or the other of two main routes to avoid having to admit that their expectations had been false. Some hurled themselves with increasing energy into their work, burying future uncertainties in the all-absorbing and often satisfying present; others argued that the Chinese had proved themselves unworthy to receive Western help—that they were corrupt, shifty, and cruel. Those Westerners who followed the first course showed by their actions how much their ambitions had been limited; those who held the second view wished to deny failure by denying that a real opportunity had ever existed.

The answer to the third question—by what right did they go?—is more difficult. A clue to the answer surely lies in the fact that the advisers themselves did not think of posing the question. They were confident. They were sure that their own civilization, whatever its shortcomings, had given them something valid to offer, something that China lacked. They had the right because they had the ability, the faith, and the drive. As they changed, so the world changed, and China with it. That was the way things were. For the Chinese to protest against this made no sense, since it was self-evident. One might as well protest the tide's rise or the sun's light.

It would be absurd to claim that this sense of superiority has totally vanished, even though absolute faith in the rightness of Western methodologies and goals was shattered for most Europeans in the years after the Second World War and has been seriously shaken in the United States in the years following the Vietnam war. Technological self-confidence has been further undermined in the late seventies by awareness of limited oil resources and the potential for disaster lurking in nuclear reactors. The Chinese, in their turn, seem strong enough now to ensure that if the Westerners come to China as advisers, they will do so on strictly Chinese terms and will not insinuate unwanted values in the pursuit of extrinsic goals. Yet it would be equally absurd to assume that the Chinese will have an easy time containing the forces they now appear to welcome. At least—if each partner in the equation has attained a new level of self-awareness—there is a chance that the old misconceptions will not be repeated.

CHAPTER NOTES

These notes give the citations for all material quoted in the text, and also the names of works that were of general relevance to each topic treated. Since few works were used for more than one chapter, there seemed no point in printing a separate bibliography. Accordingly, each book is fully listed under the note where it is first cited, and referred to thereafter by author's name and short title. In the rare cases in which a work was used in more than one chapter, the full listing has been repeated. A complete bibliography for each adviser, in other words, can be found in the notes to the chapter dealing with that adviser.

1. Schall and Verbiest: *To God Through the Stars*

1. Adapted from Fu Lo-shu, *A Documentary Chronicle of Sino-Western Relations* (1644–1820), 2 vols. (Tucson, University of Arizona Press, 1966), p. 3.
2. Adapted from ibid., p. 4.
3. For expansion of these points, cf. J. K. Fairbank and S. Y. Teng, "On the Ch'ing Tributary System," *Harvard Journal of Asiatic Studies*, 6 (1941), 135–246. Donald Lach, *Asia in the Making of Europe* (Chicago, University of Chicago Press, 1965). R. A. Skelton, *Explorers' Maps: Chapters in the Cartographic Record of Geographical Discovery* (New York, Praeger, 1958).
4. The major work on Matteo Ricci is Pasquale d'Elia, *Fonti ricciane; documenti originali concernenti Matteo Ricci e la storia della prime relazioni tra l'Europa e la Cina* (1579–1615), 3 vols. (Rome, Libreria dello Stato, 1942–1949). For biographies of Jesuits in China,

cf. Louis Pfister, S.J., *Notices biographiques et bibliographiques sur les Jésuites de l'ancienne mission de Chine, 1552–1773*, 2 vols. (Shanghai, Imprimerie de la Mission Catholique, 1932 and 1934). The best survey of early Jesuits in China is George H. Dunne, S.J., *Generation of Giants: The Story of the Jesuits in China in the Last Decades of the Ming Dynasty* (London, Burns and Oates, 1962). The best account of the Ch'ing missions is Arnold H. Rowbotham, *Missionary and Mandarin: The Jesuits at the Court of China* (Berkeley and Los Angeles, University of California Press, 1942).

5. For Mendoza's sources, cf. C. R. Boxer, *South China in the Sixteenth Century, Being the Narratives of Galeote Pereira, Fr. Gaspar da Cruz, O.P., Fr. Martin de Rada, O.E.S.A. (1550–1575)* (London, Hakluyt Society, 1953).

6. Louis J. Gallagher, S.J., *China in the Sixteenth Century: The Journals of Matthew Ricci, 1583–1610* (New York, Random House, 1953), pp. 22–23.

7. Gallagher, *Ricci Journals*, p. 154.

8. Alfons Väth, S.J., *Johann Adam Schall von Bell, S.J., Missionar in China, Kaiserlicher Astronom und Ratgeber am Hofe von Peking, 1592–1666* (Cologne, J. P. Bachem, 1933), p. 30.

9. Dunne, *Jesuits*, pp. 210–211; Väth, *Schall*, pp. 40–41.

10. Dunne, *Jesuits*, pp. 130–145; Väth, *Schall*, pp. 41–46.

11. Väth, *Schall*, pp. 54–66.

12. *Lettres et mémoires d'Adam Schall S.J.*, ed. Henri Bernard, S.J. (relation historique, texte latin avec traduction française du P. Paul Bornet, S.J.) (Tientsin, Hautes Etudes, 1942), p. 4.

13. Arthur W. Hummel, ed., *Eminent Chinese of the Ch'ing Period (1644–1912)*, 2 vols. (Washington, D.C., United States Government Printing Office, 1943), p. 453.

14. Franz Michael, *The Origin of Manchu Rule in China* (Baltimore, Johns Hopkins Press, 1942). Charles O. Hucker, *The Censorial System of Ming China* (Palo Alto, Stanford University Press, 1966).

15. Schall, *Memoirs*, p. 6.

16. Ibid., p. 10; and Pasquale M. d'Elia, S.J., *Galileo in China, Relations through the Roman College between Galileo and the Jesuit Scientist-Missionaries (1610–1640)*, trans. Rufus Suter and Matthew Sciascia (Cambridge, Mass., Harvard University Press, 1960), p. 34.

17. Dunne, *Jesuits*, p. 200.

18. Pfister, *Notices biographiques*, p. 163; Hummel, *Eminent Chinese*, pp. 807–809; Väth, *Schall*, pp. 74–75.

19. Hummel, *Eminent Chinese*, p. 317.

20. d'Elia, *Galileo*, pp. 27–32; Dunne, *Jesuits*, p. 214; Joseph Needham, *Science and Civilization in China* (Cambridge, Cambridge University Press, 1954), vol. 3, pp. 437–438; Henri Bernard, "L'encyclopédie astronomique du Père Schall," *Monumenta Serica*, 3 (1938), 35–77, 441–527.

21. Schall, *Memoirs*, pp. 14–16; Pfister, *Notices biographiques*, p. 180; Dunne, *Jesuits*, p. 309.
22. Schall, *Memoirs*, pp. 76, 92, 46.
23. Ibid., pp. 50–60.
24. Dunne, *Jesuits*, pp. 252–253.
25. Pfister, *Notices biographiques*, p. 165; Dunne, *Jesuits*, p. 312.
26. Schall, *Memoirs*, p. 84.
27. Ibid., pp. 86, 90, 102.
28. Ibid., p. 134.
29. Ibid., p. 114.
30. Ibid., p. 132.
31. Ibid., p. 142.
32. Ibid., pp. 190, 216, 238; Fu Lo-shu, *Documentary Chronicle*, p. 4.
33. Schall, *Memoirs*, p. 192.
34. Ibid., p. 242.
35. Ibid., p. 362.
36. Ibid., pp. 210, 246–248; Pfister, *Notices biographiques*, pp. 170–171.
37. Schall, *Memoirs*, pp. 272–284.
38. Yuan Tschen, "Johann Adam Schall von Bell S.J. und der Bonze Mu Tschen-wen," trans. D. W. Yang, *Monumenta Serica*, 5 (1940), 316–328.
39. Schall, *Memoirs*, p. 98.
40. John Nieuhoff, *An Embassy from the East-India Company of the United Provinces to the Grand Tartar Cham, Emperor of China*, trans. John Ogilby (London, John Macock, 1669), pp. 117–118.
41. Dunne, *Jesuits*, p. 333.
42. Ibid., pp. 325–328; Kenneth Scott Latourette, *A History of Christian Missions in China* (New York, Macmillan, 1929), pp. 131–138; François Bontinck, *La lutte autour de la liturgie chinoise aux XVII et XVIII siècles* (Louvain, Editions Nauwelaerts, 1962).
43. J. S. Cummins, ed., *The Travels and Controversies of Friar Domingo Navarrete, 1618–1686*, 2 vols. (Cambridge, Cambridge University Press, 1962), II, p. 190.
44. Anastasius van den Wyngaert, ed., *Relationes et Epistolas Fratrum Minorum Saeculi XVII, Sinica Franciscana* (Florence, 1936), III, p. 90; Dunne, *Jesuits*, p. 229.
45. Condensed from Fu Lo-shu, *Documentary Chronicle*, pp. 35–36.
46. Cummins, *Navarrete*, p. lxxvii.
47. Schall, *Memoirs*, p. 136.
48. Ibid., p. 302. Written before the final persecution, but typical of his views.
49. H. Josson, S.J., and L. Willaert, S.J., eds., *Correspondence de Ferdinand Verbiest de la compagnie de Jésus (1623–1688), directeur de l'observatoire de Pékin* (Brussels, Palais des Académies, 1938), p. 15.
50. Ibid., p. 5. H. Bosmans, S.J., "Ferdinand Verbiest, directeur de l'observatoire de Peking (1623–1688)," *Revue des Questions Scien-*

tifiques, 71 (1912), pp. 195–273 and 375–464; Quotation, pp. 203–204.

51. The biographical data is drawn from Bosmans, *Verbiest;* Pfister, *Notices biographiques,* pp. 338–362; Rowbotham, *Jesuits.*
52. Josson and Willaert, *Verbiest Correspondence,* p. 123.
53. Fu Lo-shu, *Documentary Chronicle,* p. 43.
54. Adapted from ibid., p. 44.
55. Ibid., p. 45.
56. Bosmans, *Verbiest,* p. 256.
57. Needham, *Science in China,* vol. 3, pp. 451–452.
58. Bosmans, *Verbiest,* p. 265.
59. Ibid., p. 269.
60. Ibid., p. 383.
61. Ibid., pp. 385–387.
62. For a sceptic, cf. Matteo Ripa, *Memoirs of Father Ripa, During Thirteen Years' Residence at the Court of Peking in the Service of the Emperor of China,* trans. Fortunato Prandi (London, J. Murray, 1844).
63. Fu Lo-shu, *Documentary Chronicle,* p. 48.
64. Ibid., p. 58; Bosmans, *Verbiest,* p. 390.
65. J. B. du Halde, *Description géographique, historique, chronologique et physique de l'Empire de la Chine* (Paris, Le Mercier, 1735), IV, p. 75.
66. Ibid., p. 77.
67. Ibid., p. 80.
68. Fu Lo-shu, *Documentary Chronicle,* p. 69. Henri Bernard, "Ferdinand Verbiest, continuateur de l'oeuvre scientifique d'Adam Schall," *Monumenta Serica,* 5 (1940), 103–140; cited activities on pp. 116–119.
69. *Sinica Franciscana,* III, p. 486; IV, p. 277; V, p. 115.
70. Cited Rowbotham, *Jesuits,* pp. 100–103.
71. Joseph Sebes, S.J., *The Jesuits and the Sino-Russian Treaty of Nerchinsk (1689)* (Rome, Institutum Historicum S.I., 1961); Jonathan Spence, *Ts'ao Yin and the K'ang-hsi Emperor, Bondservant and Master* (New Haven, Yale University Press, 1966); Walter Fuchs, "Materialen zur Kartographie der Mandju-Zeit," *Monumenta Serica,* 1 (1935), 386–427, and 3 (1937–38), 189–231.
72. Antonio Sisto Rosso, O.F.M., *Apostolic Legations to China of the Eighteenth Century* (South Pasadena, P. D. and Ione Perkins, 1948); Francis A. Rouleau, S.J., "Maillard de Tournon, Papal Legate at the Court of Peking," *Archivum Historicum Societatis Iesu,* 31 (1962), 264–323.
73. Bernward H. Willeke, O.F.M., *Imperial Government and Catholic Missions in China During the Years 1784–1785* (St. Bonaventure, New York, The Franciscan Institute, 1948); J. J. M. de Groot,

Sectarianism and Religious Persecution in China, 2 vols. (Leiden, E. J. Brill, 1901); Ishida Mikinosuke, "A Biographical Study of Giuseppe Castiglione (Lang Shih-ning), a Jesuit Painter in the Court of Peking under the Ch'ing Dynasty," *Memoirs of the Research Department of the Toyo Bunko*, 19 (1960), 79–121.

74. G. F. Hudson, *Europe and China, A Survey of their Relations from the Earliest Times to 1800* (Boston, Beacon, 1961); Adolf Reichwein, *China and Europe; Intellectual and Artistic Contacts in the Eighteenth Century* (New York, Knopf, 1925); *Lettres édifiantes et curieuses concernant l'Asie, L'Afrique et l'Amérique* (Paris, various eds., 1713–1843); Basil Guy, *The French Image of China Before and After Voltaire* (Geneva, 1963).

75. Arthur Waley, *The Opium War Through Chinese Eyes* (New York, Macmillan, 1958), p. 97.

76. Bosmans, *Verbiest*, p. 386.

2. Peter Parker: *Bodies or Souls*

1. Peter Parker, *Statements Respecting Hospitals in China, Preceded by a Letter to John Abercrombie, M.D., V.P.R.S.E.* (Glasgow, James Maclehose, 1842), p. 5.

2. Ibid., p. 15.

3. George B. Stevens, *The Life, Letters, and Journals of the Rev. and Hon. Peter Parker, M.D., Missionary, Physician, Diplomatist, The Father of Medical Missions and Founder of the Ophthalmic Hospital in Canton* (Boston and Chicago, Congregational Sunday-School and Publishing Society, 1896), p. 13.

4. Ibid., p. 31.

5. Ibid., pp. 34–37.

6. Ibid., p. 29.

7. Ibid., p. 37.

8. Ibid., pp. 44–48.

9. Ibid., pp. 50–52.

10. Ibid., p. 54.

11. *Encyclopaedia Americana, A Popular Dictionary of Arts, Sciences, Literature, History, Politics and Biography*, Vol. III, "Catholic Epistles" to "Cranmer, Thomas" (Philadelphia, Carey and Lea, 1830), pp. 142–150, article on "China."

12. Ho Ping-ti, *Studies on the Population of China, 1368–1953* (Cambridge, Mass., Harvard University Press, 1959); David S. Nivison, "Ho-shen and His Accusers: Ideology and Political Behavior in the Eighteenth Century," in David S. Nivison and Arthur F. Wright, eds., *Confucianism in Action* (Palo Alto, Stanford University Press, 1959); John K. Fairbank, *Trade and Diplomacy on the China Coast,*

the Opening of the Treaty Ports, 1842–1854, 2 vols. (Cambridge, Mass., Harvard University Press, 1953); W. C. Costin, Great Britain and China, 1833–1860 (Oxford, Clarendon, 1937).

13. Hosea Ballou Morse, The International Relations of the Chinese Empire, 3 vols. (London, New York, Longmans, Green, 1910–1918), I, pp. 82–84, 89–91.
14. Fairbank, Trade and Diplomacy, p. 69.
15. Stevens, Parker, p. 73.
16. Ibid., p. 71.
17. Ibid., p. 73.
18. Ibid., pp. 75–76.
19. Ibid., p. 78.
20. Ibid., pp. 82–83.
21. Ibid., pp. 87–88.
22. Ibid., p. 92.
23. Ibid., p. 93.
24. Ibid., p. 94.
25. "The Journals of Peter Parker," 10 vols. MSS. in the Medical Library of the Yale School of Medicine, entry under June 13, 1834.
26. Morse, International Relations, I, pp. 69–74. An engaging account of life in Canton at this time is The 'Fan Kwae' at Canton Before Treaty Days, 1825–1844, by "An Old Resident" [William C. Hunter] (Shanghai and Hong Kong, Kelly and Walsh, 1911).
27. Kenneth Scott Latourette, A History of Christian Missions in China (New York, Macmillan, 1929), pp. 217–219.
28. Parker to Rev. Leonard Bacon, Singapore, Feb. 15, 1835; Bacon Family Papers, Yale Historical MSS.
29. Stevens, Parker, pp. 111–112.
30. "Parker Journals," entries under June 12 and August 15, 1835.
31. Ibid., entry under October 18, 1835.
32. Stevens, Parker, p. 117.
33. The Chinese Repository, 4 (1836), 461–462.
34. W. W. Cadbury and Mary H. Jones, At the Point of a Lancet, One Hundred Years of the Canton Hospital, 1835–1935 (Shanghai and Hong Kong, 1935); Eugene M. Blake, "Yale's First Ophthalmologist, the Reverend Peter Parker, M.D.," Yale Journal of Biology and Medicine, 3 (1931), 387–396; Samuel C. Harvey, "Peter Parker: Initiator of Modern Medicine in China," Yale Journal of Biology and Medicine, 8 (1936), 225–241. Some of the paintings of Parker's patients done by the Chinese artist Lamqua are reproduced in C. J. Bartlett, "Peter Parker, the Founder of Modern Medical Missions, a Unique Collection of Paintings," Journal of the American Medical Association, 67 (1916), 407–411. The originals of these paintings are now preserved in the Yale Medical Library; another set is in The Gordon Museum of Guy's Hospital Medical School, London.
35. The Chinese Repository, 4 (1836), 467–469.

36. "Parker Journals," entry under May 1, 1836.
37. Parker, *Statements Respecting Hospitals*, pp. 22–23.
38. S. Wells Williams to Parker, Canton, August 27, 1835; Williams Family Papers, Yale Historical MSS.
39. Stevens, *Parker*, p. 130.
40. Ibid., p. 134.
41. Chang Hsin-pao, *Commissioner Lin and the Opium War* (Cambridge, Mass., Harvard University Press, 1964). Lengthy translations from Lin's diary are given in Arthur Waley, *The Opium War Through Chinese Eyes* (New York, Macmillan, 1958).
42. Stevens, *Parker*, p. 167.
43. Ibid., p. 172.
44. *The Chinese Repository*, 8 (1840), 634–637.
45. Chang Hsin-pao, *Commissioner Lin*, p. 137.
46. Immanuel Hsü, *China's Entrance into the Family of Nations, the Diplomatic Phase, 1858–1880* (Cambridge, Mass., Harvard University Press, 1960), pp. 123–124.
47. S. Wells Williams to Parker, August 1, 1839; Williams Family Papers, Yale Historical MSS.
48. Stevens, *Parker*, p. 174.
49. Ibid., p. 175.
50. "Parker Journals," entry under June 3, 1840.
51. Stevens, *Parker*, p. 180.
52. Ibid., p. 190.
53. Ibid., pp. 194–197.
54. Ibid., p. 197.
55. Ibid., p. 201.
56. Ibid., p. 229.
57. Treaty terms in Morse, *International Relations*, I, pp. 299–301; cf. also Teng Ssu-yü, *Chang Hsi and the Treaty of Nanking* (Chicago, University of Chicago Press, 1944).
58. An extremely good account of events around Canton in this period is Frederic Wakeman, Jr., *Strangers at the Gate, Social Disorder in South China, 1839–1860* (Berkeley and Los Angeles, University of California Press, 1966). Quotation from ibid., p. 61.
59. Stevens, *Parker*, p. 235.
60. Ibid., pp. 239–240.
61. Tong Te-kong, *United States Diplomacy in China, 1844–1860* (Seattle, University of Washington Press, 1964), pp. 32–33. Fairbank, *Trade and Diplomacy*, pp. 165–166.
62. Stevens, *Parker*, p. 252.
63. Tong, *U.S. Diplomacy*, pp. 1–5.
64. Stevens, *Parker*, p. 259.
65. S. Wells Williams to Parker, Macao, February 26, 1829 [sic.? 1839]; Williams Family Papers, Yale Historical MSS.
66. Stevens, *Parker*, p. 261.

67. Ibid., p. 265.
68. Morse, *International Relations*, I, p. 388. Tong, *U.S. Diplomacy*, pp. 90, 115–116.
69. Stevens, *Parker*, p. 277.
70. Edward H. Hume, "Peter Parker and the Introduction of Anesthesia into China," *Journal of the History of Medicine*, 1 (1946), 670–674.
71. Stevens, *Parker*, p. 287.
72. Ibid., p. 299.
73. Tong, *U.S. Diplomacy*, p. 174.
74. Stevens, *Parker*, p. 305.
75. Morse, *International Relations*, I, pp. 417, 684. Tong, *U.S. Diplomacy*, pp. 173–181.
76. Eldon Griffin, *Clippers and Consuls: American Consular and Commercial Relations with Eastern Asia, 1845–1860* (Ann Arbor, Edwards Brothers, 1938), pp. 128–133; Tong, *U.S. Diplomacy*, pp. 102–103, 142, n. 93.
77. Earl Swisher, *China's Management of the American Barbarians, 1841–1861* (New Haven, Yale University Press, 1953), pp. 314, 323, 316–317.
78. Morse, *International Relations*, I, p. 416, n. 71.
79. Ibid., p. 433.
80. Tyler Dennett, *Americans in Eastern Asia: a Critical Study of the Policy of the United States with reference to China, Japan and Korea in the Nineteenth Century* (New York, Macmillan, 1922), p. 286.
81. Ibid., pp. 279–291; Tong, *U.S. Diplomacy*, pp. 193–207.
82. Latourette, *Christian Missions*, p. 453. An interesting account of medical mission development in Shanghai during this period is William Lockhart, *The Medical Missionary in China: a Narrative of Twenty Years' Experience* (London, Hurst and Blackett, 1861).
83. Stevens, *Parker*, p. 144.

3. Ward and Gordon: *Glorious Days of Looting*

1. Mary Harrod Northend, *Memories of Old Salem, Drawn from the Letters of a Great-Grandmother* (New York, Moffatt, Yard, 1917), p. 50.
2. Frederick Wells Williams, *Anson Burlingame and the First Chinese Mission to Foreign Powers* (New York, Scribner, 1912), p. 44.
3. Franz Michael in collaboration with Chang Chung-li, *The Taiping Rebellion, History and Documents*, vol. I, *History* (Seattle and London, University of Washington Press, 1966). Miyazaki Ichisada, "The Nature of Taiping Rebellion," *Acta Asiatica*, 8 (1965), 1–39.
4. Theodore Hamberg, *The Visions of Hung-Siu-tshuen, and Origin of*

the *Kwang-si Insurrection* (Hong Kong, China Mail Office, 1854), p. 12.

5. Michael, *Taiping*, Part II.
6. Charles Macfarlane, *The Chinese Revolution, With Details of the Habits, Manners and Customs of China and the Chinese* (London, Routledge, 1853), p. 224.
7. Father Brouillon, *Mémoire sur l'état actuel de la mission de Kiangnan (1842–1855) suivi de lettres relatives à l'insurrection (1851–1855)* (Paris, 1855), pp. 272, 266, 314.
8. Dona Torr, ed., *Marx on China 1853–1860: Articles from the New York Daily Tribune* (London, Lawrence and Wishart, 1951), p. 50.
9. Mary C. Wright, *The Last Stand of Chinese Conservatism; The T'ung-chih Restoration, 1862–1874* (Palo Alto, Stanford University Press, 1957); Stanley Spector, *Li Hung-chang and the Huai Army: A Study in Nineteenth-Century Chinese Regionalism* (Seattle, University of Washington Press, 1964); Chiang Siang-tseh, *The Nien Rebellion* (Seattle, University of Washington Press, 1954); Chu Wen-djang, *The Moslem Rebellion in Northwest China, 1862–1878: A Study of Government Minority Policy* (The Hague, Mouton, 1965).
10. Robert S. Rantoul, *Frederick Townsend Ward* (Historical Collections of the Essex Institute, vol. XLIV, 1908), p. 17.
11. Rantoul, *Ward*, p. 29.
12. E. A. Lyster, ed., *With Gordon in China; Letters from Thomas Lyster, Lieutenant Royal Engineers* (London, Fisher Unwin, 1891), p. 79.
13. Holger Cahill, *A Yankee Adventurer, The Story of Ward and the Taiping Rebellion* (New York, Macaulay, 1930), p. 45.
14. Hosea Ballou Morse, *The International Relations of the Chinese Empire*, 3 vols. (London, New York, Longmans, Green, 1910–1918), II, p. 71, n. 27.
15. Ibid.
16. Michael, *Taiping*, Part V.
17. Admiral Hope's policies and the changes in attitudes are discussed in John S. Gregory, "British Intervention Against the Taiping Rebellion," *Journal of Asian Studies*, 19 (1959), 11–24. Quotation, p. 18.
18. Rantoul, *Ward*, p. 33. Cahill, *Ward*, p. 147.
19. Cahill, *Ward*, p. 148.
20. Lin-le [A. F. Lindley], *Ti-ping Tien-kwoh; The History of the Ti-ping Revolution, Including a Narrative of the Author's Personal Adventures*, 2 vols. (London, Day, 1866), II, p. 450.
21. Gregory, "British Intervention," p. 15.
22. J. C. Cheng, *Chinese Sources for the Taiping Rebellion, 1850–1864* (Hong Kong, Hong Kong University Press, 1963), pp. 95–96.
23. Rantoul, *Ward*, pp. 17 and 51.

24. Samuel Mossman, *General Gordon's Private Diary of his Exploits in China* (London, Sampson Low, 1885), pp. 86–87.
25. Edward Forester [sic], "Personal Recollections of the Tai-ping Rebellion," *The Cosmopolitan*, 22 (1896–97), 37.
26. Ibid., p. 214.
27. Cited in Lin-le, *Ti-ping*, II, pp. 452–453.
28. Cited ibid., p. 511.
29. Cited ibid., p. 507.
30. This was reported on February 25, 1862. Cf. *Ch'ou-pan i-wu shih-mo*, T'ung-chih chuan 4, pp. 25–27.
31. Rantoul, *Ward*, p. 37.
32. Morse, *International Relations*, II, p. 72, n. 28.
33. Cheng, *Chinese Sources*, p. 94.
34. Ibid., p. 103.
35. Rantoul, *Ward*, pp. 55–56.
36. Cheng, *Chinese Sources*, p. 101.
37. Forester, "Personal Recollections," p. 214.
38. Ibid., p. 216. Hallett Abend, *The God from the West, A Biography of Frederick Townsend Ward* (Garden City, N.Y., Doubleday, 1947), p. 245 citing Rev. W. B. Burke.
39. *Letters from Thomas Lyster*, p. 112.
40. Demetrius C. Boulger, *The Life of Gordon*, 2 vols. (London, Fisher Unwin, 1896), I, p. 46. Background on the allied expedition is in Morse, *International Relations*, I, pp. 589–617.
41. Gordon to Augusta, "Camp near Pekin," Nov. 2, 1860; British Museum Manscripts, Gordon Papers, Moffitt Collection, 51291/14.
42. Boulger, *Gordon*, I, p. 45.
43. Ibid., I, p. 31.
44. Ibid., I, pp. 36–37.
45. Anthony Nutting, *Gordon of Khartoum, Martyr and Misfit* (New York, Potter, 1966), p. 12.
46. Boulger, *Gordon*, I, p. 43.
47. Gordon to Augusta, Tientsin, Oct. 11, 1861, and Tientsin, Dec. 6, 1861, Moffitt Collection, 51291/21, 22.
48. Nutting, *Gordon*, p. 79.
49. Boulger, *Gordon*, I, p. 61.
50. Ibid., I, p. 53.
51. Ibid., I, pp. 53–54.
52. Cited in Raymond Dawson, *The Chinese Chameleon: An Analysis of European Conceptions of Chinese Civilization* (London, Oxford University Press, 1967), p. 133.
53. Boulger, *Gordon*, I, p. 52.
54. Ibid., I, pp. 53 and 54.
55. Stanley Lane-Poole, *The Life of Sir Harry Parkes, K.C.B., G.C.M.G., Sometime Her Majesty's Minister to China and Japan*, 2 vols. (London, Macmillan, 1894), I, p. 500.

56. Nutting, *Gordon*, p. 84.
57. Ibid., p. 318.
58. Boulger, *Gordon*, I, pp. 57-58.
59. Cheng, *Chinese Sources*, p. 107.
60. Ibid., p. 109.
61. Morse, *International Relations*, II, pp. 91-92.
62. Boulger, *Gordon*, I, p. 79.
63. Ibid., I, pp. 78-79.
64. Andrew Wilson, *The "Ever-Victorious Army," A History of the Chinese Campaign under Lt.-Col. C. G. Gordon, C.B., R.E., and of the Suppression of the Tai-Ping Rebellion* (Edinburgh and London, William Blackwood and Sons, 1868), p. 127.
65. Jenny Lewis, "The Gordon Papers," *The British Museum Quarterly*, 28 (1964), 75-81. Quotation p. 77.
66. Wilson, *Ever-Victorious Army*, p. 144.
67. Mossman, *Gordon's Diary*, p. 183.
68. A. Egmont Hake, *The Story of Chinese Gordon* (New York, Worthington, 1884), p. 63.
69. Boulger, *Gordon*, I, p. 114.
70. Cheng, *Chinese Sources*, p. 111.
71. Ibid., p. 112.
72. Nutting, *Gordon*, pp. 41-42.
73. Ibid., p. 41.
74. Mossman, *Gordon's Diary*, p. 191.
75. Bernard M. Allen, *Gordon in China* (London, Macmillan, 1933), p. 105.
76. Cheng, *Chinese Sources*, p. 112.
77. Ibid., p. 120.
78. Mossman, *Gordon's Diary*, pp. 219-220.
79. Hake, *Chinese Gordon*, p. 84.
80. Lewis, "Gordon Papers," 77-78.
81. Boulger, *Gordon*, I, p. 107.
82. Ibid., p. 107.
83. Ibid., pp. 111-112.
84. Cheng, *Chinese Sources*, p. 129.
85. Hake, *Chinese Gordon*, p. 123.
86. Nutting, *Gordon*, p. 63.
87. Hake, *Chinese Gordon*, p. 146.
88. Cheng, *Chinese Sources*, pp. 131 and 132.
89. Ibid., p. 135.
90. Lane-Poole, *Parkes*, I. p. 498.
91. Nutting, *Gordon*, pp. 70-71.
92. Boulger, *Gordon*, p. 120.
93. Lewis, "Gordon Papers," p. 78.
94. Nutting, *Gordon*, p. 70.
95. Hake, *Chinese Gordon*, p. 153.

96. Nutting, *Gordon*, pp. 77–78.
97. Lane-Poole, *Parkes*, I, p. 501.
98. Boulger, *Gordon*, I, p. 124. For Gordon's brief return to China, cf. Immanuel C. Y. Hsü, "Gordon in China, 1880," *Pacific Historical Review*, 33 (1964), 147–166.

4. Lay and Hart: *Power, Patronage, Pay*

1. Robert Hart to W. Williams, Peking, Feb. 8, 1869; Williams Family Papers, Yale Historical MSS.
2. Paul King, *In the Chinese Customs Service: A Personal Record of Forty-seven Years* (London, Fisher Unwin, 1924), p. 246.
3. W. A. P. Martin, *A Cycle of Cathay, Or China, South and North, With Personal Reminiscences* (Edinburgh, and London, Anderson and Ferrier, 1896), p. 415.
4. Stanley F. Wright, *Hart and the Chinese Customs* (Belfast, Mullan, 1950), p. 221, n. 6; Juliet Bredon, *Sir Robert Hart: The Romance of a Great Career* (New York, Dutton, 1909), p. 25.
5. Wright, *Hart*, p. 167.
6. Bredon, *Hart*, p. 19.
7. Martin, *Cycle*, pp. 425–426.
8. Wright, *Hart*, p. 178, n. 40.
9. Bredon, *Hart*, pp. 24–25.
10. Jacob J. Gerson, "Horatio Nelson Lay, His Role in British Relations with China, 1849–1865" (Ph.D. dissertation, University of London, 1967), pp. 41, 42.
11. Ibid., pp. 57, 60.
12. Ibid., p. 105.
13. Ibid., p. 118.
14. Andrew Wilson, *The "Ever-Victorious Army," A History of the Chinese Campaign under Lt.-Col. C. G. Gordon, C.B., R.E., And of the Suppression of the Tai-Ping Rebellion* (Edinburgh and London, Blackwood, 1868), pp. 309–310.
15. Wright, *Hart*, pp. 111–112.
16. Earl Swisher, *China's Management of the American Barbarians: A Study of Sino-American Relations, 1841–1861, With Documents* (New Haven, Conn., Far Eastern Publications, 1951), p. 522.
17. Gerson, *Lay*, p. 158.
18. Wright, *Hart*, pp. 112–113.
19. Developments discussed in Immanuel C. Y. Hsü, *China's Entrance into the Family of Nations: The Diplomatic Phase, 1858–1880* (Cambridge, Mass., Harvard University Press, 1960).
20. Gerson, *Lay*, p. 190.
21. Hosea Ballou Morse, *The International Relations of the Chinese*

Empire, 3 vols. (London, New York, Longmans, Green, 1910–1918), I, p. 521.
22. Gerson, *Lay*, p. 215.
23. Swisher, *China's Management*, p. 485.
24. Hsü, *China's Entrance*, p. 52.
25. Gerson, *Lay*, p. 214, n. 105.
26. Hsü, *China's Entrance*, pp. 40–42.
27. Swisher, *China's Management*, p. 505.
28. Wright, *Hart*, p. 155, n. 50. The Chinese formally ratified this title in January 1861.
29. Ibid., p. 240.
30. Swisher, *China's Management*, p. 522.
31. Gerson, *Lay*, p. 484.
32. Wright, *Hart*, pp. 157–158, n. 118.
33. Ibid., p. 152.
34. Ibid., p. 221, n. 6.
35. Gerson, *Lay*, p. 507.
36. John L. Rawlinson, "The Lay-Osborn Flotilla: Its Development and Significance," *Papers on China*, vol. 4, Harvard University, April 1950, pp. 58–93. Quotation, p. 71.
37. Gerson, *Lay*, p. 505.
38. Ibid., p. 339.
39. Morse, *International Relations*, II, p. 37.
40. Rawlinson, "Lay-Osborn," p. 68.
41. Morse, *International Relations*, II, p. 46.
42. Ibid., p. 45.
43. Bernard M. Allen, *Gordon in China* (London, Macmillan, 1933), p. 124.
44. Gerson, *Lay*, p. 533.
45. Wright, *Hart*, p. 287, n. 3.
46. Ibid., pp. 261–262.
47. King, *Customs Service*, p. 246.
48. Martin, *Cycle*, p. 417.
49. Ibid., p. 416.
50. Wright, *Hart*, p. 286; p. 350, n. 28.
51. Ibid., pp. 268–269.
52. Charles Drage, *Servants of the Dragon Throne, Being the Lives of Edward and Cecil Bowra* (London, Dawnay, 1966), pp. 67–68.
53. Wright, *Hart*, p. 269.
54. Ibid., p. 262.
55. Ibid., p. 822.
56. Ibid., p. 601.
57. Ibid., p. 788, n. 128.
58. Ibid., p. 789, n. 130.
59. Ibid., pp. 289–290, n. 30.
60. Martin, *Cycle*, p. 424.

61. Wright, *Hart*, p. 541.
62. Ibid., pp. 857–858.
63. Ibid., p. 858.
64. Ibid., p. 370.
65. Ibid., p. 395.
66. Ibid., pp. 167–168.
67. Ibid., p. 601; p. 788, n. 129.
68. Ibid., p. 833.
69. Ibid., p. 538.
70. Ibid., p. 859.
71. Bredon, *Hart*, pp. 157–158.
72. Martin, *Cycle*, p. 417.
73. Bredon, *Hart*, p. 118.
74. King, *Customs Service*, p. 238.
75. Bredon, *Hart*, p. 188.
76. Wright, *Hart*, p. 651.
77. Ibid., p. 711, for both Quotations.
78. Ibid., p. 730.
79. For bibliography on the Boxer Rebellion cf. notes 86 and 88 to Chapter 5 below.
80. Wright, *Hart*, p. 737.
81. Bredon, *Hart*, p. 216.
82. Robert Hart, *"These from the Land of Sinim." Essays on the Chinese Question* (London, Chapman and Hall, 1901), pp. 52, 54–55.
83. Ibid., p. 59.
84. Bredon, *Hart*, pp. 248–249.
85. Wright, *Hart*, p. 864.

5. Martin and Fryer: *Trimming the Lamps*

1. On the examination system, cf. Ho Ping-ti, *The Ladder of Success in Imperial China, Aspects of Social Mobility, 1368–1911* (New York, Columbia University Press, 1962); and Chang Chung-li, *The Chinese Gentry, Studies on their Role in Nineteenth-Century Chinese Society* (Seattle, University of Washington Press, 1955).
2. Peter Duus, "Science and Salvation in China: The Life and Work of W. A. P. Martin (1827–1916)," in Kwang-ching Liu, ed., *American Missionaries in China, Papers from Harvard Seminars* (Cambridge, Mass., Harvard University East Asian Research Center, 1966), pp. 11–14.
3. W. A. P. Martin, *A Cycle of Cathay, or China, South and North, With Personal Reminiscences* (Edinburgh and London, Anderson and Ferrier, 1896), p. 24.

4. Ibid., pp. 54–55.
5. Ibid., pp. 55–56.
6. Ibid., p. 58.
7. Duus, *Martin,* pp. 17–19.
8. Ibid., pp. 21–24.
9. W. A. P. Martin, *Hanlin Papers, or Essays on the Intellectual Life of the Chinese* (London, Trübner, 1880), pp. 359–360.
10. W. A. P. Martin, *The Awakening of China* (London, Hodder and Stoughton, 1907), p. 138.
11. Immanuel C. Y. Hsü, *China's Entrance into the Family of Nations, The Diplomatic Phase, 1858–1880* (Cambridge, Mass., Harvard University Press, 1960), p. 126.
12. Ibid., p. 128.
13. Ssu-yü Teng and John K. Fairbank, *China's Response to the West, A Documentary Survey, 1839–1923* (Cambridge, Mass., Harvard University Press, 1954), p. 98.
14. Hsü, *China's Entrance,* pp. 134–135.
15. Ibid., p. 136; Martin, *Cycle,* p. 297; Duus, *Martin,* p. 25.
16. Teng and Fairbank, *China's Response,* p. 51.
17. Ibid., p. 76.
18. Hosea Ballou Morse, *The International Relations of the Chinese Empire,* 3 vols. (London, New York, Longmans, Green, 1910–1918), III, p. 473. On the founding of the school, cf. Knight Biggerstaff, *The Earliest Modern Government Schools in China* (Ithaca, New York, Cornell University Press, 1961), pp. 94–107.
19. Martin, *Cycle,* p. 298.
20. Duus, *Martin,* p. 26.
21. Martin, *Cycle,* p. 293.
22. Biggerstaff, *Government Schools,* pp. 119–120, n. 47; 146.
23. Martin, *Hanlin Papers,* p. 298.
24. Ibid., p. 69; Morse, *International Relations,* III, p. 471.
25. Biggerstaff, *Government Schools,* pp. 127–128.
26. Martin to William Dwight Whitney, Dec. 4, 1874; W. D. Whitney Collection, Yale Historical MSS.
27. Martin, *Cycle,* p. 300.
28. Adrian Arthur Bennett, "John Fryer: The Introduction of Western Science and Technology into Nineteenth Century China" (Master's thesis University of California at Berkeley, 1966), p. 7. This thesis has been revised for publication as No. 24 in Harvard's East Asian Monograph Series. Citations are to the original thesis, which has slightly fuller quotations on Fryer's early life.
29. Ibid., p. 6. "The Letter Journals of John Fryer" (4 vols. of MSS, Bancroft Library of the University of California at Berkeley), Fryer to Cousin Susy, July 11, 1868.
30. Bennett, *Fryer,* p. 10.
31. Ibid., p. 8.

32. "Fryer Letters," to Cousin Susy, July 11, 1868.
33. Rhoads Murphey, *Shanghai, Key to Modern China* (Cambridge, Mass, Harvard University Press, 1953).
34. "Fryer Letters," to Carrman (?), Mar. 13, 1868.
35. Ibid., to Parents, Mar. 9, 1867.
36. Ibid., to Brother, Nov. 23, 1867.
37. Ibid., to Cousin Susy, Mar, 1867; to Cousin Susy, July 18, 1867; and to Sister, Jan. 10. 1867 [sic 1868].
38. Ibid., to Brown, Mar. 1, 1867; and to Stewart, Mar. 4. 1867.
39. Ibid., to Gamwell, July 5, 1867.
40. Ibid., to Gamwell, Dec. 1865; July 5, 1867; June 6, 1867.
41. Ibid., to Brown, Mar. 13, 1867.
42. Ibid., to Brown, Mar. 13, 1867; to "Dear old friend," Good Friday, 1867; to Cousin Susy, Mar., 1867.
43. Ibid., to Kennett, Mar. 20, 1867.
44. Ibid., to Cousin Susy, Mar., 1867.
45. Ibid., to Cousin Susy, July 18, 1867.
46. Ibid., to Sister, Jan. 10, 1867 [sic 1868].
47. Bennett, *Fryer*, p. 24; "Fryer Letters," to Parents, Mar. 9, 1867.
48. Bennett, *Fryer*, pp. 25–27.
49. "Fryer Letters," to Tootal, Apr. 28, 1868.
50. For accounts of the Arsenal cf. John Fryer, "Science in China," *Nature*, 24 (May–Oct. 1881), 9–11; Gideon Chen, *Tseng Kuo-fan, Pioneer Promoter of the Steamship in China*, (Peiping, Yenching University, 1935); Biggerstaff, *Government Schools*, pp. 154–199.
51. Teng and Fairbank, *China's Response*, p. 62.
52. Ibid., p. 65.
53. Ibid., p. 71.
54. Ibid., p. 73.
55. "Fryer Letters," to Muirhead, Dec. 1, 1867. Feng was probably Feng Chun-kuang, Shanghai Prefect.
56. Ibid., to Cousin Susy, July 11, 1868.
57. Ibid., to Father and Sister, May 9, 1868.
58. Ibid., to Bishop Williams, Jan. 22, 1868.
59. Ibid., to Cousin Susy, July 11, 1868; to Brother, Mar. 15, 1870.
60. Ibid., to Cousin Susy, July 11, 1868.
61. Ibid., to Brother, Sept. 28, 1869.
62. Ibid., to Wherry, May 4, 1869.
63. Ibid., to Kennett, June 3, 1869.
64. Ibid., to Brother, Aug. 28, 1869, and to Father and Mother [of Anna], Sept. 28, 1869.
65. A detailed and graphic account of this anti-Christian background is in Paul A. Cohen, *China and Christianity: The Missionary Movement and the Growth of Chinese Anti-foreignism, 1860–1870* (Cambridge, Mass., Harvard University Press, 1963).
66. Martin, *Cycle*, p. 445.

67. "Fryer Letters," to Brother, Aug. 11, 1870.
68. Ibid., to Brother, Mar. 15, 1870.
69. Ibid., to Brother, Mar. 15, 1870, and to Cousin Susy, July 11, 1868.
70. Ibid., to Brother, July 15, 1869.
71. Ibid., to Brother, Sept. 28, 1869.
72. Ibid., to Aunt Maria, Nov. 8, 1870.
73. Bennett, *Fryer*, pp. 55–59. The appendices to Bennett's work give a full listing and analysis of all books translated by Fryer.
74. Ibid., p. 65. Fryer, "Science in China," *Nature*, 24 (1881), p. 57.
75. Fryer, "Science in China," p. 56.
76. Knight Biggerstaff, "Shanghai Polytechnic Institution and Reading Room: An Attempt to Introduce Western Science and Technology to the Chinese," *Pacific Historical Review*, 25 (1956), 127–149. Quotation, p. 137.
77. Ibid., p. 141.
78. Ibid., pp. 143–145. Bennett, *Fryer*, p. 80.
79. "The Educational Association of China," *The Chinese Recorder*, 23 (1892), 30–36.
80. The best analysis of "official supervision and merchant management" is Albert Feuerwerker, *China's Early Industrialization: Sheng Hsuan-huai (1844–1916) and Mandarin Enterprise* (Cambridge, Mass., Harvard University Press, 1958). Other "self-strengtheners" are discussed by Samuel Chu, *Reformer in Modern China, Chang Chien, 1853–1926* (New York, Columbia University Press, 1965); C. John Stanley, *Late Ch'ing Finance: Hu Kuang-yung as an Innovator* (Cambridge, Mass., Harvard University Press, 1961); Gideon Chen, *Tso Tsung T'ang, Pioneer Promoter of the Modern Dockyard and the Woolen Mill in China* (Peiping, Yenching University, 1938). Ch'ing finance is analyzed in Frank H. H. King, *Money and Monetary Policy in China, 1845–1895* (Cambridge, Mass., Harvard University Press, 1965).
81. Teng and Fairbank, *China's Response*, pp. 159–160.
82. Fryer, "Science in China," p. 56.
83. "Fryer Letters," to Brother, Mar. 15, 1870.
84. Fryer, "Science in China," p. 11. (Fryer spelt Schall as Schaal.)
85. Martin, *Cycle*, p. 411.
86. Victor Purcell, *The Boxer Uprising, A Background Study* (Cambridge, Cambridge University Press, 1963), p. 294.
87. Ibid., p. 224.
88. On the Boxers and the siege, cf. also Chester C. Tan, *The Boxer Catastrophe* (New York, Columbia University Press, 1955); and Peter Fleming, *The Siege at Peking* (New York, Harper, 1959).
89. W. A. P. Martin, *The Siege in Peking: China Against the World* (New York, Revell, 1900), pp. 96–97.
90. Martin, *Awakening*, p. 177n.
91. Martin, *Siege*, p. 15.

92. Ibid., pp. 20–23, 146–147.
93. Ibid., pp. 154–156.
94. Martin, *Awakening*, p. 280.
95. Martin, *Siege*, p. 161.

6. Edward Hume: *Yale for China*

1. Reuben Holden, *Yale-in-China: The Mainland, 1901–1951* (New Haven, The Yale-in-China Association, 1964), pp. 11–12.
2. Ibid., p. 9.
3. Ibid., p. 23.
4. Ibid., p. 78.
5. Edmund S. Wehrle, *Britain, China, and the Antimissionary Riots, 1891–1900* (Minneapolis, University of Minnesota Press, 1966), p. 66.
6. Despatches from United States Consuls in Hankow, 1861–1906 (file microcopies of records in the National Archives, no. 107), William Martin, Consul General, Hankow, Feb. 8, 1906, p. 2.
7. United States Department of State, Records Relating to the Internal Affairs of China, 1910–1929; 893.00/847.
8. A detailed study of Hunan in this period is Charlton M. Lewis, "The Opening of Hunan: Reform and Revolution in a Chinese Province, 1895–1907" (Ph.D. dissertation, University of California at Berkeley, 1965).
9. Hsüeh Chun-tu, *Huang Hsing and the Chinese Revolution* (Palo Alto, Stanford University Press, 1961), p. 18.
10. Despatches Hankow 1861–1906, William Martin, Hankow, Feb. 8, 1906, p. 5.
11. Ibid., William Martin, Hankow, Mar. 7, 1906, p. 5.
12. Holden, *Yale-in-China*, pp. 30–31.
13. Ibid., p. 28
14. Ibid., p. 32.
15. Ibid., p. 34.
16. Ibid., pp. 49 and 103.
17. Edward H. Hume, *Doctors East Doctors West, An American Physician's Life in China* (New York, Norton, 1946), pp. 20–21.
18. Yale-in-China Archives, Sterling Memorial Library, New Haven, Conn.; enclosure in Hume to A. C. Williams, Kuling, Mar. 27, 1906.
19. Ibid., Hume to A. C. Williams, Kuling, Dec. 27, 1905.
20. Ibid., Hume to E. B. Reed, Kuling, Sept. 11, 1905.
21. Edgar Snow, *Red Star over China* (New York, Grove, 1961), p. 134.
22. Yale-in-China Archives, Hume to E. B. Reed, Kuling, Sept. 11, 1905.
23. William Reeves, Jr., "Sino-American Cooperation in Medicine: The Origins of Hsiang-Ya (1902–1914)," in Liu Kwang-ching, ed.,

312   NOTES TO PP. 161–183

American Missionaries in China, Papers from Harvard Seminars (Cambridge, Mass., East Asian Research Center, Harvard University), p. 139.
24. Hume, *Doctors East*, pp. 40–48; John 5, 2–9.
25. Hume, *Doctors East*, p. 210.
26. Ibid., p. 187.
27. Ibid., pp. 132–140.
28. Department of State, 893.00/380, pp. 4–5.
29. Hume, *Doctors East*, p. 235.
30. On Sun Yat-sen and the background of the revolution cf. Lyon Sharman, *Sun Yat-sen, His Life and Its Meaning, A Critical Biography* (New York, Day, 1934); Michael Gasster, "Currents of Thought in the T'ung-Meng-Hui" (Ann Arbor, University Microfilms, 1964); Shelley Hsien Cheng, "The T'ung-Meng-Hui: Its Organization, Leadership and Finances, 1905–1912" (Ann Arbor, University Microfilms, 1964); Hsüeh, *Huang Hsing*. A collection of essays on the revolution, edited by Mary Wright, is now being prepared for publication by Yale University Press.
31. Edward Hume, "The Chinese Rebellion and Yale's Educational Opportunity," *Yale Alumni Weekly, 21* (1911–12), 181.
32. Hume, *Doctors Last*, p. 177.
33. Reeves, "Hsiang-ya," p. 153.
34. Ibid., p. 151.
35. Ibid., p. 152.
36. Ibid., p. 154.
37. Ibid., p. 158.
38. Lotta Carswell Hume, *Drama at the Doctor's Gate: The Story of Doctor Edward Hume of Yale-in-China* (New Haven, The Yale-in-China Association, 1961), p. 123.
39. Department of State, 893.00/1576. Consul Greene discusses arrangements with the Governor to turn off current if looting starts, in 1913.
40. An excellent discussion of the warlord world is in the first chapter of James E. Sheridan, *Chinese Warlord: The Career of Feng Yü-hsiang* (Palo Alto, Stanford University Press, 1966); cf. also Jerome Ch'en, *Yuan Shih-k'ai (1859–1916)* (Palo Alto, Stanford University Press, 1961).
41. Two good accounts of Hunan in this period are "Political Conditions in Hunan, 1911–1923," prepared by George Atcheson and submitted by Consul C. D. Meinhardt in Department of State 893.00/5394, 5410, and 5665; and "General Historical Sketch of Political Conditions in the Hankow Consular District from the Revolution of 1911 to March 1925," submitted by Consul J. C. Huston, ibid., 893.00/6206, 153 pp. The quotation is from 893.00/5665, p. 8.
42. Department of State, 893.00/5394, p. 11.

43. Hume, *Doctors East*, p. 230; Department of State, 893.00/1478, p. 9.
44. Hume, *Doctors East*, p. 242.
45. Ibid., p. 253.
46. A very detailed account of these developments is Chow Tse-tsung, *The May Fourth Movement: Intellectual Revolution in Modern China* (Cambridge, Mass., Harvard University Press, 1964).
47. Snow, *Red Star*, p. 139.
48. Ibid., p. 142.
49. Ibid., pp. 147–148.
50. Jerome Ch'en, *Mao and the Chinese Revolution* (New York, Oxford University Press, Galaxy Books, 1967), pp. 64, 72; Stuart Schram, *Mao Tse-tung* (New York, Simon and Schuster, 1967), p. 55.
51. Holden, *Yale-in-China*, p. 81.
52. Ibid., p. 79.
53. Yale-in-China Archives, Hume to Palmer Bevis, Changsha, Dec. 13 and Dec. 24, 1924; Suiwo en route to Shanghai, Jan. 8, 1925.
54. Ibid., Bevis to Wilcox, New Haven, July 18, 1925.
55. Ibid., Hume to Trustees, Changsha, Oct. 23, 1925.
56. Ibid., Hume to Bevis, Changsha, Dec. 24, 1924, and Hong Kong, Jan. 22, 1925.
57. Holden, *Yale-in-China*, pp. 118–122, 134–135.
58. Yale-in-China Archives, Hume to Bevis, Shanghai, Jan. 10, 1925.
59. Ibid., Hume to F. W. Williams, Shanghai, Jan. 19, 1925; Hume to Bevis, Changsha, May 21, 1925.
60. Ibid., Hume to Bevis, Hankow, June 25, 1925, and Changsha, June 21, 1925.
61. Ibid., Hume to Anson Phelps Stokes, Changsha, Feb. 6, 1925, to Williams, Feb. 16, 1925, to Stokes, Apr. 24, 1925.
62. Ibid., Hume to Bevis, Changsha, Mar. 25, 1925.
63. Ibid., Hume to Bevis, Changsha, Mar. 28, and Apr. 7, 1925.
64. Hume, *Doctors East*, p. 264.
65. Yale-in-China Archives, Changsha, June 9, 1925; Holden, *Yale-in-China*, pp. 153–155.
66. *New York Times*, Monday Oct. 26, 1925, p. 2, col. 6.
67. Department of State, 893.00/5391, pp. 1–5.
68. Ibid., 893.00/5665, pp. 10–11. The original has countries [sic] for counties.
69. Ibid., 893.00/6480.
70. Ibid., 893.00/5410, p. 3; 893.00/6206, p. 45; 893.00/6273.
71. Yale-in-China Archives, Hume to Bevis, Shanghai, May 17, 1925 with enclosure by M. K. Hsiao; Hume to Williams, Changsha, Feb. 16, 1925.
72. Ibid., Edwin Harvey to Bevis, Changsha, Nov. 15, 1926.
73. Ibid., Dr. O. H. Robertson to Secretary Yale-in-China, Peking, Mar. 20, 1925.

74. Ibid., Hume to Bevis, Changsha, May 26, 1925.
75. Ibid., Hume to Henry Houghton, Changsha, Sept. 25, 1924; Hume to Bevis, Changsha, Feb. 23, 1925.
76. Ibid., Hume to Houghton, Changsha, Sept. 25, 1924; to Williams, Oct. 16, 1924; to Bevis, Oct. 23, 1924.
77. Ibid., Hume to Bevis, Changsha, May 21, 1925; Dec. 24, 1924; June 9, 1925.
78. Ibid., Hume to Bevis, Changsha, Dec. 9, 1924.
79. Ibid., Hume to Bevis, Changsha, June 21, 1925.
80. Ibid., Hume to Bevis, Changsha, Dec. 24, 1924; Hong Kong, Jan. 22, 1925.
81. Ibid., Hume to Stokes, en route Hong Kong to Changsha, Jan. 31, 1925.
82. Receipt acknowledged in Ibid., Hume to Bevis, Changsha, Mar. 30, 1925. A good summary of Hume's various suggestions is in Hume to Bevis, "Between Shanghai and Hankow," Feb. 4, 1925.
83. Ibid., Hume to Bevis, Shanghai, May 17, 1925.
84. Ibid., Hume to Trustees, New Haven, June 24, 1926.
85. Ibid., Hume to Bevis, New York, Jan. 3, 1927.
86. Holden, *Yale-in-China*, pp. 156–162; Yale-in-China Archives, Harvey to Bevis, Feb. 22, 1927.
87. Hume, *Doctors East*, p. 272; Lotta Hume, *Drama*, pp. 149–150. In 1928 Yale-in-China joined with Boone College, the Wesleyan Mission, the London Mission, Huping College and Lutheran College to form Hua-chung University in Wuhan, agreeing to abide by the registration laws of the new Nationalist government. From 1929 onward the Hziang-ya hospital, the Nursing School and the Medical College were gradually resurrected under Chinese direction and performed considerable service. Hume was made a Yale-in-China trustee. Details are in Holden, *Yale-in-China*.
88. Yale-in-China Archives, Harvey to Ralph, Changsha, Nov. 6, 1926.
89. Ibid., Hail, Harvey, and Leavens to "the Committee considering Dr. Hume's resignation," Changsha, Sept. 30, 1926.

7. Mikhail Borodin: *Life in the Sun*

1. Vincent Sheean, "Some People from Canton," *Asia*, 27 (Oct. 1927), 812.
2. Vera Vladimirovna Vishniakova-Akimova, *Dva Goda v Vosstavshem Kitaye, 1925–1927* [Two Years' Service in China] (Moscow, 1965), pp. 175–177; *New York Times*, Sept. 3, 1953, p. 21, obituary of Borodin; Conrad Brandt, *Stalin's Failure in China* (Cambridge, Mass., Harvard University Press, 1958), pp. 195–196n.
3. James W. Hulse, *The Forming of the Communist International* (Palo Alto, Stanford University Press, 1964); Jane Degras, ed., *The*

Communist International, 1919–1943, vol. I, "1919–1922" (Oxford University Press, 1956); Hugh Seton-Watson, *From Lenin to Khrushchev: The History of World Communism* (New York, Praeger, 1960), pp. 68–77.

4. Allen S. Whiting, *Soviet Policies in China, 1917–1924* (New York, Columbia University Press, 1954). Quotation p. 22.

5. Ibid., 243–244; C. Martin Wilbur and Julie Lien-ying How, eds., *Documents on Communism, Nationalism, and Soviet Advisers in China, 1918–1927* (New York, Columbia University Press, 1956), pp. 143–144. Cf. also Robert C. North, *Moscow and Chinese Communists* (Palo Alto, Stanford University Press, 1963), pp. 73–75.

6. James Shirley, "Political Conflict in the Kuomintang: The Career of Wang Ching-wei to 1932" (Ph.D. dissertation, University of California at Berkeley, 1962), Chap. 3. Ellsworth Tien-wei Wu, "The Chinese Nationalist and Communist Alliance, 1923–1927" (Ph.D. dissertation, University of Maryland, 1965), pp. 168–179. Edward Hallett Carr, *Socialism in One Country, 1924–1926* (London, Macmillan, 1964), III, pt. 2, p. 774; Louis Fischer, *The Soviets in World Affairs: A History of Relations Between the Soviet Union and the Rest of the World* (London, Cape, 1930), II, pp. 637–638.

7. Lyon Sharman, *Sun Yat-sen, His Life and Its Meaning, A Critical Biography* (New York, Day, 1934), pp. 267–268; Fischer, *Soviets in World Affairs*, II, p. 633; Wu, *Nationalist and Communist Alliance*, p. 175.

8. Sharman, *Sun Yat-sen*, pp. 270–272; Wilbur and How, *Documents 1918–1927*, pp. 144–148; North, *Moscow and Chinese Communists*, pp. 75–76.

9. United States Department of State, Records Relating to the Internal Affairs of China, 1910–1929: 893.00/5762; Wilbur and How, *Documents 1918–1927*, pp. 154–157, 171–173.

10. Aage Krarup Nielsen, "Borodin's Swan Song," *The Living Age*, 333 (July–Dec., 1927), pp. 1000–1001.

11. Randall Gould, "Borodin Opposed Expedition from Canton as Premature," *The Trans-Pacific*, 14 (Apr. 9, 1927), p. 15.

12. Department of State, 893.00/7088, Jan. 14, 1926, enclosure.

13. Stuart Schram, *Mao Tse-tung* (New York, Simon and Schuster, 1966), pp. 66–68, 73–82; Wu, *Nationalist and Communist Alliance*, p. 216.

14. Akimova, *Two Years' Service*, pp. 247–250; M. I. Kazanin, *V Shtabe Bliukera* [In Blyukher's Staff] (Moscow, 1966), p. 54.

15. Kazanin, *In Blyukher's Staff*, p. 124; Akimova, *Two Years' Service*, pp. 253–255.

16. Kazanin, *In Blyukher's Staff*, p. 70.

17. John Erickson, *The Soviet High Command* (London, St. Martin's, 1962), pp. 225–230, 836; Kazanin, *In Blyukher's Staff*, pp. 49–51; Akimova, *Two Years' Service*, p. 182.

316   NOTES TO PP. 184–204

18. Chiang Chung-cheng (Chiang Kai-shek), *Soviet Russia in China: A Summing-up at Seventy* (New York, Farrar, Straus and Cudahy, 1957), pp. 51–52; Akimova, *Two Years' Service*, pp. 250–253, 311; Kazanin, *In Blyukher's Staff*, p. 114.
19. F. F. Liu, *A Military History of Modern China, 1924–1949* (Princeton, Princeton University Press, 1956), pp. 20–21, 34; Akimova, *Two Years' Service*, p. 280.
20. Department of State, 893.00/6393, May 29, 1925, enclosure.
21. Wu, *Nationalist and Communist Alliance*, pp. 256–257.
22. Liu, *Military History*, pp. 15 and 25.
23. Wu, *Nationalist and Communist Alliance*, p. 766.
24. Sharman, *Sun Yat-sen*, pp. 306–309. Cf. also James R. Shirley, "Control of the Kuomintang after Sun Yat-sen's Death," *Journal of Asian Studies*, 25 (1965), 69–82.
25. Harold Isaacs, *The Tragedy of the Chinese Revolution* (Palo Alto, Stanford University Press, 1961), p. 103.
26. Randall Gould, *China in the Sun* (New York, Doubleday, 1946), p. 65.
27. For elaboration of these complex developments cf. Wilbur and How, *Documents 1918–1927*, pp. 228–230, 266–270; North, *Moscow and Chinese Communists*, p. 87; Brandt, *Stalin's Failure*, pp. 76–77; Wu, *Nationalist and Communist Alliance*, pp. 456–457; Carr, *Socialism in One Country*, III, pt. 2, p. 792n.
28. Wilbur and How, *Documents 1918–1927*, pp. 251–252; Fischer, *Soviets in World Affairs*, II, p. 661, for Borodin's Taiping studies.
29. Stuart Schram, *The Political Thought of Mao Tse-tung* (New York, Praeger, 1964), pp. 183, 182, 180.
30. Wu, *Nationalist and Communist Alliance*, pp. 515–516.
31. Ibid., p. 501.
32. Ibid., p. 524; Wilbur and How, *Documents 1918–1927*, pp. 386–387.
33. Department of State, 893.00/8502, Feb. 16, 1927, report from Canton Consul General Douglas Jenkins; and 893.00/8427, Minister MacMurray to State, Mar. 24, 1927. A colorful account of Cohen's extraordinary career is Charles Drage, *Two-gun Cohen* (London, Cape, 1954).
34. Isaacs, *Tragedy*, pp. 130–185; André Malraux has a dramatic fictional recreation of these events in *La Condition Humaine* (*Man's Fate*).
35. So recorded in Victor Serge, *Memoirs of a Revolutionary, 1901–1941* (London, Oxford University Press, 1963), p. 217.
36. Isaac Deutscher, *The Prophet Unarmed: Trotsky: 1921–1929* (London, Oxford University Press, 1959), pp. 331–336.
37. Akimova, *Two Years' Service*, p. 312; Isaacs, *Tragedy*, passim; Department of State, 893.00/8787, Apr. 26, 1927, Consul General F. P. Lockhart, Hankow. Allegedly inside information is given by

"Eugene Pick" in *China in the Grip of the Reds: Sketches of the Extravagant Effort Made by Soviet Russia to Set up and Control a Red Regime in China, with Strong Light upon the Ruthless Character of Borodin and His Agents* (Shanghai, North China Daily News and Herald, 1927), pp. 15–21.

38. Sheean, "Some People," p. 813.
39. Vincent Sheean, "Moscow and the Chinese Revolution," *Asia*, 27 (1927), p. 104.
40. Department of State, 893.00/9103, May 9, 1927, Lockhart to MacMurray.
41. Ibid., 9106, June 15, 1927, Lockhart to MacMurray.
42. Isaacs, *Tragedy*, pp. 245–246.
43. Robert North and Xenia Eudin, *M. N. Roy's Mission to China: The Communist-Kuomintang Split of 1927* (Berkeley and Los Angeles, University of California Press, 1963), pp. 111–113.
44. Nielsen, "Borodin's Swan Song," pp. 1002–1003.
45. Anna Louise Strong, *China's Millions. The Revolutionary Struggles from 1927 to 1935* (New York, Knight, 1935), p. 242.
46. Karl Marx and Friedrich Engels, *Selected Works*, 2 vols. (Moscow, 1958), I, p. 247.
47. Nielsen, "Borodin's Swan Song," p. 1004.

8. Todd and Bethune: *Overcome All Terrors*

1. W. A. P. Martin, *Hanlin Papers, or Essays on the Intellectual Life of the Chinese* (London, Trübner, 1880), p. 368.
2. O. J. Todd, *Two Decades in China, Comprising Technical Papers, Magazine Articles, Newspaper Stories and Official Reports Connected with Work Under His Own Observation* (Peking, The Association of Chinese and American Engineers, 1938), p. 88.
3. Ibid., p. 320.
4. John R. Freeman, "Flood Problems in China," *Transactions of the American Society of Civil Engineers*, 85 (1922), 1405–1460. Quotation p. 1405. Cf. also Vannevar Bush, "John Ripley Freeman, 1855–1932," *National Academy of Sciences, Biographical Memoirs*, 17 (1937), 171–187; Samuel C. Chu, *Reformer in Modern China, Chang Chien, 1853–1926* (New York, Columbia University Press, 1965).
5. Andrew James Nathan, *A History of the China International Famine Relief Commission* (Cambridge, Mass., Harvard University East Asian Research Center, 1965); O. Edmund Clubb, *20th Century China* (New York, Columbia University Press, 1964), pp. 186–188.
6. Todd, *Two Decades*, pp. 10–12.
7. Ibid., pp. 21, 81–82.
8. Ibid., pp. 25–26.

9. Ibid., p. 69.
10. Cf. accounts in *Hunger Fighters*, no. 55, San Francisco, Mar. 1967; *Time*, June 17, 1946, p. 15.
11. Todd, *Two Decades*, p. 42.
12. O. J. Todd to author, Sept. 13, 1967.
13. Todd, *Two Decades*, p. 73.
14. O. J. Todd to author, July 12, 1967.
15. O. J. Todd, "Recollections," *Hunger Fighters*, 55 (1967), p. 9.
16. Todd, *Two Decades*, p. 393.
17. Ibid., pp. 327–328.
18. Ibid., p. 244.
19. Ibid., pp. 229–241.
20. Ibid., pp. 78–79.
21. Ibid., p. 343.
22. O. J. Todd to author, July 12, 1967.
23. Ibid.; also Todd to author, Aug. 6, 1967.
24. Todd, *Two Decades*, p. 1.
25. Ibid., p. 19.
26. Harold Isaacs, *The Tragedy of the Chinese Revolution* (Palo Alto, Stanford University Press, 1961), p. 207. On growth of anti-imperialism, cf. Akira Iriye, *After Imperialism: The Search for a New Order in the Far East, 1921–1931* (Cambridge, Mass., Harvard University Press, 1965).
27. Todd, *Two Decades*, p. 328.
28. Ibid., p. 109.
29. Ibid., p. 305; also pp. 263–264, 318.
30. Norman Bethune, "Wounds," *The China Weekly Review*, 92 (Apr. 27, 1940), 292–294. Quotation, p. 293.
31. Gabriel Nadeau, "A T. B.'s Progress, The Story of Norman Bethune," *Bulletin of the History of Medicine*, 8 (Oct. 1940), 1135–1171. Quotation p. 1143.
32. Ted Allan and Sydney Gordon, *The Scalpel, the Sword: The Story of Dr. Norman Bethune* (Boston, Little, Brown, 1952), p. 35. This book is the major source for this section.
33. Ibid., p. 67.
34. Ibid., p. 87.
35. Ibid., p. 106.
36. Ibid., p. 167.
37. On this period, cf. John E. Rue, *Mao Tse-tung in Opposition, 1927–1935* (Palo Alto, Stanford University Press, 1966); Robert McColl, "The Oyüwan Soviet Area, 1927–1932," *The Journal of Asian Studies*, 27 (Nov. 1967), 41–60; and works by North, Schram, and Schwartz cited in footnotes to Borodin chapter.
38. Lyman van Slyke, *Enemies and Friends: The United Front in Chinese Communist History* (Palo Alto, Stanford University Press, 1967); Mark Selden, "Yenan Communism: Revolution in the

Shensi-Kansu-Ninghsia Border Region, 1927–1945" (Ph.D. dissertation, Yale University, 1967); Edgar Snow, *Red Star Over China* (New York, Random House, 1938, 1944; and Grove Press, 1961).

39. Allan and Gordon, *Bethune,* p. 186.
40. Ibid., p. 191.
41. Ibid., p. 193.
42. Ibid., p. 198.
43. For analysis of resistance and border governments cf. Chalmers A. Johnson, *Peasant Nationalism and Communist Power: The Emergence of Revolutionary China, 1937–1945* (Palo Alto, Stanford University Press, 1962); and George Taylor, *The Struggle for North China* (New York, Institute of Pacific Relations, 1940). Firsthand accounts of guerrilla methods are: Claire and William Band, *Two Years with the Chinese Communists* (New Haven, Yale University Press, 1948); Evans F. Carlson, *Twin Stars of China* (New York, Dodd, Mead, 1940); Harrison Forman, *Report from Red China* (New York, Henry Holt, 1945); Michael Lindsay, *A Study of Chinese Guerrillas in Action* (London, China Campaign Committee, 1944).
44. Allan and Gordon, *Bethune,* p. 214.
45. Ibid., p. 225.
46. "Dr. Bethune's Last Report—A Saga of a Heroic China," *Daily Worker* (New York, Monday, Dec. 11, 1939), p. 5.
47. Ibid.; Allan and Gordon, *Bethune,* pp. 256–259, 282–286.
48. Bethune, "Wounds," p. 293.
49. Allan and Gordon, *Bethune,* p. 298. The legend and the practical results are spelled out in two pamphlets: Chou Erh-fu's "No-erh-man Pai-ch'iu-en tuan-p'ien" [Notes on Norman Bethune] written in 1944, which was used as a source by Allan and Gordon; and "In Guerrilla China, Report of the China Defence League" by Mme. Sun Yat-sen et al. (New York, The China Aid Council, 1943[?]).
50. Allan and Gordon, *Bethune,* pp. 311–312.
51. Bethune, "Wounds," pp. 293–294.
52. Ibid., p. 293.

9. Chennault, Stilwell, Wedemeyer: *A Compass for Shangri-La*

1. Claire Lee Chennault, *Way of a Fighter* (New York, Putnam, 1949), pp. 10–11.
2. Ibid., p. 35.
3. Ibid., pp. 38–39. For the background to U.S. policy, cf. Herbert Feis, *The Road to Pearl Harbor: The Coming of the War Between the United States and Japan* (New York, Atheneum, 1965); Dorothy Borg, *The United States and the Far Eastern Crisis of 1933–1938,*

320   NOTES TO PP. 228–278

from the Manchurian Incident Through the Initial Stages of the Undeclared Sino-Japanese War (Cambridge, Mass., Harvard University Press, 1964); James B. Crowley, *Japan's Quest for Autonomy: National Security and Foreign Policy, 1930–1938* (Princeton, Princeton University Press, 1966).

4. Chennault, *Fighter*, pp. 44–45.
5. Ibid., pp. 55 and 59.
6. Ibid., pp. 73–75.
7. Wesley Frank Craven and James Lea Cate, eds., *The Army Air Forces in World War II*, 7 vols. (Chicago, University of Chicago Press, 1948–1958), I, p. 488. John Morton Blum, *From the Morgenthau Diaries*, 3 vols. (Boston, Houghton Mifflin, 1959–1967), II, pp. 366–368.
8. Chennault, *Fighter*, p. 103.
9. Russell Whelan, *The Flying Tigers: the Story of the American Volunteer Group* (New York, Viking, 1942), p. 54. Robert Lee Scott, Jr., *Flying Tiger: Chennault of China* (New York, Doubleday, 1959), pp. 25–26.
10. Quotations in order: Whelan, *Flying Tigers*, p. 33; Scott, *Chennault*, p. 21; Robert Lee Scott, Jr., *God Is My Co-Pilot* (New York, Scribner, 1943), p. 143; Whelan, *Flying Tigers*, p. 90.
11. Craven and Cate, *Army Air Forces*, I, p. 506. Whelan, *Flying Tigers*, p. 211.
12. Craven and Cate, *Army Air Forces*, I, pp. 490–506.
13. Charles F. Romanus and Riley Sunderland, *Stilwell's Mission to China* (Washington, D.C., Department of the Army, 1953), p. 188.
14. Herbert Feis, *The China Tangle* (New York, Atheneum, 1965), pp. 4–13. Quotation p. 11.
15. Romanus and Sunderland, *Stilwell's Mission*, p. 253.
16. Ibid., pp. 254, 263, 277. *Foreign Relations of the United States: Diplomatic Papers, 1942: China.* (Washington, D.C., U.S. Government Printing Office, 1956), pp. 128, 150.
17. Theodore H. White ed., *The Stilwell Papers* (New York, Sloane, 1948), p. 183.
18. Chennault, *Fighter*, p. 226.
19. *Stilwell Papers*, p. 204.
20. Romanus and Sunderland, *Stilwell's Mission*, pp. 322–323.
21. General Albert C. Wedemeyer, *Wedemeyer Reports!* (New York, Holt, 1958), p. 202.
22. Chennault, *Fighter*, p. 226.
23. Romanus and Sunderland, *Stilwell's Mission*, p. 367.
24. Robert E. Sherwood, *Roosevelt and Hopkins, an Intimate History* (New York, Harper, 1950 ed.), p. 731. Similar views by others are in *Foreign Relations of the United States: Diplomatic Papers, 1943: China.* (Washington, D.C., U.S. Government Printing Office, 1957), pp. 36–38.

25. Craven and Cate, *Army Air Forces*, IV, pp. 521–527.
26. Chennault, *Fighter*, p. 78.
27. Ibid., p. xix.
28. Blum, *Morgenthau Diaries*, III, pp. 114–115; Feis, *Tangle*, pp. 121–125.
29. Sherwood, *Roosevelt and Hopkins*, p. 739.
30. Craven and Cate, *Army Air Forces*, V, p. 46.
31. Henry L. Stimson and McGeorge Bundy, *On Active Service in Peace and War* (New York, Harper, 1948), p. 538.
32. *Foreign Relations of the United States: Diplomatic Papers, 1944: China.* (Washington, D.C., U.S. Government Printing Office, 1967), pp. 58, 158.
33. Charles F. Romanus and Riley Sunderland, *Stilwell's Command Problems* (Washington, D.C., Department of the Army, 1956), pp. 316, 322–326.
34. Ibid., p. 364.
35. Ibid., p. 382.
36. Ibid., pp. 374–377; 385, n. 51; *Wedemeyer Reports!*, pp. 201–202; Elliott Roosevelt, ed., *F.D.R.: His Personal Letters, 1928–1945*, 2 vols. (New York, Duell, Sloan and Pearce, 1950), II, p. 1544.
37. Craven and Cate, *Army Air Forces*, V, pp. 270–271.
38. Ibid., pp. 568–569, 614–617.
39. Chennault, *Fighter*, p. 350.
40. Romanus and Sunderland, *Stilwell's Mission*, p. 6. Quotation is authors' composite of reports by Stilwell and others.
41. *Stilwell Papers*, p. 19.
42. Romanus and Sunderland, *Stilwell's Mission*, p. 66.
43. Ibid., pp. 15, 26–27, 40.
44. Blum, *Morgenthau Diaries*, II, p. 370.
45. Feis, *Pearl Harbor*, p. 60, n. 8.
46. *Stilwell Papers*, p. 25. Stimson, *Active Service*, p. 530.
47. *Stilwell Papers*, p. 26.
48. Romanus and Sunderland, *Stilwell's Mission*, p. 74.
49. Quotations in order: *Stilwell Papers*, p. 30; Winston S. Churchill, *The Hinge of Fate* (Boston, Houghton Mifflin, 1950), p. 169; *Stilwell Papers*, p. 36 (last two).
50. Chennault, *Fighter*, p. 142; Romanus and Sunderland, *Stilwell's Mission*, pp. 87, 90, n. 22.
51. *Stilwell Papers*, p. 49.
52. Ibid., p. 56.
53. Chennault, *Fighter*, p. 143.
54. Quotations: *Stilwell Papers*, pp. 76–80.
55. Romanus and Sunderland, *Stilwell's Mission*, pp. 123–139.
56. Ibid., pp. 143, 148.
57. Quotations in order: Churchill, *Hinge of Fate*, p. 134; Blum, *Morgenthau Diaries*, III, pp. 91–92; *Foreign Relations of the U.S. 1942*:

China, p. 93. For general discussion of the "quid pro quo" problem, cf. Tang Tsou, *America's Failure in China, 1941–50* (Chicago, University of Chicago Press, 1963), pp. 90–109. On the Chinese Army at the time, cf. Romanus and Sunderland, *Stilwell's Mission*, pp. 33–43, 153–154.

58. *Stilwell Papers*, pp. 113–116.
59. Quotations in order: *Stilwell Papers*, pp. 124, 133, 147, 157.
60. Romanus and Sunderland, *Stilwell's Mission*, pp. 171–172.
61. *Stilwell Papers*, p. 125.
62. Romanus and Sunderland, *Stilwell's Mission*, p. 279.
63. Ibid., p. 282.
64. Chennault, *Fighter*, pp. 310–311.
65. Romanus and Sunderland, *Stilwell's Mission*, p. 313; Scott, *Chennault*, pp. 128–133.
66. *Stilwell Papers*, p. 199.
67. Ibid., p. 207.
68. Ibid., p. 237.
69. Romanus and Sunderland, *Stilwell's Mission*, pp. 368, 376–378. On earlier use of Communists, cf. ibid., p. 121, n. 8. For Chiang Kai-shek's views on Stilwell and Communists, cf. Chiang Chung-cheng (Chiang Kai-shek), *Soviet Russia in China: A Summing-up at Seventy* (New York, Farrar, Straus and Cudahy, 1957), p. 118.
70. Romanus and Sunderland, *Stilwell's Mission*, p. 385.
71. Feis, *Tangle*, p. 109.
72. Churchill, *Hinge of Fate*, p. 780.
73. *Stilwell Papers*, pp. 251–253.
74. Feis, *Tangle*, pp. 103–125; Romanus and Sunderland, *Command Problems*, pp. 53–77.
75. *Stilwell Papers*, p. 256.
76. Ibid., pp. 277–278.
77. Fred Eldridge, *Wrath in Burma: The Uncensored Story of General Stilwell and International Maneuvers in the Far East* (New York, Doubleday, 1946), p. 193.
78. Field Marshal Sir William Slim, *Defeat into Victory* (London, Cassell, 1956), p. 256.
79. Scott, *Chennault*, pp. 210–211.
80. Chennault, *Fighter*, p. 310.
81. *Stilwell Papers*, pp. 306–307.
82. Romanus and Sunderland, *Command Problems*, pp. 213, 306–312, 371–374.
83. Ibid., p. 346.
84. Ibid., p. 352.
85. Ibid., pp. 380–382.
86. *Stilwell Papers*, p. 307.
87. Romanus and Sunderland, *Command Problems*, p. 383.
88. Ibid., pp. 385–386.

89. Ibid., pp. 409, 412.
90. *Foreign Relations of the U.S. 1944: China*, p. 154.
91. Romanus and Sunderland, *Command Problems*, pp. 426–428.
92. Ibid., pp. 429–430.
93. *Stilwell Papers*, p. 330.
94. Romanus and Sunderland, *Command Problems*, p. 435.
95. Ibid., p. 437.
96. Ibid., pp. 445–446.
97. *Stilwell Papers*, p. 333.
98. Romanus and Sunderland, *Command Problems*, pp. 453, 459, 456, 460–462, 469. The American Ambassador sent a report on Chiang's views received from a confidential informant; cf. *Foreign Relations of the U.S. 1944: China*, pp. 265–266.
99. *Stilwell Papers*, p. 339.
100. Romanus and Sunderland, *Command Problems*, p. 470.
101. *Stilwell Papers*, p. 237.
102. *Wedemeyer Reports!*, p. 23 n.
103. Ibid., p. 10. The investigation is described in ibid., Ch. 3, "Investigated by the FBI."
104. Ibid., p. 81.
105. Ibid., p. 17.
106. Ibid., pp. 269–270.
107. *Foreign Relations of the U.S. 1944: China*, pp. 178–179.
108. Ibid., p. 191.
109. Charles F. Romanus and Riley Sunderland, *Time Runs Out in CBI* (Washington, D.C., Department of the Army, 1959), p. 52.
110. Ibid., pp. 64–70.
111. E.g., *Wedemeyer Reports!*, pp. 312–316, 394–395, 403.
112. Romanus and Sunderland, *Time Runs Out*, p. 166.
113. Ibid., p. 176.
114. Ibid., p. 152.
115. Ibid., p. 156.
116. Ibid., p. 166; *Wedemeyer Reports!*, p. 332.
117. Romanus and Sunderland, *Time Runs Out*, p. 232.
118. Ibid., pp. 237–238.
119. Ibid., p. 242.
120. Ibid., pp. 242–246.
121. Ibid., pp. 254–256.
122. Ibid., pp. 74–75, 251–253.
123. *Wedemeyer Reports!*, p. 285.
124. Romanus and Sunderland, *Time Runs Out*, p. 254.
125. On Yalta agreements, cf. Feis, *Tangle*, and Tsou, *America's Failure*. Some of the Foreign Service Officers' reports are printed in *United States Relations with China, with Special Reference to the Period 1944–1949* (Washington, D.C., Department of State, 1949), pp. 564–576. Many more are in *Foreign Relations of the U.S.*

1942, 1943, 1944: China. Wedemeyer's estimate is in Romanus and Sunderland, *Time Runs Out*, p. 338.

126. *Wedemeyer Reports!*, pp. 331–332; Romanus and Sunderland, *Time Runs Out*, pp. 330–336.
127. *Wedemeyer Reports!*, pp. 340–341.
128. Romanus and Sunderland, *Time Runs Out*, p. 337.
129. Ibid., pp. 278–285; Feis, *Tangle*, 307, 324.
130. Romanus and Sunderland, *Time Runs Out*, pp. 389–390.
131. Ibid., pp. 386–387.
132. Feis, *Tangle*, pp. 333–337; Craven and Cate, *Army Air Forces*, V, pp. 732–733.
133. Romanus and Sunderland, *Time Runs Out*, p. 390.
134. Scott, *Chennault*, p. 280.
135. Senator Joe McCarthy, *The Story of General George Marshall* (privately printed, 1952), p. 78.
136. Romanus and Sunderland, *Time Runs Out*, pp. 368–373.

10. The Last Rounds: *U.S.A. and U.S.S.R.*

1. Cf. Tang Tsou, *America's Failure in China, 1941–1950* (Chicago, University of Chicago Press, 1963), especially pp. 305–311.
2. *United States Relations with China, with Special Reference to the Period 1944–1949* (Washington, D.C., Department of State, 1949), p. 131.
3. Ibid., pp. 607–609.
4. Ibid., pp. 381–382.
5. For analyses of this period cf. Cheng Chu-yuan, *Economic Relations Between Peking and Moscow: 1949–63* (New York, Praeger, 1964); and Franz Schurmann, *Ideology and Organization in Communist China* (Berkeley and Los Angeles, University of California Press, 1966).
6. Cheng Chu-yuan, *Scientific and Engineering Manpower in Communist China, 1949–1963* (Washington, D.C., National Science Foundation, 1965), pp. 186–192.
7. Ibid., pp. 192–208. Quotation, pp. 206–207.
8. Ellis Joffe, *Party and Army: Professionalism and Political Control in the Chinese Officer Corps, 1949–1964* (Cambridge, Mass., Harvard University East Asian Research Center, 1965), pp. 1–43.
9. Mikhail A. Klochko (Andrew MacAndrew transl.), *Soviet Scientist in Red China* (New York, Praeger, 1964), pp. 23–24.
10. Alexander Eckstein, *Communist China's Economic Growth and Foreign Trade: Implications for U.S. Policy* (New York, McGraw-.ill, 1966), pp. 168–182.

11. Donald S. Zagoria, *The Sino-Soviet Conflict, 1956–1961* (Princeton, Princeton University Press, 1962), p. 68.
12. Cheng, *Scientific Manpower*, p. 189.
13. Raymond L. Garthoff, ed., *Sino-Soviet Military Relations* (New York, Praeger, 1966), pp. 89–90, 166–169; Morton H. Halperin, *China and the Bomb* (New York, Praeger, 1965), p. 73.
14. United States Joint Publications Research Service, No. 4530 (Apr. 12, 1961), *Soviet-Chinese Friendship — Stronghold of Peace and the Security of Nations*, p. 3. Cf. also ibid., No. 8501 (June 28, 1961).
15. Halperin, *China and the Bomb*, pp. 84, 88.
16. Walter C. Clemens, Jr., "Chinese Nuclear Tests: Trends and Portents," *The China Quarterly*, 32 (Oct.–Dec. 1967), 111–131.
17. Ibid., p. 127.
18. *Peking Review*, 26 (June 23, 1967), p. 7.

INDEX